$

$

$

THE WOMAN'S DAY BOOK OF FUND RAISING

$

Perri and Harvey Ardman

ST. MARTIN'S PRESS, NEW YORK

THIS BOOK is dedicated to Rose Ardman, one of those committed and energetic women who managed to combine volunteer fund raising with motherhood and a career. She's been with us from the beginning of this project, full of encouragement and advice. She's shared her knowledge and experience with us and given us countless good suggestions. For all of this, we say: "Thanks, Mom."

The Authors

Library of Congress Cataloging in Publication Data
Ardman, Perri.
  The Woman's day book of fund raising.

1. Fund raising—Handbooks, manuals, etc.
I. Ardman, Harvey, joint author. II. Woman's day.
III. Title. IV.Title: Book of fund raising.
HV41.A72   361.7   79-26737
ISBN 0-312-88650-0

CONTENTS

PART THREE

Indirect Solicitation

PART FOUR

Direct Solicitation

PART FIVE

Ending a Campaign

ACKNOWLEDGMENTS

A BOOK like this cannot be written without the help and cooperation of many, many people. To all the professional and volunteer fund raisers listed below, we say thank you. Thanks for being so generous to us—with your time, your knowledge, your experience, your ideas—so that others, also in search of funds, can benefit from what you've learned.

Linda Abromson, United Jewish Appeal, Portland, Maine; Dale Ahearn, fund-raising consultant, Washington, D.C.; Francis Andrews, President, American Fundraising Services, Inc., Waltham, Massachusetts; C. Lloyd Bailey, Executive Director, U.S. Committee for UNICEF; Jean Boobar, Camden, Maine; Alice Davidson, Partner, Project Specialists, Ltd., New York City; Betty Forhman, Coordinator, Women's Activities, United Cerebral Palsy; Edward A. Grefe, President, International Civics, Inc., New York City; Jan Holloway, League of Women Voters, San Francisco, California; Kurt Johnson, Executive Director, Campaign Associates, New York City; Aline Kaplan, Executive Director, Hadassah, New York City; Chris Kurtz, League of Women Voters, Columbus, Ohio; Linda Lese, Partner, Project Specialists, Ltd., New York City; Ruth

Logan, Development Director, Federation of Protestant Welfare Agencies, New York City; George H. Martens, Jr., Camden, Maine; Fannie M. Munlin, Director, CARE Tri-State (New York, New Jersey, Connecticut) Regional Office; Gayle Palmer, Camden, Maine; John J. Schwartz, President, American Association of Fundraising Counsel; Victor O. Swanson, Assistant Vice President for Crusade, American Cancer Society; Lynnette Teich, President, Oram Group Events, Oram Group, Inc., New York City; Diane Terman, Partner, Project Specialists, Ltd., New York City; Dave Walsh, Executive Director, Runyan-Winchell Cancer Fund, New York City; Rita Wasmuth, Staff Specialist, League of Women Voters of the United States, Washington, D.C.; Irene Wolf, Rockport, Maine; and to the thousands of *Woman's Day* readers who responded so warmly and enthusiastically to our call for fundraising stories. This book wouldn't have been possible without them.

We would also like to thank our editors, Dina Von Zweck of *Woman's Day* and Barbara Anderson of St. Martin's Press for all their help and their patience.

And a very special thanks to Camden *Herald* staff writer Tobey Levine, for joining our team as research assistant, who helped coordinate and organize the massive amount of material; and to Channa Eberhart, our dedicated typist, who, on a moment's notice, threw everything else to the wind to meet our deadline. We couldn't have done it without both of you.

We would also like to thank the many others, too many to name, who gave us their help and support. We are very grateful.

INTRODUCTION

MONEY makes the world go 'round—as the saying goes.

But there's another saying, too: The best things in life are free.

Now, you can't have it both ways, can you?

Well, the fact is, you can. In fact, it could be said that fund raising is a blending of exactly these two ideas.

In fund raising, money certainly *does* make the world go 'round. It's what you seek. It's what you need, if you're to accomplish your philanthropic purpose. It's at the heart of all your plans.

On the other hand, the qualities you need in order to get this money—idealism, determination, energy, dedication, persistence, caring, noble purpose—are all free. And we think that in many ways, these qualities are the best life has to offer.

Fund raising—and philanthropy, which is the institution it supports—is a uniquely American concept. Of course, it exists elsewhere and it always has. But it's here in the United States that it has been developed to its present state.

In 1977, the most recent year for which we have complete figures, Americans gave $35 billion to various philanthropic causes. And this $35 billion changed the lives of both the givers and the recipients—for the better.

That doesn't mean that we automatically give to charity. To get that $35 billion, fund raisers had to employ every device at their command. They had to make visits, write letters, give speeches, sell tickets, bake cakes, make quilts, run marathons, hold house tours, make telephone calls, hold parties, put on shows—well, the list is endless.

If you're reading this book, you probably have two major questions in your mind: (1) Which method should I use to raise funds? (2) Once I've chosen a method, what do I do to pull it off successfully?

We have some good news for you—and some bad news. First the bad: We can't choose a method for you—not without knowing your exact circumstances (your needs, your resources, your community, just to name a few). Also, we can't tell you everything you need to know to pull it off successfully. That's also a matter of circumstance.

But—and now it's time for the good news—we *can* tell you what factors go into deciding on a particular method. And we *can* tell you how to find out what you need to know to make a success out of it.

Where does our information come from? Mostly from two main sources:

First, it comes from women like you, community-minded women who've raised funds themselves, who've lived through the process, who know its problems and pleasures.

Second, it comes from professional fund raisers—that is, from people who routinely raise hundreds of thousands of dollars annually for a wide variety of organizations.

To our knowledge, no other fund-raising book has ever tapped the expertise of the professionals. And expertise is exactly what they have. They know what it takes to raise substantial amounts of money. They've used every known method, in every imaginable circumstance.

We've asked these professionals to apply what they've

learned raising large amounts of money to situations like yours. We asked them to translate their institutional-level knowledge to fund raising on the community or service club level. And they responded with enthusiasm.

Just what will you learn in this book?

To start with, we'll tell you about the science of fund raising and the art of fund raising. Both can be learned. In fact, both must be learned, if you hope to succeed in your enterprise.

Next, we'll tell you how to develop your case—how to put together the elements of your sales pitch, for that's your chief fund-raising tool. It's what will convince people to give to your cause.

Of course, before you can start a fund-raising campaign of any sort, you need leadership. Should you be the leader? Should that honor—and that task—go to someone else within your organization? Should you get an outsider? How about co-chairpersons? We address all these questions—and more—in the leadership chapter.

What good is a leader without followers—without volunteers? Not much. So we next talk about how to recruit the volunteers needed in almost any fund-raising effort.

Then there's the question of donors, perhaps the most crucial subject of all. We explore it in our chapter on constituency. Here, you'll learn how to determine who belongs to your constituency—and how you can broaden it, if necessary.

Next, we'll talk about campaigns. They come in a number of shapes and sizes. There are capital campaigns, annual campaigns, special gifts campaigns, and many others. Which is right for your purpose? This chapter will help you decide.

After that, we'll go into the issue of publicity. One of the best ways to assure a successful fund-raising campaign is to get it written up in the newspapers. But publicity goes far beyond that, as you'll see in the publicity chapter.

Viewed in the broadest perspective, there are two main

types of fund raising: direct solicitation, in which you ask for the money directly; and indirect solicitation, in which you have some sort of event—a bake sale, a car wash, a dinner-dance, or whatever—and put the proceeds toward your philanthropic purpose.

The next three chapters deal with *indirect* fund raising. The first discusses when and why to use this approach. The second describes in detail the thirteen categories of indirect fund raising (like sales, raffles, etc.). The third talks about the steps in planning such an event.

The following three chapters address the subject of *direct* fund raising. They talk about person-to-person solicitation, about telephone solicitation, and about direct mail solicitation.

The book's final chapter concerns a subject often neglected by fund raisers: ending a campaign. Believe it or not, how you wind things up can be the difference between success and failure.

After this, you'll find the book's appendix. This is where you go if you want more information. It's a list of essential books and magazines, merchandise sources, and other useful names and addresses.

The one thing we won't do here is to remind you to bring the cord to the coffee pot when you're having a pancake breakfast, or remind you to mow the lawn if you're having a lawn party. We've found fund raisers to be intelligent, creative, and imaginative people. So we won't insult your intelligence by telling you the obvious.

In the end, of course, successful fund raising depends on more than information, no matter how inclusive, no matter from what source. It depends on the dedication and energy of the fund raiser. In short, it depends on you—and on others in your organization.

Without your commitment, without your hard work, there'll be no hot lunches in the day-care center; the overgrown vacant lot will never be a neighborhood park; there won't be enough beds in the hospital; your church won't have a pastor; your candidate won't be elected; cancer research will slow; the university will close; your library will get no new books; your Little League won't have uniforms.

But . . . with your commitment, with your dedication, almost anything is possible.

If you have that commitment and that willingness to work to raise money for whatever nonprofit cause you believe in, and you want to:

Increase the amount of money your group can earn;

Raise more money in less time;

Put to work the trade secrets of the professional fund raisers;

Give your organization new prestige;

Increase your cause's visibility;

Learn how to identify and nurture your most likely sources of funds;

Strengthen your organization with better leadership and more committed, more active volunteers;

Insure that today's efforts not only pay off today, but also help build your organization for the future. . . .

Then, this is the book for you.

Read on.

$

$

$

PART ONE

*The Art and Science
of Fund Raising*

1
THE SCIENCE OF
FUND RAISING

LIKE practically everything else you can name, fund raising is both an art and a science. The science of fund raising—and it's hardly an exact science—involves certain principles, methods, and techniques which work in *all* fund-raising programs. By learning them and applying them to your fund-raising efforts, you can substantially increase your chances of success. In fact, you're probably using some of them right now without knowing it and without any plan. So you're not getting the most money you could be getting for your cause.

The artistic aspect of fund raising—which can also be learned to some extent—has to do with the creative application of these principles, methods, and techniques to your own situation. It also has to do with how you deal with other people—how you communicate with them, inspire them, motivate them, persuade them. In one sense, the art of fund raising is the art of helping people feel good and right about what they are doing when they give to your cause. It is also the art of helping others feel a sense of personal pride, recognition, and accomplishment when they join you in your endeavor. Chances are that you are already somewhat of an artist in fund raising. If you've ever done it successfully, you've had to be.

Let's talk first about the scientific aspect of fund raising. What do we actually know for certain about fund raising?

1. We know where money comes from.
2. We know that giving follows a pattern.
3. We know that large amounts of money can be raised more easily and more quickly than small amounts.
4. We know that fund raising is selling and that there are two basic selling techniques. Except under certain circumstances, one is always better.
5. We know that every worthy cause is composed of five elements.

You say you *don't* know some of these things? Let us explain.

WHAT WE KNOW ABOUT FUND RAISING

1. *Where money comes from.* According to *Giving U.S.A.*, published annually by the American Association of Fundraising Counsel, donations come from four different sources: *individuals, bequests, foundations,* and *corporations.* "Many people have the mistaken idea that it's business that supports philanthropy," says Kurt Johnson, Executive Director, Campaign Associates, fund-raising arm of the National Y.M.C.A. in New York City. "This just isn't true. People give the money. Individuals."

How much do *individuals* give, in relation to other sources? Quite a bit. In 1977, a whopping 83.8 percent of all philanthropic dollars—$29.50 billion of the $35.20 billion raised—came from individuals.

The next largest source is *bequests*—money left by individuals in their wills. Bequests accounted for 6 percent, or $2.12 billion, in 1977. *Foundations* ran third, with 5.7 percent, or $2.01 billion, and *corporations* gave the least amount of money to philanthropic causes in 1977—4.5 percent, or $1.57 billion.

Hopefully, corporations will someday make a better showing. They could right now if they wanted to. As of this writing, they're permitted to deduct up to 5 percent of pretax corporate profits for charitable donations. Had the corporate world taken the permitted maximum deduction in 1977, its contribution would have been about $8 billion—more than four times the actual contribution. But of course some individual businesses do live up to their philanthropic responsibilities.

Whatever efforts you make to enlist business support are more likely to succeed with small businesses, not big corporations—especially if the money raised will stay within your own community. Says Mrs. Mary Beth Crisco, Special Gifts Chairperson of the Bel Air, Maryland, "Band Bash Week," a weeklong festival of fund-raising events to buy new band uniforms, "It was the hometown folk and the 'little guy' who had the biggest hearts. Large businesses and branch offices gave the poorest response."

Since *most* of the charitable contributions come from individuals (and will continue to come from individuals even should corporations plant both feet on the philanthropic bandwagon), you should direct *most* of your fund-raising efforts toward individuals. There are two ways to do this:

1. Work toward getting meaningful amounts of money from people who now give token sums;
2. Find more people who are interested in supporting your cause.

We'll talk more later about how to interest more people in your cause. Professional fund raisers call this *broadening the base*. Broadening the base is important to the future of your organization. Your old reliable donors won't be around forever. Eventually, you'll need replacements, committed and loyal people who can be depended upon as a continuing base of financial support. An individual contributor is a nonprofit organization's most valuable financial resource. The more individuals you have, the more secure your organization's financial future.

We'll also talk more later about what "meaningful amounts" of money are, and how to get them. Don't let this scare you—this book isn't a course in arm-twisting or bugging. Although we're encouraging you to raise funds scientifically, we haven't for a moment forgotten that fund raising must always be a humanitarian means to a humanitarian end, and that it must always be done with dignity and respect for others. We believe this should lead to what professionals call *thoughtful and proportionate giving*—that is, contributions that are in proportion to a person's *interest* in your cause, and in proportion to his *ability* to give.

2. *Giving follows a pattern.* People give at all different levels according to their ability and interest in the cause. A sound fund-raising plan calls for support from all of them, with most of the money coming from those few most able to give. "You can predict the kind of giving that has to be accomplished to raise a certain amount of money," says John J. Schwartz, president of the American Association of Fundraising Counsel.

One of the most deadly mistakes an inexperienced fund raiser can make, according to Schwartz, is to try to calculate fund-raising potential by the multiplication method—that is, to divide the amount needed into an equal number of contributions—rather than by the *pattern-giving* method.

We know of one dreadful failure, which could have been avoided if it had been organized for pattern giving. A midwestern community had been promised a $20,000 federal grant to build tennis courts costing a total of $40,000, if it could raise the other $20,000 and maintain the courts. The town officials agreed to cover the maintenance costs out of the town budget—on the condition that the $20,000 was raised from voluntary contributions from the public.

A community-minded tennis enthusiast, long eager to have courts near his home, located an overgrown vacant lot that couldn't be used as a homesite because of soil problems. Together with town officials, he persuaded the owner to donate the lot to the town. All that was left to do was to raise the $20,000.

Easy, our citizen figured. He was willing and able to donate $1,000, and he was sure there were nineteen others like him, anxious for a nearby tennis court and to see something nice done with the ugly vacant lot. Furthermore, they'd even save money in the long run, because they could give up their memberships in a private club half an hour away.

Letters were written, telephone calls made, personal visits paid. After four months, it became apparent that this approach wasn't working. About $6,000 had been raised, and nearly all the people who could afford to give $1,000 had been contacted. With $14,000 left to go, our fund raiser decided to look for people who could afford to contribute $500. Now, instead of needing an initial twenty donors, he had to find an additional twenty-eight.

Another four months passed, and he did manage to come up with $6,000 more—mainly because he was able to interest some new people who had moved into town. But he was still $8,000 short.

Then, he tried "everything" else he could think of—a raffle, a children's door-to-door canvas, and a concert benefit held in the community. A couple of thousand more dollars dribbled in that way, but one year after the campaign had begun, it was still $6,000 short.

Could the entire $20,000 have been raised in the first four months? Yes, most likely it could have been—if there had been some kind of a plan that took into account pattern giving—a planned appeal to people who could and would give at all levels—well above $1,000 and far below $500.

"No matter how much money you're trying to raise, it's always best to have a dollar goal," says Ruth Logan, Director of the Department of Development, Federation of Protestant

Welfare Agencies, New York City. "But, no matter what the sum, it's raised on the principle of a triangle. Up at the top, where you have your highest gift, you'll have maybe one big gift, maybe $100 if you're going to raise $1,000. Then, at the bottom, you may have one hundred $1.00 gifts, and a certain number of other gifts in between."

When you apply the principle of pattern giving to your fund raising, you need to get "about 90 percent of your money from 10 percent of your donors," according to John J. Schwartz, president of the American Association of Fundraising Counsel.

What does this mean to you? You have to have several different giving levels, or giving ranges, in mind. It is not reasonable to expect that *all* your gifts will be top-level gifts. In the case of our tennis buff, he estimated the top-level gift at $1,000, and anyone who knows about fund raising could have told him right away that there was very little hope of getting twenty people out of twenty people to give—and no chance at all that twenty people would give at the top level. His plan should have depended on one, or possibly two, top-level gifts of maybe *several* thousand dollars each, a larger number of medium-level gifts, and an even larger number of small-level gifts.

3. *Larger amounts are as easy to raise as smaller amounts.* Let's go back to our tennis friend. He set his top-level gift at $1,000, even though he knew—or should have known—that five of his twenty original prospects could afford $2,000 as easily as $1,000. He never separated them out, and he should have.

Your top-level gift (and remember, there will probably be only one or two of them) becomes the *pace-setting* gift. Everyone else at the upper and middle levels *uses* the top-level gifts, to gauge what *they* will give.

Professionals usually look for a pace-setting gift that amounts to roughly 10 percent of the goal. They've found that if you can get 10 percent or more in a lead gift from one or two people, or from one group of people (such as the board of directors of the organization), then you're likely to be able to raise the full amount. If you can't get such a pace-setting gift, it may be an indication that you're going to have trouble.

Since the pace-setting gift is the first donation you'll seek, it gives you an early clue as to the likelihood of success. Starting off with a pace-setter is "the safest way not to end up with egg on your face," says Ruth Logan.

This principle holds true regardless of the amount of money you're looking to raise—anywhere from $100 to $100,000 or more.

Our tennis buff double-faulted here. He was afraid to reach out for a really meaningful contribution—one that would have inspired other sizeable gifts. He needn't have been so afraid. People who can give pace-setting gifts like to do it—it makes sense to them. And what better reason can you give them than to tell them others' donations will be based on theirs?

Here's what happened in the tennis campaign. Mr. A was one of the five capable of giving $2,000. He was asked for $1,000, and he wrote out a check.

Mr. B was one of the fifteen who really couldn't give more than $1,000. He was asked for $1,000. He knew that Mr. A had also given $1,000, and he also knew that Mr. A was more capable of giving than he. He figured that he and Mr. A were equally interested in seeing these courts built, so Mr. B gave $500. If Mr. A had given $2,000, Mr. B would have felt that a proper gift for him was $1,000.

Chances are that if our man in charge had tried to get a pace-setting gift in the $2,000 range, one of his five richest tennis enthusiasts would have said yes, and the rest would have given proportionately.

4. Fund raising is selling. There are two basic ways to do it, and one of them is better, all other things being equal.

In fund raising for nonprofit organizations or institutions, what you're really doing is selling an idea, although that idea must always be translated into something specific, like books for the library, a new dorm for the college, a hot-lunch program, or whatever.

The fastest, easiest, and cheapest way to sell an idea is to sell it directly. You present your idea, your project, or your program to a potential donor and give that person the opportunity to contribute toward it. The potential donor is not buying anything else, except possibly a certificate, a plaque, a pin, et cetera.

This approach is called *direct solicitation*. It's usually most effective when done in person, but it can also be done by mail or telephone. We'll talk more about direct solicitation later—when and how to do it. For now, it's enough to know that most big-money fund raisers use this method. In fact, each one we spoke with felt that even people trying to raise modest sums could increase their chances of success and raise more than ever before by incorporating some direct solicitation into their fund-raising efforts.

The second approach is *indirect solicitation.* That's what you're doing when you raise money through bake sales, spaghetti suppers, house tours, art auctions, Las Vegas nights, dinner-dances, or any other fund-raising activity or event. You are not selling your idea directly. You are selling something else—with the proceeds going to the idea or the cause. You have to use this approach when you're very committed to the idea, but others are not. Or when you're raising funds in an area where people can't afford to buy ideas alone.

"Then you have to find something that they *can* and *will* spend money on," says Dale Ahearn, of Washington, D.C., a professional fund raiser whose clients include political candidates and professional societies. "Having an event is the toughest way to raise funds," she says. "It takes lots of time and money. You're going into business, and you have to compete with all the other businesses—commercial restaurants, clothing stores, entertainment, and all the other charity events, too."

In indirect fund raising, you're marketing an event or activity first, and a cause, second. People are going to buy what you're selling because they need it or want it—not just because the money goes to a worthy cause.

In the following chapters, we'll tell you what makes an event a smashing success. You need a worthy cause, but worthy causes don't sell tickets all by themselves. Worthy causes don't guarantee attendance. Worthy causes don't sell themselves. People sell them.

Sometimes an organization chooses the indirect method because it not only raises funds, but it's also an opportunity to improve the organization's image within the community, or to boost the spirits of the members, or just to have fun.

So, we have the direct approach and the indirect approach. But, there's one other possibility: combining them.

If you use both approaches, you can set your sights higher than ever before. In combining a direct solicitation campaign with a fund raising event (maybe to kick off or close the campaign), you are more likely to reach donors at *all* giving levels and have more people give meaningful contributions.

Combine direct + indirect

The Bel Air (Maryland) High School Band Uniform Committee used this combination approach recently in an effort to raise $3,000 for new uniforms. Their "Band Bash Week" included a band concert, a spaghetti dinner/bake sale, a roller skating evening, an auction, a square dance, a car wash, and a dinner dance. Raffle tickets, booster buttons, tee shirts, and souvenir program booklets were also sold throughout the fund-raising week.

Says Mrs. Elizabeth Wilson, the campaign's overall director, "One special committee—the Gifts Committee—was handled by one very determined woman. She contacted social and fraternal organizations as well as banks and selected large businesses. This effort alone raised more money than we had set as our goal—$4,876."

In all, they raised $11,446. The direct solicitation effort brought in nearly $5,000. All the indirect fund-raising activities—nearly a dozen of them—raised the rest. That's a demonstration of what we meant when we said that all things being equal, one fund-raising method is more efficient than the other.

Many national charities rely on both methods for raising

funds. The American Cancer Society, for example, directly solicits funds from people on all giving levels. And it also holds indirect fund-raising events, such as the Walter Hagen Golf Tournament (on the national level), or giant garage sales, among other things, on the local level.

Actually, there's an element of direct solicitation in almost every fund-raising event, no matter how indirect it may seem. When you ask the local grocer to donate paper plates to your spaghetti supper, that's direct solicitation. When you ask someone to buy a raffle ticket—well, that's direct solicitation, too.

5. *Every worthy cause is composed of five elements.* What we really mean is that if a fund-raising campaign is to be successful, it needs to have five things going for it, according to John J. Schwartz:

i. *The case.* That's the fund raiser's term for what you're selling or marketing, be it your worthy cause or your chocolate cake—or both. To make it work for you, you have to identify it, describe it, package it, and put a price tag on it.

ii. *Leadership.* By leadership, we mean someone capable of handling the main responsibility, someone able to get the whole thing organized, someone who is committed to the case, and, most of all, someone who can inspire others to work—and give.

iii. *Volunteers.* These are the people who make it happen, who contribute their talent and time, who serve on committees, who are dedicated to getting the job done, to reaching the goal.

iv. *Constituency.* This is another fund raiser's term. It refers to the people who want to buy what you have to sell, the people who support your idea or cause, the people who know about and respect your group and the work it does (or will, after they've heard your story).

v. *The campaign.* This is what raises the money. It's a logical, organized, structured plan—an absolute necessity in every fund-raising effort, whether minuscule or mammoth.

In the chapters that follow, we'll take these fundamental elements, one by one, explain them thoroughly and show you how you can make them work for you.

In brief, this is the science of fund raising—success by design, not by accident. It's all a matter of putting what we *know* to work, and we know that . . .

- Most money comes from individuals.
- Your best sources for donations are those who have given before.
- People give in a distinct pattern, gauging their donations by the contributions of others.
- Large amounts of money can be just as easy to raise as small ones.
- Fund raising—in essence—is selling.
- There are two basic ways to raise funds: (1) direct solicitation, which is perhaps the most efficient method; and (2) indirect solicitation—fund-raising events—which can raise not only funds, but also your organization's image and spirit.
- If one or more of the following elements is missing (or weak), your cause, no matter how worthy, is in trouble: a good case, capable leadership, willing volunteers, an able constituency, and a well-organized campaign.

Of course, there is more to fund raising than the science of it. There's also the art. . . .

2
THE ART OF
FUND RAISING

HAVE you ever been involved in a project and accomplished something that everyone else thought was "impossible"? Maybe you managed to get the tickets to the hospital follies printed for free—and the year before, your group had to pay. Maybe you convinced the local florist to do the centerpieces *gratis*. What about the wealthy widow in the big white house on the hill? Were you able to persuade her to open it for your house tour—after others had tried and failed? What made you so lucky? Or was it really luck?

Chances are that you started out with plenty of hope, determination, and convincing reasons. But there's also a good chance that there was some intangible factor at work, a certain chemistry between you and the printer, or the florist, or the woman on the hill.

Do you know just what it was that did the trick? Your winning personality? Your sincerity? Your persuasiveness? The free tickets you gave out to your event? The mood of the person you were talking to? Maybe you know and maybe you don't have the slightest idea. Maybe the other person doesn't either.

But, whatever you did, you did it with some grace and artistry. You struck a responsive chord in your dealings with the other individual. And that is the essence of the art of fund raising—the art of dealing with other people.

It's no easy matter to deal well with people, as we all know. And one of the reasons is that the same approach won't work with everyone. People are different—and it's an art to know which approach to use with what person.

Harold J. Seymour, known in professional fund-raising circles as "the guru of fund raising," says in his book *Designs for Fundraising* that in the world of fund raising there are four kinds of people.

The rarest kind are the genuine leaders, Seymour says. They make up about 5 percent of any group. Next are people who are responsible. These are the people "who can be depended upon to play a thoughtful and proportionate part in any program engaging their advocacy and support." Responsible people make up about 25-30 percent of the total, Seymour says.

The largest group of people are what Seymour calls "responsive." If they are handled just right, they'll respond in some favorable way. These people, Seymour says, are the "principal target" of most fund raisers.

Lying underneath everyone else, like the coffee grounds in the bottom of the cup, are what Seymour calls the "inert" category. These are the people who are simply not reachable. They are unreliable, unable to make up their minds, and in favor of nothing. They are chronic complainers, and, Seymour says, "they are always the first to threaten to cut off the support they have hardly ever given."

You know all four types of people. And if you've decided to become involved in fund raising, you're up there somewhere in Seymour's top two categories. You've served on committees, and you've probably been a chairman of a committee, if not the organizer of the whole campaign. You know very well that some of the people working with you can be depended upon to do a good job without much goading. And you know that you have to stay right on top of others and practically do the job for them or it won't get done. And know that some people, no matter what, are going to sit back and let everyone else do the work, and then they're going to complain about how it was done, and you'll never satisfy them, no matter what. You also know that some people will practically grab those raffle tickets out of your hand, or volunteer before they're asked. And you know that other people will have to be sold on the idea of buying the tickets. And then there are others who will just say, "Selling raffle tickets is really a bad idea," but they won't come up with anything better.

There's really not much you can do about that inert group, but you *can* do something to stir the largest group—which Seymour calls responsive. You need them, so you've got to develop the art of dealing with them. They're the ones who will actually bake the one hundred cakes you need to make your sale successful. They're the ones who really will go into their attics and pull out their white elephants for your rummage sale. They're the hotel owners who, in fact, *will* give you the ballroom for your banquet, the merchants who will buy space in your journal, the people who will give you as much as they can truly afford—if you can sell them.

What does that take? Let's assume the cause is genuinely worthwhile. That's one of the reasons you're involved—you believe in it, and you're willing to support it with your time, talent, and dollars.

You are personally committed. Furthermore, you're enthusiastic.

Enthusiasm is probably the number one key to successful salesmanship, regardless of what's being sold—a new car, a brand of house paint, a raffle ticket, or an idea.

"I couldn't raise funds for something I don't believe in," says Ruth Logan, of the Federation of Protestant Welfare Agencies. "If you're enthusiastic, then probably some of that will rub off on the other person."

Dale Ahearn, a professional, free-lance fund raiser, agrees

about the importance of enthusiasm. "You either must *be* enthusiastic, or have the ability to *act* enthusiastic. The way I charge up my own enthusiasm is to select my clients very carefully. First, *they* must already be committed and enthusiastic. Second, they must be raising money for something I feel I can support."

"Genuine enthusiasm is really crucial," says Kurt Johnson of Campaign Associates. "There's so much competition for that dollar, or even for membership or clients to use your services, that you've got to be out all the time telling people how great you are. But, even some people who are really committed to the organization often don't realize how important that is."

But, is your enthusiasm enough? By itself, will it get people to contribute to your cause, or to attend your bazaar, instead of giving to some other cause equally worthwhile?

Other philanthropies aren't your only competition. There are hundreds of television commercials for everything from junk food to vacation condominiums, all competing for the same dollars that go to philanthropic causes. Disposable income, the professionals call it. What you've got left over after you've bought all the necessities. Lots of people don't have very much left over these days—and usually they're spending it on things to make themselves more beautiful, more desirable, or more comfortable, or on things that will make them forget their troubles, like liquor or movies. Can you compete? Can your enthusiasm alone make someone feel good about giving?

Probably not. Your enthusiasm is essential—but it's not enough. You must also appeal to something inside the other person if you want him to choose your cause over everything else that's beckoning for his money.

So, where do you start this complex process called fund raising? What's involved in the art of convincing people to respond to your cause? What can you use to persuade them, besides enthusiasm? What did you do, perhaps by accident, to get those tickets, or those flowers, or that house, or that check—none of which the person had any intention of giving to you? Consciously or unconsciously, you employed one or more of the following five fund-raising arts:

1. *The art of communication.* Communication, as we all know, but sometimes forget, is a two-way street. You can't just look at the other person and think only of the check he'll write, or the ticket he'll buy, or the house he'll add to the house tour. If you think of yourself as a collection box, you're also off on the wrong track. You're not a machine, and neither is the other person.

When you approach someone in search of funds, or help, or support, you should begin by getting some communication going—a dialogue. This is important, because the more you learn about the other person, the more likely you are to elicit the response you're hoping for.

Is someone saying no because you asked at the wrong time? Because they don't like the design of the hospital's new wing? Because they don't agree with your organization's goals? Because the president of your club had a feud with the person's mother-in-law ten years ago? Listen, listen, listen. It's a fine art and one that will take you far toward your goal if you use it wisely.

One organization we know of in the South was holding a benefit for a new alcoholism treatment center that was called a "treatment facility." One potential donor refused to attend the dinner, or to support it in any way, because she didn't like the word "facility." It reminded her of the days when she was a child, who, when taken visiting, was always asked, "My dear, do you need to use the facilities?"

We know of one lady in a small town in Illinois who was in charge of raising money to put an addition onto the hospital. One of the most unlikely contributors was a man named Mr. L, whose mother had died in that same hospital some years earlier. It was widely known that Mr. L held a grudge against the hospital and felt that if it had just done something different, something better, something right, his mother would still be alive.

Our lady had walked by Mr. L's jewelry store countless times but hadn't gone in because she knew that Mr. L would attack her for supporting the hospital with her time and money. She knew he wouldn't contribute, but she felt uncomfortable about avoiding him.

Finally, she got up the courage to pay a visit to Mr. L, and she walked into his store. She asked to see Mr. L. As soon as he spotted her, he let her have it with both barrels, ranting and raving about the hospital.

What did our fund raiser do? She listened. Just listened. When Mr. L was through, she said, "I understand how you feel. If I were you, I'd probably feel the same way. Thank you for telling me how you feel."

Two weeks later, she received a check for $100 from Mr. L. The note said, "I hope you reach your goal. Thank you for listening to me. The hospital does need a new wing, doesn't it?"

Moral: It never hurts to listen to the other guy. Sometimes listening will do things that no amount of talking can accomplish. Remember that communication means a dialogue—not just you talking.

When people know you're genuinely interested in how *they* feel, they're much more likely to listen to what *you* have to say. That's why an approach with room for the other person's questions is good. Dialogue, remember.

2. *The arts of persuasion, inspiration, and motivation.* Unless they're of the "inert" variety, people generally like to give to philanthropic causes. But they rarely give meaningful donations to causes that don't interest them on both the emotional and intellectual levels.

"If you only appeal to the emotions," says Edward A. Grefe, a political campaign consultant and President of International Civics, Inc., a public affairs consulting firm in New York City, "you're doing what some fund-raising professionals call 'tin-cupping.' You're basically appealing to some fear, and maybe getting a small donation because the donor is saying to himself, 'There but for the grace of God go I.'"

People *do* give for emotional reasons all the time. You do it yourself, when you drop coins in the Animal Shelter can that's stationed underneath the poster of the little, sad-eyed puppy. If the need is great—say the family down the block was burned out of its home—significant amounts of money can be raised with an emotional appeal and substantial relief can be given.

But, these are one-time affairs. Appeals of this sort generally can't be sustained—even when the need remains. And that means that good continuing programs don't get the steady support they need to get started or to keep going.

The other side of the coin is the appeal to the intellect, called "investment," according to Ed Grefe. "Investment is a harder kind of fund raising," he says. "You must think it out, figure out the selling points, in order to get someone else to say, 'Yes, this is what I need.'"

Most professional fund raisers say that the best appeals are those that affect both the intellect and the emotions. You want your potential donor to say to himself, "I *want* to support this cause because it moves me, *and* I can rationalize my support because it's a sensible way to spend money."

How can you do that? By adding reason and logic to emotional content.

Nearly every cause has emotional content. "Hungry children draw immediate sympathy," one professional fund raiser told us. "Health causes, crime prevention, prevention of drug abuse, environmental issues—they all have emotional content. Who doesn't want happy kids, good health, and a safe place to live. Give people a good way to back these causes with dollars and they will."

Let's say your group wants to start a day-care center, and it's decided to get the initial funding from a raffle. The Buck

Lane Memorial Daycare Center in Haverford, Pennsylvania, started out exactly this way, incidentally.

The first problem you'll run into is that you must raise money *before* you raise money, since it costs money to print raffle tickets. It's a "Catch-22" situation. What's the way out? Get the tickets printed for nothing. That means approaching a printer (or more than one, if the first printer turns you down) and appealing not only to his emotions, but also to his sense of reason and logic. But how can you do that?

Well, you can start by telling him that in day-care centers in neighboring communities, the number of low-income or one-parent families on welfare decreased when the day-care center opened, if your research backs that up. You can tell him that your day-care center will provide jobs for teachers and teachers-aides in your own community, and will therefore cut down on unemployment in that way.

If you've mustered a logical argument, he's probably interested in supporting your day-care center by now, if he can. But, how can you convince him to print those tickets for nothing?

He may be willing, and he may not be. Maybe he's already committed himself to another charity printing and he can't afford a second. Maybe his assistant has just botched a big, expensive job, and he's had to absorb the cost of doing it all over again. Maybe his rent was just raised, and things are pretty tight for him just now. Maybe he's snowed under with work, and he can't delay paying orders to do yours first. Maybe he'd love to print your tickets for free because he needs the income tax deductions. Or, maybe his circumstances and current tax laws would make it more beneficial for him to give you an outright donation.

The donor will consider many factors other than your case and its merits. Among these are his own finances and the potential tax benefits, if you're representing an organization to which donations are legally deductible.

While tax gains are a factor in philanthropic giving, people rarely give for tax benefits alone. Someone who believes in your case will probably be willing to give you *something*. *How much*, if you're looking for high-level gifts, may well be influenced by tax considerations.

Many institutions have financial and tax experts on their fund-raising teams, so they can keep donors informed of how current tax laws affect giving to that particular institution and to design giving programs that give donors maximum tax benefits.

But, back to our printer. It's not likely that you'll know all about his current workload, cash flow situation, or tax situation, so you really can't tell him what he *should* do. You can only tell him what you hope he'll consider doing, or what your needs are.

Of course, part of the art of fund raising is knowing which approach to use with what person. Sometimes directly asking for exactly what you want is just right. Other times, you need to be a bit more subtle. "Knowing which approach to use with each person is one of the keys to good salesmanship," says George Martens, Jr., president of the Camden, Maine, Chamber of Commerce, and chairman of a successful, half-million-dollar hospital campaign.

"A good salesman has a feeling about how to deal with other people. It's intuition. It's having the person who makes the contribution think it was his own idea and not yours."

Aline Kaplan, Executive Director of Hadassah, the Women's Zionist Organization of America, Inc., told us this story about a regional Hadassah president who was looking for a way to cut expenses: "A lot of printing—invitations, monthly newsletters, and the like—comes out of a regional office. It seemed like here was a good place to save some money. The president went to the best printer in the area, whom she happened to know socially as well. 'You have great expertise in the printing business,' she told him. 'Here is what we have to print every month. How can we do this more economically?'

" 'Easy,' he told her. 'Give it to me and I will do it for you.' She didn't even have to ask."

According to Ms. Kaplan, "Hadassah women are experts in recruiting support. They make people understand that it's a privilege for them to give and participate in this wonderful work. By giving a picture of the kind of work we do, we let them know that we're raising money for a principle and a philosophy as well as a practical program, and so we can sell our product."

What else will help you make an easy sale? Most people don't give in a vacuum. They're interested in knowing what other people are giving, so they can gauge what is appropriate for themselves. Remember Mr. B and the tennis courts? He knew he couldn't give as much as Mr. A. He knows something about Mr. A's position and condition in life, relative to his own.

The printer may be quite interested in what the other business people in town are doing. When he goes to the next businessman's society lunch, how is he going to feel—generous, foolish, sensible, selfish?

When we contacted people raising funds on a community level, we discovered that most of them learned from experience how important it is to tell prospects what *others* have given. "This sometimes makes them want to compete and perhaps give or do more," says Victoria J. Denn, of Dayton, Ohio, who spear-headed a drive to pay medical expenses for an eleven-year-old girl with kidney failure.

This is especially important when you're approaching a business. Most business people within any given community want to appear to be at least as generous as their peers or competitors.

"All you really need is one 'yes' and you're well on your way," says Irene Wolf, who started a program for area businesses to support Rockport, Maine's, summer "Bay Chamber Concerts."

"I've found that offering the businesses some publicity also helps. If a business sponsors one of our summer concerts, either a whole concert at $150 or some part of a concert for less, I put the business name on the concert program. After I did this a couple of times, business people started calling me up and asking how they could get their names on the program."

But, a word of caution is in order here. Some businesses don't want publicity. They're afraid they'll become known as a "soft touch," and, as a result be bombarded by requests. One Maryland bank, for example, refused to donate anything to the Bel Air Band Bash Week because, "Past experience has shown that our participation has had a 'snowballing' effect, thereby forcing us to adopt this policy."

Just how you inspire or motivate your potential donor will depend a lot on what you already know about him or her, or what you have learned during this encounter. But the essence of it is to give your potential donor *reasons* to give, reasons he or she can accept.

3. The art of helping others feel good and right about what they are doing. One of the reasons people give donations is that, for one cause or another, it makes them feel good. And the better they feel, the more likely they are to continue to give. People don't generally make large or continuing gifts out of guilt or fear. Nor do they give just because it gives them a tax deduction.

When you ask people to support you, to join you in furthering a cause, treat them with respect, be honest with them, give them a reason for feeling good. If you don't, then you won't have a committed supporter to whom you can return.

This person has bought something from you, and you owe it to him or her—and to yourself—to see that he or she is happy about having done it. If you were selling a product, like a car, or a typewriter, or shoes, you'd want your customers to be satisfied, so they'd keep coming back to you—and bring their friends. Joe Girard, the "world's greatest salesman," and author of *How to Sell Anything to Anybody*, figures that passing in and out of the lives of nearly everyone are an average of 250 people—people who can be influenced by that person. That means every satisfied customer can potentially bring in 250 more. And every unsatisfied customer can keep that many away.

Your donor is like a customer. Is he/she satisfied enough to be a repeat customer? You have something to say about that. For one thing, you can tell him/her what is being done with the money he/she contributed.

"Credibility is an all-important word," says David G. Stern, who began an annual radio marathon for the Ashley County Sheltered Workshop in Crossett, Arkansas. "The first year . . . we raised the money on the blind faith of our listeners. Ever since then we have promised what we would do with the money, and we've always delivered more than we promised."

Knowing how his donation is used keeps the donor feeling good about it, which is no less than he deserves. It also keeps your "customer" interested and gets him involved. And that's what you need, more people who are involved and committed.

"I think how much people feel they're part of an organization is the determining factor in whether or not they're going to contribute," says C. Lloyd Bailey, Executive Director of the United States Committee for UNICEF.

Take Al and Dorothy Vait, of Monomonee Falls, Wisconsin, for example. They're the organizers of an annual benefit softball game, which raises money for the Waukesha County Association for Retarded Children.

How do they get everyone involved and committed? They throw a party after the game, at the Orchard Inn, which they own. They make it a family affair, inviting both parents and children. They also invite adults from the Adult Activity Center.

"It's hard to imagine the feeling that the party generates," say the Vaits. "It's a very emotional experience." As a result of these parties, the Vaits have seen ticket sales grow spectacularly year after year. "People who never bought a ticket in their lives now sell hundreds of ours," they say.

It's not that the cause is any worthier or the publicity any better or the game any more exciting. It's that more and more people are involved with the fund-raising project—or feel they are, which is essentially the same thing.

This is just one example of what happens when people feel a part of something. From then on, donations become a sort of investment. And the donor tells his friends, business associates, family, and acquaintances. All 250 of them, to use Girard's number. And some of these 250 are likely to join, too.

"If you permeate the life and the thinking of every potential giver," says Hadassah's Aline Kaplan, "you will have a steady base, not a one-shot gift."

4. The art of giving recognition. It should almost go without saying that every contributor deserves some kind of a thank you—a personal note, for example. There is nothing like appreciation as a final reassurance that the donor has done the right thing. But, somehow, too many people forget where the money came from once it has been collected.

Some fund-raising professionals believe that top-level donors should get more than a thank you note. Many organizations have special luncheons or dinners or awards for their big donors. Only you can decide whether you should go in for something like this.

Whatever you do, whether you have different forms of recognition for different levels of giving, or whether you treat everyone equally, what you do should be in keeping with your own personal way of doing things.

The lady who was raising funds for the hospital in Illinois believed in treating every donor equally. "One day I opened up my mail," she told us, "and I found a donation of two quarters wrapped up in a piece of old newspaper. I'm pretty sure that the people who sent them went without a loaf of bread or a quart of milk that day. Why shouldn't I have written them the same letter that I wrote the guy who sent me a

$1,000 check? I couldn't think of any reason not to. It's not for me to say whose sacrifice was greater."

5. *The art of being yourself.* Do you have to be an artistic genius, or scientific wizard, or a glib and crafty salesperson to be successful at raising money? No. There are, however, some qualities that will help you. Some of them you already have, and some you can develop, with experience.

i. *Sincere belief in the worth of your cause and a serious personal commitment to it.* If this cause honestly deserves the financial support of others, it also deserves yours. "That means a money commitment," says Ed Grefe, a political campaign consultant. "Often when I'm approached by inexperienced fund raisers and I ask to what extent they are committed, they answer, 'Well, I'm giving my time, or I'm baking a cake for the sale.' But what they're asking from me is much more. What they need to be giving, really, is time *and* money. How can you expect to convince someone else to contribute if you don't?"

"If you've given money to your cause, then that means something," says Victor O. Swanson, Assistant Vice President, American Cancer Society. "I wouldn't be working for this organization if I wasn't sold on it. And because I am sold, I contribute, and I can ask others to do the same."

If you're a contributor who asks for a donation, you're not begging. You're giving someone the opportunity to join you, to add his or her support to yours.

You don't have to be wealthy to make your own contribution, but you may need to consult with your family. And you should personally be willing to do without something else in order to make that contribution. This willingness is evidence of your commitment and will inspire other people to give as well.

We know of one woman who was elected to her school board and in the midst of her term the town voted to pay school board members a salary of $250 per year. That was found money—money she didn't expect. "Sure," she told us, "I could have used it to buy something. Everyone can use a little extra. But I didn't take the school board job to earn money. I decided I'd feel better giving it away. I really wasn't aware of this when I made that decision," she said, "but I know now that the $250 *I* give each year is worth much more than that, because I can ask other people I know to do the same thing. Could I have gotten that much satisfaction out of a couple of new dresses, or a new coat? Never."

ii. *A sense of responsibility.* When you take on the job of raising money, other people are counting on you. What will happen if that money is not raised? Who will do it if you don't? "Every volunteer I've ever worked with had a mission," says Victor Swanson. "It goes beyond commitment, beyond obligation, beyond responsibility, really. It is caring at the very deepest level possible."

Any organization or group that successfully raises funds is made up of people who care. "When a group, any group, really believes in what they're doing, then they can have a very successful money-maker year in and year out," says Mark Bullard, a cubmaster in Graterford, Pennsylvania. His cub scout pack earns about $4,500 with its annual Easter Flower Sale.

iii. *A genuine liking for other people.* If you enjoy being around people, meeting new people, talking to people, then you're probably a natural-born fund raiser. "I like to talk. It's a real high to talk about this organization and try to raise money," says Fannie Munlin, Director of the Tri-State (New York, New Jersey, Connecticut) Regional Office of CARE. "I really get a good feeling from it, even if I'm turned down." When you try to raise money, you really have an opportunity to talk to other people about something that concerns you deeply, and many people find that very satisfying.

iv. *An optimistic nature.* You've got to think that what you're trying to do can be done. First, think in terms of what the money is going to accomplish—hungry children *can* be fed, disease *can* be prevented or cured, the painting *will* hang in the museum; second, tell yourself that the money to do these things *will* be found. "I leave my office every day with the idea of making money every place I go," says Fannie Munlin, "and I am excited about those programs the money is going into. That's the way you have to approach it, and if you like it, you'll do a good job."

v. *Persistence.* Not everyone is going to say yes to you. Says Fannie Munlin, "It can drive you insane, because there are days when you've done everything and you wait for the right thing to click and nothing happens. You do make mistakes—people who say they don't are lying—and you bounce back. You need a sense of humor. You cultivate, you talk, you spend time agonizing, and then there's humanity, I find. I feel that we're all interrelated, and if I can help just one person, just one, then it's been well worth the effort."

"You have to be able to hang in if you don't have immediate successes," says Ruth Logan, of the Federation of Protestant Welfare Agencies. "You have to be able to say to yourself, 'Well, they said no this time, but I'll go back again.' "

One of the hardest lessons for any salesperson to learn is that a no-sale isn't necessarily permanent, and that it's not a personal rejection. The same lesson applies in fund raising.

Think back on it a moment. In the last five years, what have you bought—or not bought—because of whether you *liked* the salesperson? You buy something because you like it, or need it, or want it. Or you refuse it because you don't like it or need it or want it. You're not making a judgment about the salesperson. And the person who declines to give to your cause isn't judging you, either.

So, the art of fund raising is really many arts: it's the art of dealing with people—genuine leaders, responsible people, responsive people, and people who are inert; it's the art of communication; it's the art of persuasion, inspiration, and motivation; it's the art of helping others feel good and right about what they are doing; it's the art of giving recognition.

Finally, and most important, the art of fund raising is the art of being yourself—of having a sincere belief in the worth of your cause, of using your sense of responsibility, of allowing your genuine liking for people to come up, of letting your optimistic nature rise to the fore, and of persisting, despite obstacles, despite discouragement.

The art of fund raising is really a way of applying your own personal style to everything you know—or learn—about the techniques, methods, and principles of raising money. It is challenging, creative—and exceptionally rewarding and satisfying.

The first challenge, of course, is to choose a fund-raising approach. It's a bewildering task. But it can wait. In fact, it should wait until you've developed and analyzed what Jack Schwartz of the American Association of Fundraising Counsel calls the five fundamentals of fund raising: case, leadership, volunteers, constituency, and campaign. And that's what we're going to do next.

$

$

$

PART TWO

The Five
Fundamentals
of Fund Raising

3
THE CASE

IN FUND raising, the first thing you must do is to work out your *case.*

Wait a minute—your case? What in the world is a "case"?

Well, if your mind is filled with images of Samsonite and American Tourister, forget it. The word "case" is simply fund-raising lingo for sales pitch. And that makes sense, because fund raising—in its essence—is selling.

So, what do we mean when we say the first thing you must do is to work out your case? We mean this: If you expect to have any success in your fund-raising effort, whether your goal is enormous or quite reasonable, you must spend some time thinking out your case. And you have to do that before you do anything else, since everything else depends on it.

Without a case, you can't do much about getting leadership or volunteers. You can't really approach your constituency. You can't mount a campaign, at least not effectively. You can't begin fund raising, not with any hope of success.

Of course, you're not alone. Everyone who has *anything* to sell has to work out a case, whether or not they use that word. That's not only true of fund raisers, it's also true of toothpaste makers.

Let's take a look at the case for toothpaste, and you'll see what we mean. It's a lot more like a fund-raising case than you might think. What does the toothpaste case look like?

Well, first, there's the case for toothpaste itself—which is connected to the case for toothbrushing, which is connected to the case for healthy mouths and teeth, which is connected to overall good health.

Then, there's the case for each specific toothpaste that's on the market. What are the toothpaste's special features—fluoride, teeth whitener, better taste, mouthwash included, color, stripes, et cetera.

And, then there is another related case—the image and reputation of the company that makes this particular toothpaste.

And, of course, there is the toothpaste's price, the way it's packaged, and the space it has on the shelf.

The elements that go into a case seem endless—and we've only been talking about toothpaste. There's even more to consider if you're making a fund-raising case. And that's true whether you're looking for *soft money*—money to carry out a special project—or *hard money*—money to cover your organization's operational expenses.

The success of your cause depends on the strength of your case, in the long term as well as in the short term, since the very purpose of your organization may be an essential part of it. And that's true whether you're planning a rummage sale or a nationwide, door-to-door canvass.

"The critical thing is, first of all, to have a decent reason for asking for money," says Francis Andrews, president of American Fundraising Services, Inc., a firm in Waltham, Massachusetts, specializing in mail appeals. "People don't give it to you just because you're there, or because you need it, or because you overspent your budget, or because your executive director is inefficient."

So, without a strong case, you're in trouble. But do you *have* a good case? Is your cause really deserving of support? Will people be willing to contribute substantial sums to it?

The answer to all of these questions is yes—if your case meets these five criteria:

1. The need, the cause for which you want to raise funds, must extend beyond the organization itself. It must, in some way, be a community need.
2. The need must be genuine, that is, you must be able to prove it exists.
3. You must be able to demonstrate that your organization is capable of meeting this need—and that no other organization is doing it already.
4. You must be able to show that your organization is well-managed, financially sound, with trusted, dedicated, and respected leadership. In short, your organization must be well-known and reputable.
5. You must have figured out just how you'll spend the funds you raise—and have a budget to back it up.

No doubt, as you read through this list, you thought about your own fund-raising project. You probably felt that you'd have no trouble meeting some criteria, but you weren't so certain about others. And you probably realized that whether or not your fund-raising project met these criteria, you weren't really prepared to make a convincing case. Well, the purpose of this chapter is to show you how to do just that.

PUTTING YOUR CASE TOGETHER

Whether you're raising $500 or $50 thousand, preparing a case is no small task. It requires not only *your* best thinking, but also the thinking of others. What to do? Put together a "case committee."

If possible, make sure your committee includes someone who's been involved with the organization for a long time, someone who's involved in the organization's overall policies and goals, someone who's involved in organization finances, and anyone else you want to make sure is with you from the start.

Then call a meeting.

At your case meeting, go over the five criteria, one by one, each committee member adding everything that he or she can think of. Write down every point you think of, even if it takes page after page. But make sure someone plays "devil's advocate." Developing a case is a time for solid fact, not wishful thinking.

Start with need—the need that goes beyond your organization itself. List every possible direct and indirect beneficiary of your program—from those who benefit most to those who benefit least. How do you know who benefits? How do they benefit? Gather figures, facts, photographs—anything at all that will prove your point.

"People won't give you any more than a token gift unless they feel your organization is doing something worthwhile. And the only way to convince them it's worthwhile is to say it in a way that is irrefutable," says Jack Schwartz, of the American Association of Fundraising Counsel.

Are you, for example, a private college in a small town? How many jobs do you supply to residents of the town? How much additional business do you bring to town because of the jobs you provide and because of your student body's purchasing power? These things may not mean much to the alumni appeal, but they sure can make the local business community grateful for your continued existence and growth.

Think of what problems would appear if your organization or program ceased to exist, and let people know about those, too.

Then go to the genuine and proven needs of your community. You want a mini-park in your neighborhood? Where's the need? Start with fresh air and sunshine—everyone needs that. Perhaps the closest park is twenty miles away and children can't get there on their own. There is no place to play but in the street? Is that safe? Get some photos of the traffic conditions. Who will use the park? Take a poll, find out how the people in the neighborhood feel.

Now, ask yourselves if anyone else is meeting the need: Is

there any other organization with jurisdiction over your particular problem? If not, you're in great shape. But you may not be the only hospital, or school, or social welfare agency, or theatre group in your locale. Make sure they are not planning to do what you're planning to do, appealing to the very same audience. If someone else is thinking along your same lines, maybe a coalition is in order.

Then, examine your organization's capabilities. Perhaps you might go into the history of your organization: who found it and why. What has your organization done throughout its history? What do you stand for, as a group? What do you hope to accomplish in the next year, the next five years, the next ten? What kind of community visibility and prestige do you have? Do you deserve more? Why? Are you attracting new people? Are your members committed? Are meetings well-attended? Are people in your organization always moaning and groaning about something, or are they out working toward some realistic goal?

If there's not much life in your organization right now, maybe you'd better think about ways to revitalize yourself internally or improve your image in the community—or both—before you undertake a major fund-raising venture. Who is going to raise the money you need, anyway? Are you proud to be connected with your organization? Why?

Next, examine budget. Before you can start to raise money, you have to know how much you need, why you need it, and what it will cost you to raise it.

"It's pretty hard to sell someone on your idea if you say, 'Well, we need as much as we can get,'" says Dale Ahearn, a free-lance fund-raising consultant. "That implies that you don't know how much you need, or that you haven't done your homework. Really, it's very sloppy. If someone's going to invest some money in your cause, you'd better be able to show what's happening to the dollars."

Donors may want to see just a budget for the particular project that's being financed now, or they may want to see your organization's annual budget or annual report, if they have questions about your financial stability and fiscal management.

Find someone in your group who is skilled in the area of financial planning and get him or her to help you prepare a budget for the particular program you're raising money for. Remember, many donors may be business people and they'll look at your budget very critically.

The first thing you'll need to do is make a list of everything you'll need to put your program into operation and check the prices. You must come up with a figure—how many dollars you need to accomplish the task at hand—whether it's buying equipment for the Little League team, or modernizing the church, or giving away a scholarship, or landscaping the mini-park.

You can even make several different budgets—one for the bare minimum and one for a program that has everything you could possibly hope for. You can assess your prospects and figure out which budget is most realistic later on.

Suppose you've got a program that could be partially funded by someone else—the government, for example. In that case, make out a contingency plan—what you'll need to raise if the outside funds do come through, and what you'll need to raise if they don't. You can decide which budget will be the real budget later on. For now, include all possibilities.

In preparing your case this way, you'll soon have some idea of whether what you want to accomplish *can* be accomplished—and how long it will take you.

For example, if your organization is suffering from internal strife, weak leadership, and poor visibility, you'll obviously have to strengthen yourself from within, or improve your image in the community before you can begin a campaign to raise significant funds.

If you can't satisfy yourself that there is a genuine and great need for your project and programs, then you'll see that and won't struggle along to raise money for something that isn't going to "take." Instead, you'll start directing your attention elsewhere, or toward making your project fundworthy by altering it in some way.

Once you've examined your case from all angles, you'll be ready to prepare a *case statement,* a kind of position paper, a restatement of your case for public consumption. If you're contemplating a large-scale campaign with a substantial goal, this case statement could be fairly long. If you're planning a bake sale to raise a few hundred dollars, it will probably fit on a single page.

Why prepare a case statement? To use as the basis for all of your publicity and your promotional literature (see chapter on publicity). To use in recruiting a leader, if you haven't got one already (see leadership chapter). To use in attracting volunteers (see volunteer chapter). Finally, and most important, to use as a sales tool, when approaching potential donors.

Obviously, the case statement is an important piece of paper. How do you write it? Well, drawing on the work of your case committee, you make a three-part definition, as follows:

1. **Who are you?** Your organization, that is. Your organization, its membership, its leadership, and its past accomplishments, are like a product's brand name.

If you are selling typewriters, then you are IBM, or Royal, or Underwood, or Smith-Corona, or some other company that makes typewriters. Everyone knows something about you—or they've never heard of you. If they have heard of you, they have a certain picture in their minds. They either trust your product, or they don't. They think that you will stand behind your product, or they don't. They think they are getting something of value for their money. They are buying not just the product itself but the name behind it.

When someone donates money to your cause, they are buying your product—your playground equipment, or your hospital wing, or your halfway house for handicapped adults, or whatever it is you need the money for—but they are also buying your organization, which they must trust to make the product good and to stand behind it.

So, when you start to work on developing your case, even if it's a simple one, who you are is part one.

2. *What are you selling?* Maybe you are trying to sell the idea that your Little League team needs new uniforms, or new bats and balls, or money to get to the state playoffs. Maybe you're selling a dry basement for the church. Maybe you're selling a clinic for your town. There's no end to the possibilities.

If you were selling a product, perhaps china, you wouldn't just say, "Dishes for Sale" would you? No. You'd take a good, hard look at that product and do everything you could to proclaim its good features. Maybe it's very delicate. Perhaps it's all hand-painted. Or maybe it's made on some local potter's wheel. Perhaps it's chip-proof or oven-proof. Who knows what the special features are? You do.

Special features are good selling points for all products, including not-for-profit ones. Suppose you live in a small community where there is no public transportation to or from the center of town. This is fine for people who have cars, but many of the senior citizens need some kind of free transportation. So you've formed a community action group to raise money. What's your case? What are its special features?

Well, you might start with the vans or vehicles you intend to purchase. They've been geared especially toward the needs of older people, with ramps or poles or other things that make them good for senior citizens. Then there's the servicing on the vehicles. Maybe you've got a discount arrangement with a local garage. Maybe you've even managed to get an exceptional buy on these vehicles—if you pay cash. Whatever the arrangements, the particular vehicles are just one special feature of your product or your case.

Other special features would involve implementing the program: what the routes will be, what hours of operation, who will be driving, who will be scheduled, how will the drivers be trained.

Break down the package into whatever makes it interesting and exciting and special.

3. The price tag. Let's say that your organization has a good name and reputation. You've proved to the public that you have your internal affairs under firm control and that you have the talent, skill, and influence behind you to get this program underway and to keep it going. And the program looks good.

What's the next question? How much?

The budget is part of any case statement. People want to know exactly where their money is going—remember, they are going to trust you to spend it for them. So show them how much the vans will cost to buy, to maintain, to fuel. Show them what it will cost to promote the program so that all the senior citizens know how to take advantage of it, what it will cost to train and pay your drivers, what it will cost to garage the vehicles, et cetera. You've got to do a lot of homework, listing the hidden costs as well as the obvious ones.

In this new transportation system going to have a central office, with a telephone, so that people can call in to check on schedules, or to find out if you're running during a snowstorm? Then include your telephone costs. Part-time or full-time office help? Include that, too. And don't forget supplies—pencils, paper, postage. In a case where you're creating some kind of on-going program, a projected budget for the second year is a good idea.

And don't cut corners to make your program *look* less expensive than it is, just to get it sold. If you try to run any program on a shoestring that's pulled too tight, you're going to get into trouble later. If you think it will take some time—perhaps a year—to raise the money, then take inflation into account. Your potential supporters will be impressed with a realistic, well-planned budget. Too low, or too high, and they'll question your competence and financial planning ability.

If your group is a permanent institution, one with a past (or one that hopes to have a future), then you should prepare a budget not only for the program you have in mind, but also for your organization itself, on an annual basis. There's no better time than now.

William Lampton, who writes a column for *Fund Raising Management Magazine,* suggests ten questions that a prospective donor—one who may not be terribly familiar with your organization—might ask:

1. *Exactly what is the purpose of your institution?* "Tell what you are not, as well as what you are," advises Lampton. For instance, if your organization serves clients, what services does it provide, and what services does it not provide. If your organization is a college, what curriculum does it offer and what does it not offer.

2. *What proof do you have that your institution provides a real service?* "Sometimes your answer comes in the way of statistical data, and at other times, in the form of case histories you cite. . . . Personal testimony can present additional, compelling evidence of a worthwhile program," Lampton notes.

3. *How does your organization compare to similar institutions in this geographic area?* People won't be very willing to give you money if your organization duplicates what another organization is doing. "You'll be wise to know your competition," says Lampton. Then you can explain to people that the organizations are not interchangeable, but that they have differing purposes and may indeed "complement each other."

4. *Will you be expanding your services in the future?* According to Lampton, expansion in terms of new buildings or capital improvements is less important these days than it used to be. Now, he says, "To really appeal to affluent persons, you'll probably need to talk about how their lives will be healthier, safer, happier, and more enlightened because of the ways your program touches them."

5. *How do people become eligible for your institution's offerings?* Does the general public take advantage of your organization's services, and if not, who does? "Even a restrictive membership policy does not rule out substantial widely-based dollar support," Lampton says, "as long as you demonstrate that your service benefits society as a whole."

6. *What is your total operating budget?* "Keen business peo-

ple can judge very quickly (with surprising accuracy) whether a total budget figure appears skimpy, just right, or lavish. Also, I've observed that the magic word *inflation* draws sympathetic nods from almost anyone who asks about your budget total."

7. *What is your cost for serving each person who comes to your institution?* This yardstick (measuring cost by the unit method) can offer splendid comparisons," says Lampton. "If you haven't figured your unit cost lately, I recommend that you do, both for your own understanding of your cost effectiveness and as information you can share with gift prospects."

8. *What is the relationship of your staff size to the number of people served?* Potential donors will want to know that your organization is efficiently managed, and they will especially want to be sure that a nonprofit organization does not have too many paid people doing too little work. "All of us should be able to defend our organization's staffing, even down to the personnel who perform maintenance functions."

9. *How recent are the figures you have quoted?* The public, Lampton says, is genuinely sophisticated and unwilling "to accept data until they know something about how and when it was gathered."

10. *Where are you located in town?* This is a simple question, but as a representative of your organization, you are likely to assume others know when actually they don't.

Your case statement, especially if it is brief, won't necessarily answer all of these questions. But Lampton suggests that they be answered in any speech you might make as a representative of your organization, because they were frequently asked by audiences he had faced. We suggest that—at the least—the person raising funds know the answers, and indeed bring up the questions to any potential donor who does not raise them himself. A willingness and ability to answer questions before they're asked will impress an intelligent prospect.

What will your case statement look like when you're finished? Well, that depends. If you're making a direct appeal for money, your statement will talk about how you plan to spend the funds you raise. If, on the other hand, your fund raising is indirect—a raffle, a bake sale, a dinner-dance, a car wash, et cetera—how you plan to spend what you take in may be only briefly addressed.

Of course, your case statement needn't be a piece of paper at all. It could be a brochure, a slide show—even a movie. That depends entirely on your needs. And it's something you and your case committee will have to determine. You may want to prepare several case statements, to appeal to different kinds of prospects.

Here are a few examples of actual case statements:

1. Community hospital in the northeast. An inexpensive, four-page brochure stressing need, services, costs, and ways to donate was mailed throughout the community. Volunteer fund raisers also used a slide presentation, which was written and produced by the volunteer campaign leader. Among other things, the presentation illustrated the old hospital and how it would look when additions and renovations were completed. The slide presentation was made to church groups and other nonprofit organizations able to contribute.

2. Y.M.C.A. in a small town near Denver. Professional film-makers who lived in the town volunteered their talents and produced a ten-minute film showing how the Y serves the community and showing how people who use the Y feel about it. The film also shows the overcrowded conditions in the gym and swimming pool that will be alleviated when money is raised for building expansion and modernization. Volunteer fund raisers show this film by appointment to individual, top-level prospects.

3. Benefit softball game for Waukesha County (Wisconsin) Association for Retarded Citizens. This fund-raising event, sponsored by the Village Workers Union, Local 31, was promoted in part by a bright yellow flyer that advertised the date of the event, the names of the teams, the beneficiary and sponsor, the ticket price, the post-game party and door-prize

drawings, and the use of the money. The ball game theme was carried out in the flyer, which had drawings of softballs on it and the information printed within the circle that looked like a softball.

4. Morris County, New Jersey, Retired Educators. They sent a poem to all members to state their fund-raising case. The poem was called "Bakeless Bake Sale," and it encouraged members to donate what it would cost them to make an item for the group's annual food sale, instead of preparing the food.

5. Unitarian-Universalist Society, Manchester, Connecticut. This group held a quilt raffle for the church's building fund. The making of the quilt was directed by a member of the congregation, Judy Robbins, a professional quiltmaker who volunteered to help with the project. "I designed and had printed a brochure which included a line drawing of the quilt and a short text telling the purpose of its creation and sale. I believe the visual aid of the brochure made it easier for our sometimes timid membership to approach people with tickets."

Okay. You and your case committee have worked up a case. You've looked at the need, you've examined your organization's capabilities, and its reputation, you've done a detailed budget.

You've used all that to write a case statement, based on who you are, what you're selling, and how much it will cost. What's the next step? The next step is to find someone willing—and able—to *lead* your fund-raising effort.

4
LEADERSHIP

LET's say, for the sake of argument, that you write up a case statement persuasive enough to make Midas give you the keys to his treasury. Then, let's say, you choose the wrong person to head your fund-raising drive. What's the result? Disaster.

To put it mildly, choosing the right person to lead your campaign—or chair your event—is a matter of crucial importance. But who is that right person? You? Someone on the case committee? The president of the organization? A prominent member of the community?

We know what you're thinking now. You're thinking, "What are they talking about? We don't have the luxury of finding the right leader. We're darn lucky if we can get someone to volunteer for the job. And if someone does—if anyone does—it's theirs."

Well, we can't tell you about the leadership situation in your organization. That's something you know quite well. But, if you're going to be your group's fund-raising leader, we can help you zero in on what it will take to do the job. And if you're not going to be the leader, we can give you some idea

of what qualities to look for, where to look for them, and how
to enlist the best person you can find.

ATTRIBUTES OF A GOOD LEADER

We know that top leaders are rare—about 5 percent of any
given population, according to Harold J. Seymour, the
founder of the American Association of Fundraising Counsel.
However, he says in his book *Designs for Fundraising* that
leaders "are always worth looking for and worth waiting for.
They bring warmth and confidence to the cause. They have a
way of attracting the interest and the loyalty of effective and
devoted lieutenants. They give the required amount of their
talents and their time. . . . They know what the committee
system is for and how to use it. And, finally, by the example of
their own words, deeds, and gifts, they help to set high stan-
dards of campaign performance. . . . They never question the
good faith of those with other views, and they never doubt the
ultimate victory."

Let's examine these characteristics a little more closely and
see just what—and who—comes to your mind. Ask your case
committee to join you. The more suggestions the better.

1. "Bring warmth and confidence to the cause." A leader
must be enthusiastic about the project. He or she must come
with verve and zest so that other people will *want* to join in.
He or she should attract other people and make them feel
good just to be associated with such a person. The leader
should make people feel like they're on a winning team. "Yes,
we can get that park." "Sure, we can get this transportation
program going." "This town certainly can support a symphony." "It can be done, and we're all pulling together."
"Ideally, the leader will have what we call 'outreach,' " says
Ruth Logan, Director of Development for the Federation of
Protestant Welfare Agencies. "This is the ability to open
doors to people in the community who most people on the

fund-raising committee do not have access to." Can you think of anyone like this inside your organization or out? Put the names on a list.

2. "Attract interest and loyalty of effective and devoted lieutenants." The leader can't do the job alone. He or she needs help and should be the first to admit it. Even the simplest fund-raising job has many different jobs and areas of responsibility.

Can your leader inspire other people to put on an extra push when necessary, to perform beyond the call of duty, to act as leaders within their own scope of responsibility? It is an essential characteristic—because this ability alone could be the difference between success and failure.

"One thing that's important is that you find someone who has already worked for other people," says Linda Abromson, of Portland, Maine, who is a volunteer fund raiser and lecturer for United Jewish Appeal and active in community affairs. "The only way you get workers is to have people who are obligated to you. If I've turned down working on every fund-raising committee in organizations I belong to, then they're not going to work for me. So your leader will have to be someone who has already participated and who has helped others a little bit."

3. "Give required amounts of talent and time." The leader you choose should know whether a given task lies within his or her capabilities and should be able to judge with relative accuracy the amount of time it will take to do it well. Are there people you can name who seem to be setting reasonable goals for themselves, who seem willing to develop their talents and to stretch themselves a bit further every time they take something on? Do they seize an opportunity and do what's necessary to make the most of it? Are they willing to take action at the risk of being criticized?

"Leadership can be a full-time job," one Akron, Ohio, Hadassah volunteer told us. "The leader has to be willing to be available to anybody at any time, be willing to take the flak that goes along with the job."

Some people stick their necks out and get things done in spite of the fact that a day is just so long, and they do them fairly well, while others are continually frustrated and seem never to finish anything, or quit halfway through. If you can think of some "doers" or "decision-makers," put them on the list.

4. "Know and use the committee system." A leader must be able and willing to delegate responsibility and must also be able to chair a committee. This means calling meetings for well-defined purposes, conducting those meetings, getting other people involved and making them aware of their importance and their potential. This is the area where organizational talents and skill in dealing with other people count most.

"A skillful chairperson will use the committee as a resource," says Ruth Logan. "She'll get them feeling enthusiastic and involved and bring them to the point where *their* ideas are just pouring forth."

The leader you choose should be able to size up the overall situation, then break it down into orderly and manageable parts. He or she should be able to find the right person to do each task, give clear directions about what the job entails, then allow the other person to do the job freely.

If you think we're saying that the chairperson is really an organizer, decision-maker, and work delegator, you're right. In fact, Mary Webber, of Maine Savings Bank, who gives fund-raising seminars for community groups, says "A chairperson should do NO work! The chairperson's job is not to run errands or check details, but rather to coordinate the work of others. In fact, I like the term coordinator better than chairperson. . . . The wise chairperson checks in once in a while and asks, 'Is there anything I can do to help you?' "

In some ways, a good leader is like a good boss. The boss

picks the best person to do the job. The good boss tells you
what the job is and lets you know what is expected. He or she
gives you a job that's challenging enough to keep you interested.

The good boss gives you room to do the job in accordance
with your own style. He or she never gives you the feeling
you're being spied upon, but does check on your progress so
you don't get off the track or fail to identify and solve problems within a reasonable amount of time.

The good boss has an accurate picture of his or her own
strong points and weak points, and leaves you to do the things
you can do best. He or she has confidence in your ability, or
you wouldn't be hired. The good boss can criticize your work
and not undermine your confidence. The good boss recognizes
when you've done a good job and lets you know that he or she
appreciates it.

The good boss, like the good leader, is well aware that the
entire responsibility rests on his or her shoulders. He or she
will count on you to help and will give you areas of your own
responsibility, but if you fail in those areas, he or she must
take the blame. A good boss has the right to judge the quality
of the job you are doing, and a good leader, like a boss, has the
right to replace you if the job is not being done or is being
done poorly.

A good leader knows that a given percentage of committee
people will not do the work and he or she will not take it
personally when this happens. (Remember, in any given
group, some will be inert, unmoveable.)

So the good leader won't limp along with the nonworkers.
He or she will find someone else to do the job.

A small number of committed workers is far better than a
whole load of drag-alongs. One newly-elected Boy Scout
leader we know called a meeting of fathers and asked only
those truly interested in spending time with the pack to sign
on. Some fathers were relieved, because until this time they'd
been committed in name only, and they no longer had to

pretend to be involved. This pack leader ended up with half a dozen really committed people and was very pleased.

5. "Set the standard by example of word, deed, and gift." The good leader promotes the cause, but not in an offensive or damaging way. "You've got to talk freely about the campaign, but not so much that other people avoid inviting you out socially because you bore them to death. And you can't avoid mentioning the project on purpose. After all, it's the thing you are most involved in and something you believe in," one campaign leader told us.

The leader lets people know where he or she stands and does not undermine the cause or make light of it when not actively working. And the actions of the leader are visible. "A leader must have visibility," says UJA's Linda Abromson. "She must participate at every level. If I'm chairing the pot luck supper, I've got to be there with my kids buying that supper. How does it look if I'm not there?"

The leader also has to make a financial commitment to the cause. His or her support must be genuine and not hypocritical. This brings up a delicate question: Must you be well-to-do to be a leader?

"You can have leadership at every income level," says Aline Kaplan of Hadassah.

"It all depends on the project," says Linda Abromson. "If you're trying to raise $10,000, well, I can't imagine your chairman giving less than $100. She just can't be someone whose gift is going to be $5 if the job requires going to the community and asking someone to give $200.

"The woman who can give only $5 because that's all she can legitimately afford ought not to be lost in the fund-raising campaign. If she's a good worker, she's extremely valuable. Unfortunately, I don't think she can chair a $10,000 project, but she may be well-suited to chair another project."

Fortunately, there are many different types of fund-raising projects that can bring contributions at all giving levels. And these can take advantage of the leadership talent that exists at each of those levels. As you'll see in chapter 7, you can plan a campaign that appeals to every income level and that requires leadership at all income levels.

You know people who will talk one way but act another. You know people who will mouth support for some cause, but who won't contribute what they can afford to it. A responsible leader cannot behave in this way. She must set an example. Know anyone who can do this? Add her name to the candidate list.

6. "Do not question the good faith of those with other views." If a potential donor does not believe in the cause to the extent that the leader does, or is committed to something else and can't make the kind of commitment that the leader would prefer, that's the way it goes. A good leader accepts opposing views and doesn't attack those who hold them. Significant amounts of money are usually not raised by twisting arms or by making potential contributors feel guilty or afraid. When people try to raise money this way, their methods and motives are open to question.

7. "Never doubt victory." A leader must display confidence and optimism. This cannot be faked. From the start, the leader has to feel that the goals are attainable and that the people, beginning with the insiders within the organization, will rise to the challenge. The leader must feel that any problems that come up can be solved, that discouraging moments can be overcome. The leader's confidence and optimism help other people turn their own negative feelings around. A good leader must have confidence in the cause, confidence in the goal, confidence in the ability of others, confidence in their good will, confidence in himself or herself. Does that bring a name to mind? Write it down.

LOOKING FOR A LEADER

Now, take a look at that list you've been making. Divide it up into people within your organization and people outside of it. Let's look first at those within the organization.

First, is your name on the list? If not, why not? Are you being too modest? Too reluctant? Or—and this is more to the point—are you unwilling to be the leader because the case doesn't excite you all that much. If so, there's trouble ahead.

If your case doesn't excite *you,* how can you expect it to excite potential donors? How can you expect it to attract volunteer workers? Remember, a case is essentially a sales pitch. And the first person it must sell is the leader.

But, you might say, we've done it all. We *have* a strong case. What's wrong? Well, remember this: People with leadership qualities are busy people. They're in constant demand. If you expect to convince them to take charge of your project, your case must not only be strong, it must also be daring, bold, and challenging.

So, before you go any further, go back and make the necessary adjustments.

Now, let's move on. What about others from within your organization? Someone on the case committee, perhaps, or the club president, or the heir-apparent? Well, if your membership includes exactly the right person, you can end your search right now.

But, what if it doesn't?

Then, you may have to enlist someone from the outside. But whom?

All right, take a look at that list again. Chances are, it's filled with the names of busy people—community leaders, business leaders, people who've led successful fund-raising campaigns, respected people, well-known people. Which one is the right one for you?

Well, let's start by eliminating the busiest. It's true enough that busy people get things done. A person with nothing but time on his hands probably doesn't have much motivation. But you're making a mistake if you choose someone who's too wrapped up in other things. If you do, you run the risk of getting only half a leader, or worse.

That should leave you with a group of people who are lively, active, interested, and occupied—but not overwhelmed with current responsibilities. These generally can be divided into three main groups: community leaders, business people, and retirees.

Let's take community leaders first. Are there any on your list with fund-raising experience? Are there any who've headed large projects from start to finish? Are there any who seem successful at whatever they do? These are all excellent candidates for the job you're trying to fill.

What about business people? Many fund-raising experts feel that people in the business world make excellent leaders of fund-raising campaigns, especially those who have recently risen to high management positions. Why? Because they've demonstrated their energy and talent, because they're able to give middle-level money gifts themselves, at the very least, and because they have many valuable contacts.

How about retirees? Some experts tend to steer away from retirees, citing health and energy problems. And they may have a point. But we think that each of them must be judged separately. There's a very good chance that one of the retirees in your community has exactly the right combination of contacts, leadership qualities, experience, and energy.

Personally, the best fund raiser we know is a retired sales manager, with a long history of philanthropic and community service. He is extremely energetic and personable and a highly skilled marketer. Every voluntary organization in his town is after him—and any organization that can convince him to lead their campaign can be almost sure of success.

You should now have identified at least a handful of likely candidates. But that's no guarantee that you're about to get the leader of your dreams. All you know is what *they* have to offer you. What do you have to offer them?

Well, believe it or not, quite a bit. First, you're offering the chance to be associated with something meaningful and worthwhile. Second, you're offering a chance for personal fulfillment. Third, you're offering a chance for increased visibility within the community—and that can mean a lot to someone trying to get ahead professionally, maybe someone new in town. To the right person, all of this is a substantial inducement indeed.

SUBSTITUTES FOR LEADERSHIP

But what if you simply *cannot* get the kind of leader or that chairperson you really want? Then you have two other possibilities: the honorary chairperson and co-chairpeople.

What is an honorary chairperson. Or, better yet, what *good* is an honorary chairperson?

The honorary chairperson is a figurehead, some prestigious person who lends his or her name and reputation to your cause. This person may do no actual work at all, or just a little. But someone else will actually be directing the fund-raising campaign.

That's good, because the influence and contacts of the honorary chairperson will contribute a great deal to the potential success of your campaign or event. On the other hand, it means that someone within your organization (most likely) will have to assume the greatest share of the burden.

If this is the path you decide to follow, you should be very clear about telling the honorary chairperson exactly what he or she is expected to do and what you will do. You may, for example, want this person to give you a list of names to approach. You may ask him or her to sign a letter to people on their personal mailing list. He or she may have an assistant who can work with you. All these things are very valuable.

But don't expect the honorary chairperson to give you much time. Instead, you get clout. "In that case, your working chairperson must simply be a well-organized, good worker," says UJA fund raiser Linda Abromson.

We were once involved in doing a movie benefit for the restoration of an historical site in our town. The film director was going to speak in person at the showing, but we also needed some additional clout.

So we approached the founder and past president of the town's historical society—a lady of great prestige within the community, who doesn't often say yes these days, probably because too many people ask her too often. We asked her to speak at the benefit, to give a brief history of the site itself, to tell why it was important to get it restored, and to introduce the filmmakers.

We—and the other volunteers—handled all the arrangements for the theatre, the film, the filmmakers, the ticket sales, the pre-movie party, and the refreshments. But this lady's name, and the fact that she was going to speak at the benefit, were crucial to the event's success. Important people who would not ordinarily have attended a movie benefit came because they knew this illustrious woman would be there, because this benefit had her support. Our point: Don't neglect this avenue if it will help you.

There's also one other type of leadership you should consider, if necessary. This is the "co-chairship." Sometimes a co-chairship is a way for two people to share responsibility—but sometimes it's a way to avoid it. This is probably why many experienced professional fund raisers frown on the co-chairship concept.

But, we've seen too many successful partnerships to believe that's true all the time. If the co-chairpeople choose each other, if they have complementary skills, personalities, and talents, if they have worked well together before or have reason to think that they can work well together, then the team will probably be a good one.

Husband-wife teams are successful all over the country in positions of community leadership. Al and Dorothy Vait of Waukesha County, Wisconsin, and Charles and Elizabeth Wilson of Bel Air, Maryland, are two outstanding examples.

Teams of women also work well together. Nearly every community that has social fund-raising events—charity balls, bazaars, follies—has a couple of able volunteers, usually best friends, who organize these things with tremendous success.

One of the most famous teams in the annals of fund raising is the team of Sally Berger and Alice Pfaelzer, two volunteers who raised $1.4 million for Michael Reese Medical Center (Chicago).

Some kind of partnership may be just what you need. If you've got a friend, acquaintance, or husband who's just as dedicated to the cause as you are, then consider working as a team. Maybe together you'll be willing to do what neither of you would attempt alone.

But avoid any temptation to have more than two co-chair-people. If one leader is best, and two are sometimes accept-able, then three is disaster. "A triumvirate doesn't chair well," says Linda Abromson. "If you must, have a chairman and two vice-chairmen. That may be preferable to two co-chairmen."

APPROACHING A POTENTIAL LEADER

Now we come to the delicate part of the process: the actual recruitment. Let's say you've gone through your list and put it in rank order. Then you've approached your first three choices, one after another, and you've been turned down every time. What do you do now?

Well, what you don't do is approach candidate number four, whine about all the others who've turned you down and plead for help, saying "You're our last hope." That's an invita-tion to disaster.

Instead, make sure that list of candidates is confidential, even secret. Then, if a candidate turns you down, approach the next one on the list as if he or she is your top choice. If you don't, you're saying that others have seen this as a losing cause, or that you're reaching to the bottom of the barrel.

Who should do the actual recruiting? Experts recommend that candidates be approached by at least two people—and probably no more than three. One should be a member of the candidate's peer group, someone who knows the candidate personally, if possible. The other should be a crackerjack salesperson, someone who can present the case in the strongest possible light. If neither of these are bigwigs from your organization, then send one of those, too. The presence of the bigwig will underscore the prestige of the job being offered.

Before any approach is made, your organization's top leadership must make its own financial commitment to the case, as individual or as a group. That assures your candidate that all of you believe in your own cause, that there's a good chance the monetary goal can be reached, and that your candidate is not being asked to ride a dead horse out of the stable.

One last notion about finding a leader: don't dawdle. The sooner you select and recruit your campaign leader (or event chairperson), the better—since everything else depends on that person, in large part, and on who he or she knows and how he or she does things.

In fact, once your leader is recruited and on the job, he or she will take charge of developing the remaining fund-raising fundamentals. Your leader will play a key role in enlisting volunteers, analyzing the constituency, and planning the campaign.

That's why your leader is so important.

5
VOLUNTEERS

IF THE fund-raising leader or campaign chairperson is the visible key to the success of any given effort, then the hidden key is the volunteer corps.

The Blair (Nebraska) memorial community Hospital Auxiliary has held an annual rummage sale for more than twenty years. In 1958, the first year, they netted $600. In 1978, profits were nearly $13,000.

Says the Auxiliary's Mrs. Shirley E. Jipp, "How did we do it? By recruiting women from our entire town as well as other small towns and communities in surrounding Washington County. These women were from all churches, from all walks of life, ranging in age from their teens to over eighty years old."

People have many different images of what a volunteer is. What's your picture? The teenage candystriper? Your neighbor who goes door-to-door for cancer every year? The white-haired lady who collects and distributes toys among the needy children every Christmas?

Maybe it's the girl in the Salvation Army uniform collecting coins in the supermarket. Or the person who directs plays for your community theatre group, the doctor who puts in time at the free clinic on the other side of town, or the club members who put on the fashion show at the hotel ballroom. The number of images is endless.

You yourself have undoubtedly volunteered for many different jobs, especially if you're an active member of any club, organization, church, or other institution. The fact is, without volunteers, there really would not be a strong philanthropic movement in America.

The volunteer training ground is a place from which leadership can emerge. The voluntary job provides volunteers with an opportunity to serve unselfishly, to express themselves, to gain self-confidence, and to develop talents and skills that are marketable throughout both the philanthropic and business worlds.

"I talk to so many women," says Alice Davidson, a partner in Project Specialists, Inc., a New York City fund raising consulting firm, and the chairperson of the Women's Division for United Cerebral Palsy, "who are looking for paid jobs and feel they have nothing to put on their résumés. They should put 'professional volunteer.' Even the people doing it don't realize how meaningful it is and how much valuable experience they have."

There is no way that the work of the philanthropic or non-profit world could go on without volunteers, and that holds true for fund raising as well as other work. "Volunteers must be a definite part of the entire development/public relations arm of any institution," said S.G.D. Napersteck, Chief Officer, Medical Center Relations, Mount Sinai Medical Center, in a 1978 speech at the Institute for Hospital Philanthropy.

As for fund raising, in particular, it's hard to imagine a fund-raising campaign without volunteers selling raffle tickets, rounding up rummage for a giant garage sale, baking cakes for a bake sale, publicizing a dinner-dance, keeping the books, putting up the decorations, addressing the Garden Club, writing up a news item, et cetera, et cetera, et cetera.

But where do you find volunteers? How do you convince

them to join your effort? What do you do if there aren't enough? How do you match your fund-raising tasks to the volunteers' talents? How can you get the most from them? When and how should you thank them for their efforts?

Well, let's begin at the beginning . . .

IDENTIFYING POTENTIAL VOLUNTEERS

You need volunteers—maybe dozens of them, depending on exactly how you intend to raise the funds you're after. Where do they come from?

If your organization is running smoothly, if you have good internal communication and enthusiastic participation from people at all levels, then you won't have to search far for a nucleus of volunteers. They're the people who are involved already.

So, when you begin searching for volunteers, start close to home.

First, look at the inner family of your organization—the officers, past and present, the committee heads, the board of directors, those who've made the greatest commitments in the past, in terms of both time and money. This group will very likely provide your best and hardest-working volunteers.

Second, look at others in the organization—dues-paying members (if you have them), those who come to meetings regularly, those who come sporadically, those who used to come, those who have volunteered in the past.

Third, look at those who are in some way connected with the group *benefiting* from the funds you raise.

Fourth, consider everyone's relatives and friends. Everyone knows someone else willing to help. So if your need for volunteers is large, ask each initial volunteer to recruit one or two others.

Fifth, don't forget children. You can get a kids' division going for nearly any kind of campaign. Kids are terrific fund raisers. They're caring and enthusiastic and creative.

"I once had a nine-year-old boy call me up," Fannie Munlin

of CARE told us. "He said he'd seen a CARE commercial on TV, and he called to tell me that he liked the commercial. 'You really got the point across,' he told me. 'I'm going to do something about those people being hungry. I'm going to have a car wash. Please send me some of your brochures.'

"Well, I sent him brochures, and a coin collection box, and a certificate of permission that his mother had to sign. And this boy and his friends raised $50.

"Then we have a little girl who designed Christmas cards and sold them and raised $200."

Children's groups and teen youth groups all over the country are involved in fund raising. The Church of God Youth Department (Crisfield, Maryland) held a Valentine King and Queen contest. Winners were the boy and girl in each age group (four groups, ranging in age from 2–25) who collected the most votes (pennies). Winner in the youngest age group was a three-year-old who collected $256.91 in pennies. The total amount raised in this project was more than $1,200, which was used to purchase a wheelchair for a lady in a nursing home, with remaining funds going to a mission project.

Make a list of *every* potential volunteer. Then study it, with the help of the case committee, or your organization's inner family. Try to identify who are *responsible,* those who are *responsive,* and those who are *inert.* Then, apportion your recruiting efforts accordingly, putting the most time into those likely to provide the most help.

RECRUITING

In a very real way, your fund-raising campaign or event begins at the moment you start asking for volunteers. Why? Because when you ask for help, you're actually asking for a contribution—of time and energy. And, whether you say it or not, you're also asking for a monetary contribution—because all volunteers must contribute, or face some embarrassing moments when they start asking *others* for money.

And, speaking of asking for money, when you approach people to volunteer to help out, you may be asking not only for time and money, you may also be asking them to take on a task they find difficult and unpleasant. After all, it's the volunteers who do the actual fund raising, who ask the toughest question of all: Will you give money to our cause?

Asking people to volunteer, then, is no small matter, either from your point of view or theirs. Therefore, in most cases, it isn't something you can do without thought or planning. Before you start asking, you have to answer this question: Why should someone volunteer to help out? What can I say to motivate someone to volunteer?

You can start looking for the answer within yourself. Why did you join your organization?

Chances are that you didn't join to become a fund raiser. "I don't believe that very many people sit down and do a philosophical study of organizations before they decide to join," says Linda Abromson of United Jewish Appeal. "We join for all kinds of reasons—our social group belongs, or our neighborhood belongs, or there's an affiliation through our kids.

"Now, before you can raise money for this organization— which you joined not to raise money for, but for some other reason—and before you can get anyone else to raise money for it, you've got to go back and learn everything you can about the organization. Learn it inside out.

"Learn it, because when people ask you why you're raising money, you can say more than 'Well, I joined because my neighbor joined.' Raising money is something you do because you believe in it. You didn't join because you believed, but you learned all about it, and now you believe. And that's what motivates you in fund raising."

Once you're aware of your own reasons for being involved in fund raising, you can do a better job of motivating others to join you. Maybe your reasons will convince them.

Or maybe your reasons won't be enough. So what you also have to know is why *others* have joined your organization or why they've gotten involved in the fund-raising process. Then you can better tailor your appeal to the motivations of potential volunteers.

Why *do* people volunteer, anyway? According to the National Center for Voluntary Action, there are many reasons. They include: reaching out to people in need; helping others trying to solve a societal problem; doing something for a cause or advancing the cause of others; learning and growing; making new friends; belonging to a group; developing new interests; using particular skills; testing out career possibilities; coming to terms with one's conscience.

Also important, according to Joan Flanagan, author of the *Grass Roots Fundraising Book,* is "the feeling that there is upward mobility in the group. In other words, I know that if I come in and volunteer to work in the bake booth this year, next year or the year after I can run the whole fall fair."

"The reason I got so interested in fund raising," says Victor Swanson of American Cancer Society, "was the dedication of the volunteers. They weren't just joiners. They had a mission."

Here are just a few comments that indicate the deep sense of personal satisfaction volunteers feel when they get involved in fund raising:

"All proceeds (from the Spring Fair) go to the Lexington Library Association. We have built a building, but we have done more than that. We have given this community a closeness, a fellowship, that it never had before."—Rose Wilkins, Lexington (South Carolina) Woman's Club.

"I have been chairman of our (antique) show for two years. Last year, our profit was $6,200. All of our monies go back into the community via contributions and scholarships. To me, the most wonderful part of our show is the many friendships made through members working together."—Trudy Hannam, Cedarburg (Wisconsin) Woman's Club.

"When you are sitting behind a table for five hours and your head is spinning from the loud, continuous roar of the music and the dull, continuous roar of the skates (at a fund-raising skate-a-thon), take a minute to watch . . . one hundred twenty-two individuals have possibly donated just as much time as you have. They are doing this for diabetic people they don't know and probably never will meet. Take a really good look. I personally guarantee it will make your world a little more meaningful."—Nancy Hydall, Noblesville-Carmel (Indiana) unit of the American Diabetes Association.

"Twins were born prematurely to a young couple, members of St. Paul's United Church of Christ in Lakewood, Colorado. One twin was released after four months in the hospital. The other died after nearly a year in the hospital, never having been released. The hospital costs had been enormous—far beyond the ability of the young couple to pay. So we decided to help, with a Super Sidewalk Sale. The total amount raised was $4,200. This project had to have been one of the most fulfilling and rewarding experiences of my life and the life of our church. This was indeed an outpouring of love from everyone involved."—Dolores E. Bohlmeyer, Sale Chairman, Commerce City, Colorado.

According to the American Cancer Society, the best way to recruit a volunteer is through personal communication. If you don't know him or her well, bring someone with you who does—if possible, another volunteer.

Keep in mind what your potential volunteer's motivation might be for saying yes. Give that person a clear picture of what you expect of him or her. And, if, after everything, you are turned down, don't give the person a hard time. He or she might be one of those inert people you're better off without. Or he/she might be so overwhelmed with other projects that he/she wouldn't really be able to help. Again, remember that busy people are people who get things done—so they should be asked. Most volunteers we know have paying jobs *and* children to raise *and* a household to manage. People who are really interested and concerned *make* time to volunteer.

When asking volunteers to help, you're likely to hear one major objection (aside from the question of time or other interests): "I don't think I could ask someone for money." Well, let's face it—it's not easy. And for some people, it's impossible. But what do you say when someone raises this objection? Talk about yourself, and how you overcame your own fears, if you had them.

Then, if you're talking to someone who lacks confidence and technique, but not willingness, tell him or her that all volunteers will be carefully trained, so they'll know exactly what to say in all circumstances.

If you're talking with someone who simply can't ask for money—and it's obvious to both of you—tell that person what other types of jobs may be available. If you're having a party or some other event, many volunteers will not have to make a straight-out request for funds.

When you approach a potential volunteer, use the case you've developed; it is, or it should be, a very powerful, persuasive tool. And show them your own involvement and commitment. Both of these qualities—thank Heaven—are contagious.

WHEN THERE ARE TOO FEW VOLUNTEERS

It is possible to identify many potential volunteers, approach them, and wind up with too few to carry off your plans. What then?

Well, the first thing to do is to review those plans. Are they too grandiose? Are they appropriate to your cause? To your goal? To your community? Let's say, for the sake of argument, that they're quite reasonable—and everyone else agrees.

Then ask yourself these questions: Do your plans reflect the concerns, ideas, hopes, and needs of your members? Did your membership help to create them? Are they a democratic expression of the organization's policies? If not, you may have found the problem. But let's assume that you can honestly answer yes to all of these questions. Then the problem must lie elsewhere.

It's time now to start thinking about your organization or group itself. Are your programs in good shape? Are your meetings well-attended? Are your members happy? Is your leadership trusted?

The chances are, if you can't find enough volunteers to handle the program you've designed and the fault doesn't lie in the program, it lies in the organization itself.

Sometimes, you must not only define the case for an upcoming fund-raising venture, but you must also re-define your organization. Fund raising is not done in a vacuum. It occurs within the context of your organization—its past, present, and future.

If you intend to create an ambitious fund-raising program, you must make sure your membership is ready and willing to take on the task. If it isn't, you must find out why—or risk never being able to do anything that is really successful.

The problem may be simpler than you think. We know of one California recreation-youth center that was about to begin a major fund-raising campaign to refurbish the interior and to add a swimming pool.

The fund-raising leader started asking members to volunteer to help and ran into a stone wall. So, the leader asked a series of questions—What is your attitude toward the youth center? Toward its leadership? Toward the way it is run? Toward the services it offers? Toward your family's use of it? And the leader discovered what the problem was. It turned out that the membership was disgruntled with the organization's leadership. Those in a position to spend considerable time on the campaign were unwilling to do so because discipline at the center was poor and repeated complaints had brought no improvement. Initial approaches to potential donors were met with the same attitude.

Realizing that the problem had to be solved before fund raising began, the campaign leaders delayed the fund-raising drive for six months. During that time, new rules were instituted at the center, and an assistant director was replaced.

If the campaign leaders had begun fund raising before they'd solved these problems, volunteers would have been unable to answer a potential volunteer who asked, "Why should I support a swimming pool? The place is badly run. It has discipline problems and vandalism. A swimming pool will just create more discipline problems. And, as for new furniture, wouldn't it be wrecked by the same people who wrecked the old furniture? Since no one is likely to take care of the pool or the furniture, why should I give money to the center?"

On the other hand, if you find it hard to get enough volunteers from within your organization, it may be your organization that needs the refurbishing. It may be time for a re-statement of goals or a revision of basic policies. It may be time to change the leadership, if present leaders don't have the respect and cooperation of the rank-and-file. It may be time for a membership drive, to add some new blood to your ranks.

Our point: Getting commitment from volunteers, especially those within your organization, is crucial. And if you're unable to do this, there's work to be done—perhaps major surgery—before you can realistically consider *any* fund-raising campaign or event.

SKILLS, TALENTS, AND RESOURCES

Let's say you have volunteers coming out of your ears. Now what? Well, your thoughts should be turning to how to get the most out of them, how best to harness that eagerness, that willingness to serve.

By the time you put out the call for volunteers, of course, you should not only know how many warm bodies you need, but also just what you want them to do. That is, you should have a job list. And your aim should be to fill each job with the volunteer most suited to it.

How to do that? Ask. Ask your volunteers about their work

experience, their hobbies, their interests (and ask them about their spouses, too—a lot of knowledge rubs off). Ask about skills, education, and talents. Ask about fund-raising experience with other organizations. Ask what they're *willing* to do. And what they'd *like* to do.

If your volunteer group is small, you can always ask these questions face-to-face (individually, of course). If it is somewhat larger, a written questionnaire is definitely in order.

And, while you're asking these questions, here are some others to consider: "Do you have access to a copying machine?" "Can you get anything wholesale?" "Do you have a typewriter or an adding machine?" "Do you have any friends or relatives not in the group who may be able to help?" Chances are you'll be surprised at the resources these questions turn up, even if you think you know the volunteers quite well already.

Once you have the answers, you can start to assign jobs. Naturally, you'll want to take advantage of your volunteers' experiences and talents as much as possible. But be prepared for some resistance. The volunteer who's a columnist for the local paper may want nothing to do with publicity or any other kind of writing because he/she wants to try something different. But a homemaker or secretary might jump at the chance.

Your job list will be especially useful when you come across volunteers who are absolutely (they think) unable to ask people for money. In such an event, use them elsewhere, in bookkeeping, publicity, or any one of a dozen other jobs not related to money.

If you don't have enough nonfund-raising jobs, pair off your reluctant fund raisers with someone else who's confident and capable. Many times, people find it easier to raise money if they have a partner. Ideally, the team should consist of a good salesperson and someone who knows the donor.

Do your best to match the job to the volunteer, but don't be rigid about it. If it doesn't look like the matchup is working out, make a switch. Be prepared to make a change and you'll find yourself riding over the bumps and rough spots with ease.

TRAINING

It isn't enough simply to assign jobs, not by any means. If you expect your volunteers to do a good job now and in the future, then you've got to give them some job training. Not only will training build self-confidence and help them perform better, but training will also help replenish your supply of leaders. Some of the volunteers you train for this year's campaign will be able to train new volunteers next year. And some of those will eventually be capable of a campaign chairpersonship.

Whenever possible, train groups of volunteers together. The American Cancer Society found that its Crusaders (door-to-door solicitors) accomplished more in both the public education and fund-raising areas when training was held in group meetings where open discussion was encouraged.

Your training sessions may be anything from a short meeting to review check-out procedures at your upcoming charity garage sale, or a series of meetings where the history and future of your organization are discussed and where board members are trained in high-level gift solicitation techniques.

How extensive and how formal your training program needs to be will depend on the money goal and complexity of your campaign, the number of volunteers, their knowledge and experience within the organization, the method of fund raising you're using, and the amount of fund-raising experience that the volunteers have had.

Ideally, training sessions should provide volunteers with the following opportunities:

1. To increase their knowledge of the organization—history, purposes, programs, policies, growth.

2. To fully understand campaign goals, campaign plans, campaign procedures.
3. To express their own anxieties about fund raising.
4. To contribute their own ideas.
5. To ask questions.
6. To practice their sales technique.
7. To get to know each other so that a group spirit has the chance to develop.

The American Cancer Society gives these tips to leaders training door-to-door Crusaders, and we think they will work well for nearly any trainer of fund-raising volunteers.

1. "Avoid using a classroom seating arrangement with the 'teacher' up front. It is best to seat people in a circle so that everyone can see and hear each other.

2. "Your job is NOT to give a lecture, but rather to introduce discussion questions and to encourage everyone to express their ideas or concerns.

3. "Don't feel you must have the 'right' answer to every question. If a question is directed to you, re-direct it to some other member by saying, 'Mrs. Jones, how would you deal with this problem?'

4. "One way to facilitate discussion is to ask 'drawing out' questions, such as: 'Mary, how do you feel about approaching relative strangers to discuss cancer?' "

Discussing the plan for reaching a goal, and how to put that plan into action, will probably be a major portion of a training session.

Every plan has several aspects, but the essence of it is, in what order and by what method should things be done to reach the goal.

Let's say your goal is to sell 1,000 raffle tickets in the next ten days. What's the first step?

Well, if you're going to sell tickets by plan (and not at random), which is a sensible idea, the first step is perhaps to come up with a prospect list. And, if you also want to sell to the general public, then you might want to come up with a list of sales locations (busy downtown corners, in front of supermarkets, in malls, in commuter railroad stations).

Prospect lists have probably been compiled in planning meetings. Sales locations (if you have them) may also be determined already (perhaps based on last year's experience). Now you're ready to assign specific jobs and responsibilities and talk about the ways in which volunteers might carry them out.

The next step is to divide your prospect list (or sales locations) among your volunteers. The object here is to avoid duplication and to make each volunteer responsible for seeing only a specific number of prospects. Each volunteer should also be responsible for selling only a certain number of tickets. If you want to sell 1,000, for instance, and you have twenty volunteers, each should have a goal of selling fifty apiece. If you have ten days to sell the tickets, then each volunteer should have a personal goal of selling at least five tickets per day.

After you've divided up the work and the goals, volunteers should examine their prospect lists, jotting down what they know about potential ticket buyers. Can this one afford to buy several? Does that one want the prize? Does the other one support the cause without caring about the prize? Who are the toughest nuts? Who are the prospects most likely to say yes?

Then your volunteers—with your help, or helping each other—should arrange their prospect lists so that they start with the person most likely to buy.

"If I could give just one piece of advice, to any fund raiser for any project at any level, that advice is *start with a success,*" says U.J.A.'s Linda Abromson, who trains women volunteers.

"I don't care what it is you're doing. If you've got a bake sale going, put out a few better things at inexpensive prices and get them sold. If you're doing a telephone solicitation for donations up to $35, first call the woman who gives you $25 every year.

"If my kids are running a car wash, I always show up at nine o'clock if it opens at nine. Then they can go an hour with no customers. As long as they have an early success.

"Get a success immediately. You can use it later, but that's a secondary by-product. The important thing is that inside you, you know you've done it. Whatever it is you've set out to do—sell the cake, get the donation, sell the ticket—you know you can do it."

An early success is very important, and volunteer morale is not the only reason. Every donation really does help you get another donation, and one sale does lead to another. And, of course, each volunteer makes his or her own donation, or buys his or her own tickets, first.

Then, you can visit Mrs. Jones and say to her, "I've bought five raffle tickets, and Mr. Hill just bought five. Won't you consider buying five for yourself?" If she says no, you can then suggest a smaller number, greatly increasing your chances of a sale—thanks to that early success.

One woman we know, who always volunteers to solicit merchandise for her local public television station's fund-raising auction, has gotten this "early success" method down to a science.

"I plan out my route when I go to the merchants," she says, "always starting with someone I know will donate something good because he gave last year and the year before. Then I move on to the next most likely donor, making sure he knows what's already been given. By the time I get to the 'doubtfuls,' I can point to previous contributions and be pretty darn convincing. Even the local Scrooges have trouble refusing when they find out almost everyone else has given.

"If I started with an unlikely prospect—and got a no answer," she continues, "I wouldn't have anything to build on. In fact, I'm sure that would inspire other no answers—partly because my confidence would have been undermined, partly because prospective donors would feel less of an obligation. So I don't do it that way."

You (or your volunteer leader or trainer) can help assure initial success by giving each volunteer some sure prospects to start with, if the volunteer doesn't have any of her own. You might even call up your friend, Mrs. Ames, say, and tell her that Susie Q. will be calling on her, selling raffle tickets, and ask her to buy some from Susie Q. But you shouldn't tell Susie Q., because that would undermine her confidence.

Have some doubts about prearrangements like this? Don't. True, it's manipulative, but it's benevolently manipulative, a phrase which could be used to describe the whole notion of fund raising. Besides, it leads to more successes, which is exactly what you need.

Your plan should also include some provision for keeping a fairly continuous check on how your volunteers are doing. For example, if the person responsible for selling ten raffle tickets a day is having trouble, you can't wait until the end of the sales period to find out about it. Work out a system for volunteers to report in every three or four days.

The early success principle, and the reporting system, are as important for volunteers soliciting large contributions as for someone selling $1.00 tickets. Sandie Fauriol, Resource Development Officer of Planned Parenthood of Metropolitan Washington (D.C.), tells, in *Fundraising Management Magazine,* this story about a volunteer in their recent capital campaign:

"One of our Board members, although terrified of asking someone for money, was determined that she would do her part to help.

"She attended a training session and left with five names of people she did not know but who were in her neighborhood. A week later, she called me to say she still didn't have enough courage to make the first phone call.

"I then wrote her a list of instructions, detailing step-by-step how to solicit her first prospect. A few days later, I received a very enthusiastic call from this Board member, telling me that the very first person she called, after having tea with her this afternoon, decided to pledge $15,000 to the Building Fund. Needless to say, it was smooth sailing for this solicitor from then on."

From time to time, you'll almost certainly find that some volunteers aren't meeting their goals. Fortunately, you're also likely to find out that some volunteers have more than met their quotas. But these two findings may be more complex than they look. For instance, the volunteer in trouble may have a prospect list full of grouches. Or the high-seller may have a list of very willing donors.

In any event, some action will be required now. You have three main choices: First, turn over some prospects or unsold tickets to the volunteer who's already met his or her goal; second, give the volunteer who's in trouble a "helper"; third, give the volunteer who can't meet his or her sales goal some other job, one within his or her capabilities.

But, a word of caution is in order here. Several words, in fact. Remember that you're dealing with people who are *giving* you—the cause, actually—their time and their energy, not to mention their money. Remember, too, that it's very easy to hurt the feelings of someone who doesn't have much confidence in the first place. Tread gently. Emphasize the positive. Find a better way if you must, but do it in a manner that retains your volunteer's good will and maintains his or her dignity.

Keep in mind that it's possible that your volunteer has the necessary skills, but simply doesn't know how to use them. Some personal instruction might help here. Or, if that's not feasible, you may be able to temporarily pair off a "weak" volunteer with a "strong" one, to give the less productive person the opportunity to see how it's done.

So much for planning. More details can be found in the campaign chapter.

Another major aspect of training is practice. Nothing contributes more to the confidence of a volunteer. If possible, have your volunteers practice their sales pitch on each other. It's the ideal way to decrease nervousness and to learn what to say when something unexpected happens. It also promotes group spirit.

If you can't manage group training sessions, you might try practicing with each volunteer on a personal basis. You act the part of the prospect. Let the volunteer try to convince you to give. This role playing will give you an opportunity to gently correct any flaws in the sales pitch and it will also help you assess your volunteers' salesmanship, information you can use when dividing up prospects.

And, if group and personal sessions are both impossible, there's still the telephone. It's better than no training at all.

In training your volunteers, you should have two main aims. The first is to give them the information they need and make sure they master it. The second is to show them that you're behind them all the way, that they can count on you to allow them to express their fears, and to give them the encouragement they need. If you do this, you're going to have a hard time failing.

One final note on training: Be sure to prepare your volunteer fund raisers for failure, for rejection. They're sure to have some, however successful they may be in the end. Remind them that, since history began, no cause has ever gotten a yes answer from everyone. And, more often than not, the person who says no is really saying something about him or herself, not about the volunteer fund raiser or about his or her cause.

REWARDS AND RECOGNITION

A lot of people think that "thank you" is what you say to your volunteers once the campaign or event is over and the money is in the bank. Thanks are certainly in order then. But you shouldn't wait that long.

Every working volunteer on your staff needs continual reassurance and recognition. How to do this? It depends on the size of your organization and on the size of your effort. One way involves one-to-one communication—the personal pat on the back. Another involves public compliments, during organizational meetings, for instance.

Some organizations give prizes to volunteers—an award for the most raffle tickets sold in a particular week, for example. The award could be a certificate of some sort, a blue ribbon, a first-place ribbon, even an ice cream sundae.

Recognition of this sort is essential, if you want to keep up your volunteers' morale and if you want them to keep putting forth their very best efforts, which happens to be exactly what you need, if you want your efforts to meet with success.

And, when the job is done, every volunteer should get a handwritten thank you note, at the minimum. The note should make specific mention of the job the volunteer did.

Of course, you may want to go farther than just a thank you note. You may want to take the occasion to celebrate—with a breakfast, a brunch, a lunch, or a dinner. Such events provide the perfect opportunity for public recognition.

Why so much attention to recognition? Well, that lies in the nature of the concept of volunteering. Volunteers don't get paid, not in money at least. But they do get paid—or at least they should get paid—in recognition for their efforts.

Even if the job has been difficult and time-consuming, the volunteer who is adequately thanked and recognized will be willing to do it again the next time. That may not seem so important right now, but it will be crucial when the subject of fund raising comes up again—as it almost certainly will.

CLOSE

Unless you're a one-woman band, volunteers are something you need plenty of. And you can have them, if . . .
  • You systematically identify potential volunteers;
  • You motivate them to join with you;

- Should you not get enough volunteers, you find out what's wrong—either inside your organization or in your plan—and make the necessary repairs;
- You match the tasks at hand to the talents and resources of the people you have available;
- You train them properly and give them the supervision and encouragement they need; and
- You reward them and recognize them, not only when the job is done, but while the campaign or event is underway.

So, you've chosen a leader. You've recruited a platoon of volunteers, or maybe a battalion. You're ready to go. Right? Not quite. You have yet another group of people to examine, a group easily as important as the first two.

That group is called your constituency.

6
CONSTITUENCY

WHEN a manufacturer brings out a new product, you can bet he or she has a market in mind. Everything about that product is designed to appeal to a particular market—including the product itself, its price, its package, the way it is publicized or advertised, and the manner in which it is sold. Market research is a very important part of product development and forms the basis for the sales approach.

Market research is also important in fund raising. The people who are going to buy your case are your market, your constituency. The more you know about your constituency, the better-directed your appeal for support will be.

"In fund raising, you've got to do your homework," says Ruth Logan of the Federation of Protestant Welfare Agencies. "You just don't go in like somebody with a tin cup and hope for coins to drop in. You have to have a sense of how much money you can get from your community, and you have to have a knowledge of the professional people, the corporate people, the working people, and if you're raising money for something local, you have to find out whether or not the people are willing to support it."

The first step, of course, is to identify the constituency. Just who are the people most likely to support you?

1. *Natural constituency.* These are the people whose goals seem to coincide with the goals of your organization and of your case because they have similar geographic, religious, political, professional, educational, intellectual, social, cultural, avocational, or economic ties. Keep checking the growth of your natural constituency. People move—and newcomers to the community may be good prospects.

People in your natural constituency stand to benefit from your case. These benefits may be tangible or they may not. They may take place now or in the future. But this group wants to see your program or project accomplished because it meshes with their own interests—emotional, intellectual, or philosophical. Your project may result in direct improvement in their own lives or in the lives of others close to them, or they may feel personally enriched by supporting it.

2. *Institutional constituency.* These are the people who are connected with your organization—your leaders, volunteers, your members. They are that segment of the natural constituency who is already involved. The institutional constituency also consists of people who have been connected with your organization in the past—past officers, board members, people who have retired from active affiliation. In fact, anyone who has given you support in the past—money, goods, or services.

3. *Incidental constituency.* This group includes friends, relatives, acquaintances, business associates, and anyone else who is connected to people in the institutional constituency and who may support the program because of that association. If these people are also part of the natural constituency, they are more likely to give "thoughtfully and proportionately" than if they are not. If not, they may give token support, if asked.

4. *Peripheral constituency.* These are people whose interests do not seem to mesh with your case. They're not against you, as far as you know, but are just not connected to what you are trying to accomplish. Sometimes very visible and active sup-

port and involvement from the natural constituency can serve as a stimulus to the peripheral constituency.

For example, when the natural constituency is low-income, maximum involvement and financial support from natural constituents can influence giving from a higher income peripheral constituency.

Linda Abromson, of the UJA, uses herself as an example. "Sometimes children visit my house selling candy for PTA— not children from my kids' school, but from a school in a lower-income area. These kids are driven here by their parents, who wait in the car. You can see that they really are doing their best and they deserve your support. So I buy from them, and I buy from my own, too. Now if these children were from a neighborhood like mine, I would not support their PTA, because they can get what they need right at home. But if you're from a depressed area, you need to go outside to do your fund raising."

Support for your case must begin within the institutional constituency. You've already begun to develop this support by involving the case committee, officers, and volunteers. Your case is well thought out by now, your leader chosen, a financial commitment in the higher range made by the "inner family."

And, everyone involved is feeling out the incidental constituency—letting friends and associates know of their involvement, getting some feedback, picking out those people who are also a part of the natural constituency.

The natural constituency is where you are going to find the wide range of support you need. This is where you should be concentrating most of your efforts: Who's in the natural constituency? What are the available financial resources? How can you refine the case to make it most attractive to them?

Sometimes it's easy to identify the natural constituency. Take the case of the tennis courts we mentioned earlier. This case has two natural constituencies, and they overlap. One is geographic and the other is recreational. Those people who are a part of both—who live in town and play tennis—will be the strongest supporters.

There are also people within the natural constituency who have only one interest. They include tennis players who live in outlying areas that do not have any closer tennis facilities, and nontennis players who live in the town but who would benefit if that overgrown, unattractive vacant lot became an attractive and well-maintained recreational facility.

Without the support of the strongest segment of the constituency, those on the fringes won't be moved. Therefore, the first people whose support must be enlisted are the tennis players and would-be tennis players who live in the area.

Again, list-making time. Who are the avid tennis players in town? Who are the tennis players in neighboring communities? Who is interested in improving the town? Write down names.

Real estate agents might find the tennis courts a good selling point for people thinking of moving into the town. Owners of sporting goods stores might benefit from a tennis boom in town. More names to write down.

Doctors who want their patients to be physically fit might welcome such a facility. Schools might be interested in getting a tennis team started. Keep writing.

Got skeptics? A financial commitment from the inner circle of the constituency may convince them, especially if their self-interest is involved.

If you don't know how your natural constituency feels, then find out. If the support isn't immediately visible, then you'll have to add some lead time to your fund-raising campaign, to create the support you need. But if the idea gets an enthusiastic response from the start, you can plunge in a bit faster.

Our tennis-playing friend made a mistake in assuming that all the tennis players in town felt as strongly as he did about having courts. Just because you have an easily identifiable natural constituency, doesn't mean you can be sure it will support your case automatically.

What if our tennis buff had consulted with the designer of the courts, not just for price, but for some drawings, too? What if he had taken some photographs of the vacant lot and juxtaposed them next to the tennis courts?

What if he had gone to the school board or the physical education director of the high school to ask for an indication of interest in forming a tennis team?

What if he'd gone to the town police for an authoritative opinion on how the tennis courts might decrease vandalism in the town?

What if he'd consulted with the court designer and town officials about the cost and type of maintenance that would be required and built the plan into the case to reassure everyone that the beautiful tennis courts would stay beautiful and operative?

What about the procedure that would be instituted to reserve court time? The people who want courts nearby need to be assured that they won't be hanging around waiting for a vacancy.

What about a chart showing how much time and money could be saved in a year by the average tennis player who now drives a long distance and pays to play tennis?

With a strong case on paper, our tennis buff could go to the most affluent member or the most influential member of the innermost natural constituency and say, "Here is a project we've been developing, and we'd like your opinion."

Involve this crucial part of the constituency and you're more than halfway there, not necessarily in dollars given but in the process of opening doors to the rest of the constituency.

If you want "thoughtful and proportionate" support, first give visible evidence that the project has had *your* careful thought. Then find out if others agree with you.

When Linda M. Meyer of Sloatsburg, New York, decided her community needed its own park, she planned her approach so carefully that it was difficult to refute her arguments.

"It was my dream to have a park close by . . . normally we

have to travel many miles to the nearest set of swings. There are also approximately fifty children of sand-pile-to-basketball age. I drew up plans for a mini-park, got my neighbors together, and 'attacked' our local government. I had worked everything out—costs, possible layout, sites, and even got a local artist to draw up a proposal in watercolor. Three months later, with the work of my family and neighbors, we had a safe place for our children to congregate and play. Now, to continue the growth of our mini-park, we have a committee that raises money for further expansion and enjoyment of the park."

FEASIBILITY STUDIES

Constituency identification is the beginning of a process that professional fund raisers call a feasibility study. This is an assessment you make of the most influential constituents— their financial ability to support you, their willingness, and their readiness.

Feasibility studies are most often done when institutions are looking for large amounts of dollars to invest in new buildings or equipment. But they can be just as useful for small organizations seeking more modest sums.

Direct your feasibility study to those people in your constituency who are most capable of giving or who have influence with the capable givers. You'll want their opinions about your organization and the particular case you've developed.

Ask them about their interest in your organization, their opinions about your board of directors and staff, their opinions about the need for your project, their feelings about the amount of money you have set as your goal. Give them the figures you've established for pace-setting and top-level gifts and ask if they will consider making a gift in these ranges. If not, ask if they will support you financially at all. Ask them who else they think should be involved in this campaign to help make it a success and ask them to identify potential high-level givers.

If you already know the answers to questions concerning these subjects, then you probably don't need to do a feasibility study. But, if you don't, you need this market research. It is an opportunity to test your case and to start involving high-level givers and other influential people.

The feasibility study also gives you a chance to evaluate the economic feeling in the constituency. Is the timing right? Do people have money now? How much do they have to spare?

Obviously, if much of your constituency is union-affiliated, you wouldn't get a giant fund raiser off the ground during a strike. If you include local labor leaders in your study, you can find out, for example, about upcoming contract negotiations that might make people in the community feel a bit uneasy about contributing—for the time being.

Your feasibility study not only can help you decide *when* to raise funds, but also can help you figure out how.

For example, if the money seems to be available from community and business leaders and professional people who are willing to give thoughtfully and proportionately, that's a signal to take the *direct approach*, that is, to ask for money face-to-face, by mail, or by phone.

If your case is not so popular as you'd like, or your constituency cannot afford to give the funds you need, then the signal may indicate taking an *indirect sales approach*, that is, sell something other than your case, like baked goods or a dinner-dance. Something in-between may signal a combination approach in which you sell part of the constituency directly, and sell the other part indirectly.

Your feasibility study will also give you some indication of what else you need to do if you expect to be able to raise funds. For example, if your organization has low visibility, or if people have misconceptions about what your organization does, and refuse to support you for these reasons, then you need to build some lead time into your campaign to show your constituents who you really are. After you have done this, you may be able to take a direct approach. If you don't have time to do this, then you can still use an indirect approach.

The point is that no really sensible decision can be made about *how* to raise the money you need—whether it's $1,000 or $100,000—until you have some accurate picture of what the constituency thinks about your organization, about the case, and about the available financial resources. And the best way to get that picture is to sound out the constituency's leaders, because if they give their support, it's reasonable to believe that others will support you, too.

"Wait a minute," you say. "I'm not raising half a million dollars to put a new wing on the hospital. I'm not conducting a campaign that's going to last two years with one hundred volunteers at my command. What I'm trying to do is get rid of those last few Dutch Elms in town and plant a few new trees to take their place. Does all of this apply to me, too?"

The answer is yes. The principles we've just discussed—for that matter, all of the principles in this book—are valid at every fund-raising level. But they must be scaled up—or down —in accordance with the magnitude of your effort.

Let's assume, however, that you're only after a modest sum. What then? Well, your case preparation may be less formal, but you should prepare one, even if it is only mimeographed on one page with a photo or drawing to illustrate the changes you propose.

You still need a leader or a couple of co-chairpeople to assume the overall responsibility and to get everyone else organized.

You still need volunteers to be involved, to carry out the plan, and to get other people to join in your effort.

And you still need to have some idea of who is going to buy your case.

You should still attempt to get financial contributions that are thoughtful and proportionate, because *any* good case is worth more than nickles and dimes from people who can afford a dollar. And if you are too busy to do a bake sale, a bazaar, or a house tour, you should know if you can get the money you need without selling something other than your case itself.

If you decide on an indirect approach, every principle for large-scale fund raising still holds. A good case, strong and influential leadership, involved and motivated volunteers can encourage bigger donations of free goods and services for your fund-raising affair, whatever it may be.

And you must also know your constituency, which may turn out for a square dance but not for a black-tie charity ball. You must know whether they will spend $2.00 or $5.00 or $10.00 for a ticket.

And, finally, you have to have a *campaign*—a plan that shows who does what and when they do it—if you expect your affair to be all it can be.

7
CAMPAIGN

BY NOW, you should have a pretty good idea of: (1) How to make a case for your cause; (2) How to recruit a leader or an event chairperson; (3) How to attract volunteers; and (4) How to gauge your constituency.

Now, we come to (5) the hard part. And what's that? The campaign itself.

Why is the campaign "the hard part"? Well, it's not the planning that's so hard, even carrying it out. Neither are easy, but both can be managed with hard work.

The reason we call the campaign the hard part is that it involves the single most difficult fund-raising decision you'll have to make, outside of the initial decision to raise funds at all.

That decision? *How* will you go about raising funds, that is, what method or combination of methods will you use?

"Choosing the right money-maker can seem as awesome a decision as choosing the right mate," says Ena C. Swayze, Director of Area and League Services for the Association of Junior Leagues, Inc.

But, in fund raising, there are just two basic alternatives:

1. Direct solicitation. That means asking for money di-

rectly, face-to-face, by letter, or by telephone—and selling nothing other than your cause itself.

2. Indirect solicitation. That means selling something other than your cause, but donating the proceeds to your cause. Some examples: bake sales, dinner-dances, car washes, raffles, theatre benefits.

If you want, you can use *both* alternatives. Many groups do. Unfortunately, that doesn't end your decision-making. You still have to figure out what type of direct solicitation is best— and the same goes for indirect solicitation.

It's a little like walking into a clothing store in which all the size labels have been removed. You have to try things on one at a time until you get a perfect fit. In the case of fund raising, you have to choose methods that fit the skills, interests, and capabilities of your organization, your leadership, your volunteers—and your constituency.

In this chapter, we'll describe some of the basic fund-raising methods that organizations are using today. Some of them fall into the direct solicitation category, some into the indirect solicitation category, some can be both.

We'll try to give you the whys and wherefores, so that you can start to narrow your choices. We'll also show you how to handle the elements that are common to all types of fund raising.

The important thing is not to let yourself feel negative about reaching your goal.

1. Annual Appeals. You've received dozens of annual appeals in the mail from organizations that rely on regular support to keep themselves and their programs going. Annual appeals are usually responsible for the bread and butter of an organization—the "hard" money. Of course they are not always done by direct mail. Organizations like the American Cancer Society conduct an annual Crusade, and this is done person-to-person.

The annual appeal is what fills the treasury of the organization, keeping it running and out of debt. It's like your annual income. You have to have it; you are counting on it; and very likely you are always trying to come up with ways to supplement or increase it.

For organizations with dues-paying members, annual appeals often take the form of membership drives—an appeal directed toward potential new members, as well as current member renewal.

An annual appeal is a good way to gain an ongoing constituency. Institutions like museums, symphonies, theatres, hospitals, Y.M.C.A.'s, social service agencies, churches, et cetera, all have annual fund drives.

How does your organization raise the money it needs year in and year out? Through dues? Do you have one annual fund-raising affair—maybe a rummage sale or bazaar—that pretty well covers your annual budget? Do you need more regular, ongoing support? If so, then perhaps your major effort should be towards getting that kind of support.

Annual appeals have one very big advantage. Those people who contribute, or who become members, are very likely to *keep* contributing. And they are a good source for larger amounts of money in the future. Incidentally, always keep records of who gives you money, and when, and how much. "Never, never collect money without getting the person's name and address," says Dale Ahearn, free-lance professional fund raiser. These records should be kept year after year, so you know whom to go back to and how much to ask for— usually more than last time. "Even if you think it's a one-time thing, keep a record," says Ahearn, "because you can't be sure that four years from now, there won't be something similar you want to raise money for."

Colleges and universities, for example, may find that a certain graduate started out giving $25 to the first appeal from the alumni fund—and that's what he or she is still giving ten years later. But if the graduate has risen in his or her field, $25 a year is no longer a proportionate gift. So, this graduate—and others who have achieved similar success—should be asked for more.

Well-kept records are valuable even if you're raising small

amounts. Let's say your organization is an animal shelter that finds homes for unwanted pets. Your main method of raising money has been to leave tin cans in stores around town. But it hasn't been a very efficient way to raise money and it's had the further drawback of not telling you who your contributors are. So, you're considering an annual appeal—but how should you go about it? Well, you could start by looking at those tin cans.

Which can draws the most money? If it's the supermarket can, try selling raffle tickets for a case of dog food or cat food. If it's a drug store can, try raffling off a good item like a vaporizer or an electric hair curler or dryer. The merchant will probably be willing to donate the item.

Then put one of your volunteers at the cash register, where you usually place your tin can. Have her sell raffle tickets. (Maybe the store owner will even be willing to sell them.) Now you'll get $1.00 contributions instead of loose change, and you'll also get *names*, which can be appealed to on an annual basis, in a much more efficient way.

Almost any kind of permanent organization can upgrade its entire fund raising by devising an annual appeal, or by improving its existing one.

An annual appeal plan might not be the answer you're looking for today—not if you need $750 to send three inner-city kids to camp for a week. But, remember, you should be taking a look at the overall financial health of your organization.

If you want to make your organization stronger, then you may not be able to limit your fund raising to two or three events that just help you squeak by. If you want to stay healthy and grow with the times, you'll need to build regular support that you can count on year after year.

The difficult thing about annual appeals is that it's hard to make the donors feel excited about giving year after year. This is why the annual appeal is a vital part of a good overall fundraising plan, but not necessarily the only way you should raise money.

However you receive your annual income, whether by membership dues, mail or personal requests for annual contributions, or by sponsoring one or more annual fund-raising affairs (rummage sales, gambling nights, house tours, card parties, et cetera), you should have available opportunities for givers at different giving levels.

Membership organizations, for example, may offer three or four different kinds of membership plans. There is usually a regular plan that is moderately priced, and then some kind of lower-priced membership, for students or junior members. There are also one or two membership plans that are more expensive than the regular plan—these may be called sustaining memberships or patron memberships or something similar.

2. *Capital Campaign.* Capital campaigns are what organizations do when they want to raise money for something other than their usual, ongoing necessities. Bigger institutions have them when they want new buildings, or when they need expensive new equipment, or furnishings, or other assets that require capital. These campaigns are for exciting projects. They capture the imagination and challenge the leadership, the volunteers, and the contributors.

Of course, you don't need to build a whole new building to have a capital-type campaign. Your goal can be getting some acquisition for your museum, or putting a symphony together, or buying uniforms for the team, or anything else that is bold and new and visible.

Any project or program you need additional money for, more than you can get from your annual, regular support, can be considered a capital program.

Here you have something to sell in addition to your organization's regular good works. You are doing something needed, something special, something above and beyond the usual, and it requires special contributions, larger than you normally receive from your annual supporters, and contributions from people who may not be regular supporters.

Do you have some kind of special project in mind, something your organization needs or something that may not be needed by your group itself but that should be done within the community and is in keeping with your organization's goals?

"Special projects are necessary for almost all kinds of groups," says Lynette Teich, president of Oram Group Events, a division of Oram Group, Inc., a fund raising consulting firm with offices in New York City and Washington, D.C. "A special project is a way for an organization to get money it couldn't otherwise get. For instance, if the PTA wants to start an experimental garden project for the school children, they can try to get it underwritten or sponsored by a bank or some other business, and they can put up a sign with the bank's name, so everyone knows the bank is the sponsor. Without this project, the bank wouldn't give money to the PTA—no one underwrites the PTA itself, but they will underwrite a project.

"This is just what happened with the police in New York City. The department wanted to buy bulletproof vests. No one would give money to the police department, but for this project, the bulletproof vests, everyone was very willing to donate. So a special project is really very good for fund raising."

Maybe you haven't been doing special projects because you already have trouble meeting your annual budget and you're afraid you can't get more money. Nonsense. A special project may be just what you need to breathe some new life into your fund raising.

So, look at your problems and the problems and needs of other charitable causes your organization regularly supports. Does the community theatre need new curtains, or new seats, or a decent ladies room? Does the museum have an opportunity to acquire a valuable painting? Does the swimming team need a van so the kids can get to distant meets? Does the hospital need handrails?

Any need that falls within your organization's purpose and policy can be considered as a special project. Instead of trying to scrimp from your annual budget to support it a little bit, why not take on the whole responsibility? This is a great way to get your members involved in something. If the project seems too big for your group to handle alone, why not ask another organization if it would like to join you.

The excitement of a capital campaign can be compared to the challenge of saving money for something specific that you really want, or when your son or daughter suddenly decides that new bike is really important enough to work for by getting a paper route or a regular baby-sitting job.

Of course, if you are saving for something special, the money must still come from the personal income, but you save much more vigorously with a specific goal in mind. And you might even take a temporary or part-time job to get you there faster.

Many professionals strongly believe that every organization needs an exciting and purposeful capital campaign every five years or so, not only to meet community needs, but also to keep up morale within the group.

Suppose that animal shelter we mentioned does make an attempt to discover the names of its contributors. Suppose it develops an annual campaign. Enough? The experts think not. They think something must be done to keep the donors excited about the shelter—and to raise their giving level. What? A capital campaign.

In a few years, then, the animal shelter might stage a special campaign to fund those new cages they need so desperately, or a free veterinary clinic, or free rabies shots for every animal in the community.

Professional consultants feel that capital campaigns should aim to raise about three times the amount of annual contributions. The experts have found that annual contributors to an organization or institution often keep their donations fairly low in relation to their giving ability, since they make the gift every year. So capital campaigns provide you with an opportunity to ask for a larger than average donation—because you won't be asking again soon. Also, the money contributed in capital campaigns produces visible benefits while annual appeals usually go to maintain something that already exists.

When the capital contributor goes to the theatre, he sits in the new chair. When he goes to the museum, he looks at the new painting. He can see the handrails in the hospital corridor or the new cages at the animal shelter. He can feel personal pride in having made a contribution.

Getting everyone excited about an annual contribution is more difficult. Sure, it helps keep the organization alive, but it's a lot more exciting to build the building than to pay for its upkeep, if you know what we mean.

Another advantage of capital campaigns is that they last only so long. This appeals to the leaders, who may feel bogged down by the repetitive nature of annual campaigns.

Even if a capital campaign lasts three years, the real work is done in the beginning. The latter years are mostly spent collecting pledges that have been made in the first year, and the project itself is usually begun with the funds collected in the first year. Extending a capital campaign over a three-year period is a good way to enable people to support you. Mr. Black may be capable of giving you only $45 now, but he could also give $45 the following year, and the year after that as well. You have a pledge card for Mr. Black, and the major part of your work—selling the case to Mr. Black—is all done. The second and third years you send him a polite reminder. The pledge cards and reminders, if you are going this route, are all designed when the original campaign is planned. So, after the first year, it is all record-keeping and mailing. And you have $90 more from Mr. Black than you would have had if your campaign were conducted during one year.

The pledge card should be filled out by the contributor. It has your message on it: "Yes, I want to improve the quality of life for children of our town by supporting the ABC organization."

The pledge card also contains spaces for the name and address of the contributor and a place for the amount of the pledge. If the pledge is to be paid over a period of time, that too should be on the card, together with the dates the payments will be due and the amounts.

A reminder can be mailed a week or so before the due date of any pledge payment. Or you may choose instead to send reminders only to those people who don't make a payment on time. The reminder can be a friendly note. "Your pledge to the ABC organization has helped build a new park in our town. Won't you please remember to send your (second) payment of (amount), which is (was) due on (date). Thank you for your support."

In a capital or special project campaign you'll probably want the *entire* constituency to be involved. That means making a plan to reach donors at all giving levels.

You might consider having a committee in charge of identifying and contacting each giving-level segment of the constituency, and chaired by a person who is making that level contribution, or a bit higher.

If an officer or board member or someone else in your institutional constituency gives a gift in the higher-giving range, then other similar gifts are likely to come from her or his social or professional peers. The same is true for the other giving ranges.

Let's say you've decided on the direct approach, that is, personal solicitation or mail solicitation based on the case itself—selling the *need*, not baked goods or house tours.

Solicit the higher gifts first, starting with your "inner family," jointly or individually. You may need (or expect) only one more gift in that range. When that gift is made, or when solicitation for that gift is well underway, the appeal to middle-range givers can begin.

If you have any special interest groups within your constituency—doctors or merchants or pharmacists or other charitable organizations—you can get one volunteer from each to head up special appeals to the other members of their groups.

For lower-level gifts, you might decide on a house-to-house

canvass. If constituents live far apart and this is not practical, a mail appeal might be more sensible. Or a general appeal through newspaper publicity might also work well. When Albert Karsch, of Farmington, Missouri, was campaign manager for the new Farmington Community Hospital, he established a "Dollar Brigade" publicity campaign, asking for one-dollar donations. This special appeal not only took the campaign out of a slump period, it stimulated larger givers *and* brought a big response from people on welfare and social security who could afford no more than $1.00.

Small gifts are *very* important. The $100 you get in $1.00 contributions from one hundred people are just as important as the $100 you get in a single contribution, especially if you're an organization that exists to benefit the whole community. The lower-level givers need to feel a sense of ownership in that organization, and if you don't ask them to contribute, they feel neglected. If you do ask, they respond eagerly and are genuinely glad to have the opportunity to give.

One of the ways to appeal to donors is to put together various packages in different price ranges, so they can see what their money is buying. People contributing to a hospital, for example, can "buy" the whole building, or one wing, or a bed, a television set, a picture for the wall, a wheelchair, or whatever else may be needed. In church campaigns, windows, pews, prayer books, et cetera, can be "sold." Plaques or certificates can also be issued in recognition of the gift.

One political campaign we know of needed financing to buy television time. Donors were given the opportunity to buy particular time slots, at prices ranging from $35 for a 6 A.M. slot on a sunrise classroom lecture series to more than $30,000 for a slot during a prime-time, top-rated show.

Want another example? In a northeastern city, a new civic center was built and fund raising was going on to finance the interior of the building. Individual seats were "sold" for $100 each, and a plaque engraved with the donor's name was put on each seat back: "This chair was contributed by Mrs. Jane

Doe." Your contribution also entitled you to attend the gala opening night of the center, when you could sit in your own seat.

If you are using the indirect approach, that is, selling something *other* than the case itself—you can still appeal separately to all giving levels.

How? Well, let's say you've decided to put on a theatrical show to raise the money. You can sell $5.00 tickets to everyone, invite high-level donors to come to a special pre-show dinner at $25 a ticket, and invite medium-level donors to a pre-show coffee and dessert for $15.

High- and middle-level donors should still be approached by volunteers working from prospect lists. You can also sell $5.00 tickets this way, as well as at the door or in advance at a publicized location.

3. *Deferred Giving.* Is yours a permanent organization, one with a definite future ahead of it—the YMCA, for example, or the Red Cross, or even a local group such as the Historical Society?

If so, professional fund raisers recommend that you develop some sort of deferred-giving plan to be used alone or in combination with annual appeals or capital campaigns.

Deferred giving is the technical term for what happens when someone leaves you money in his or her will—a bequest. Many times, bequests seem to happen all by themselves. But they can also be planned in advance.

You'll need professional help to set up a deferred-giving plan, since the whole idea is overflowing with legal, financial, and tax complications. But, if yours is a permanent organization, you should definitely investigate this fund-raising avenue. Begin with your organization's attorneys and accountants. If your organization does not have legal and financial advisors, start looking. You might begin with an attorney who specializes in estate planning or a tax attorney or with an accountant whose clients include other nonprofit organizations or institutions. You can check with your state university's school of law or school of business for names of professors there. The professors may or may not have private practices but, in either case, they can give you the names of reliable firms. You can also request names of attorneys from the local county Bar Association.

Creating a successful deferred-giving program depends a lot on educating your regular contributors. First, they need to know the benefits of making a will. Many people don't like to think about that. Second, they need to feel that the will is really protecting their heirs.

Protection for one's family and making charitable bequests are not mutually exclusive. They can go hand-in-hand in good estate planning. In fact, a charitable bequest can actually protect heirs from paying enormous taxes on an estate.

Deferred-giving plans actually help both the giver and the recipient. In fact, they can be a service to your regular contributors. Let attorneys, accountants, and investment brokers know about your program, since they're the people your constituents consult about such matters. It may not really seem like fund raising, since the benefits aren't immediate, but you shouldn't overlook this method of helping your organization grow and achieve financial stability.

The people most likely to leave you a bequest are your long-time contributors. But experience has shown that you can never be sure just which of your contributors will remember you in their will. So it's best to think of this program as a service to your donors, because that's what it really is.

Of course, you can't include bequests in your budget plans, since you can't be sure when and if they'll materialize. But, if you are concerned with the long-term, overall development of your organization, this type of fund raising should not be overlooked, especially if you already have a substantial number of regular donors.

4. *Special Gifts.* Professional fund raisers have discovered two giving patterns that you can make use of, even if you're a small organization.

First, they've found that some people who contribute to an organization on a regular basis may be financially able to contribute more, to make their regular contributions substantially larger than they currently are.

Second, they've also found that anyone who gives you $25 or more at one time is also a good candidate for substantially larger regular contributions.

A *special gifts program* is something your organization can use to identify and provide incentive to those members of your institutional constituency most able to give larger gifts. Even when it doesn't bring in money immediately, it's an investment in the future.

You don't have to be a huge institution to make a special gifts program work for you. "Too many small groups do not make this effort, just because they don't think they're important enough," says John J. Schwartz, of the American Association of Fundraising Counsel. "The truth of it is, with a little extra effort, this technique can work very well for them."

Schwartz advises holding a meeting of the people most involved in the organization, those who have a very firm commitment to it. The meeting's purpose: to identify those contributors who can give more. "You don't need anyone's bank statements or credit ratings," Schwartz says. "Just go over your list of donors and see which ones seem to be capable of bigger gifts. People pretty much recognize the financial position of others in their own social group."

Make a list of those contributors you think are more capable. Then select a small number of them, those whose interests most highly coincide with the goals of your organization. This is the group you should approach during the first year. There may only be five or ten people on the list, but that is enough for a start.

A personal appeal is usually the best way to attempt to get a larger contribution. If that seems inappropriate, or impossible, you might want to start off by finding a way to bring them into closer contact with the organization. If they live far away, you might begin with a special mailing, which is not a request for money but an informational mailing with photographs and human interest stories that let the people know what they are accomplishing with their support. Education is a prelude to larger-gift fund raising. "The people who give big dollars are the ones you've educated," says Linda Abromson of the UJA.

If this segment of the constituency is within easy geographic range—if they live or work in your community—try to figure out how to bring them to see you, to actually see what you are doing.

Are you a day-care center? Plan an open house of some kind, so that they can see your program in action and what kind of facilities have been made available to children because of their donations.

Are you a hospital auxiliary? How about a demonstration of those beds your group purchased last year or of the new scanner the hospital now owns?

Has your garden club been responsible for some new plantings or new trees in town? Perhaps a tea on the grounds would be in order.

Whatever kind of attention-getting or interest-sparking program you have in mind—a dinner, tour, lecture, concert, show, or something else that ties in with your group's purpose and the donor's interest—try to make sure that peers of your prospective donors, people who are involved in your organization, are included in the plans. In fact, it's a good idea to have them issue the invitation personally.

If you have prestigious board members or consultants or advisers who serve your organization, this is a chance for the prospective large donors to meet them.

It may also be a good idea to include those people who are the direct beneficiaries of your program. In one rehabilitative center for handicapped people, for example, which had begun a program to train patients to get around better in wheelchairs, some of the patients demonstrated the techniques they had learned. Others talked about how their lives had improved as a result of their new mobility.

You can also use the "visit me" approach with the *other* charitable organizations within the community that support yours. And don't just send out a flyer to all the organizations in town, announcing that you will have someone visit them if they'd like. Instead, invite the presidents or "ways and means" chairperson to visit you on some specific, special occasion.

You can also use this approach with the budget committees of your community, if you are supported by local tax dollars as well as private contributions.

All prospective larger donors who accept your invitation should be personally approached sometime afterward for an increased contribution. Those who respond with more money join a very select club—your special gift contributors. Needless to say, you should do everything you can to maintain communication with them. Don't overwhelm them with invitations and literature, of course, but make sure they receive some kind of annual report, at least, to keep them abreast of what's happening.

Next year, you can repeat this process by approaching another ten people or so who may be capable of upgrading their contributions.

Organizations that have a substantial number of givers in the special gifts category often plan special donor functions, which are really ways to solicit more gifts, give special recognition, honors, and thanks, and to promote a comradeship among the donors and between donors and the organization.

5. Memorial Gifts Program. Many organizations large and small have created plans whereby contributors can give gifts in someone else's name—memorial gifts, which are lasting tributes to a deceased loved one. This is a big selling point, and many a hospital wing or university classroom has been financed this way.

Your organization may not be able to handle contributions on that level, but there's no reason it can't make a memorial gift program available to contributors who would like to give smaller sums.

What is a memorial gifts program? It's an arrangement by which a donation is made to your organization in memory of a deceased person and your organization sends notice of the gift to the family.

Easy as it sounds, however, a memorial campaign must be designed and planned. You can't just take up a collection in someone's memory without a plan, or without great need. People won't give substantial amounts simply to honor someone, no matter who that someone is. They must know how the money is going to be used—and why.

According to Harold Seymour, author of *Designs for Fundraising*, if you want to have a memorial campaign, you should begin it as soon as possible after the person's death—and you should emphasize what the money is going to accomplish, rather than its tribute aspects.

Here's an example:

When the star of a high school basketball team in Minnesota was killed in an automobile accident, the boy's family, friends, and various civic organizations joined together to raise money in his name.

They created an "open fund," which was used in two ways. First, it was used to train and provide expenses for a local retarded person to participate in the Special Olympics. This was particularly appropriate, since the boy had been a volunteer physical education instructor at the local facility for retarded people.

Second, it was used to provide a college scholarship for a graduating senior in the boy's high school, also an appropriate use of the money.

The campaign committee was formed just a few days after the young man died. A single teacher headed up fund raising among all the town's teachers. The president of the city's largest business conducted a drive among business people. One of the pastors headed the drive for contributions from all the churches. Doctors raised money from other doctors, lawyers from other attorneys, and students from other students.

The boy's family did not want to ask for donations to the fund in lieu of flowers because they did not want the local florists' business to suffer. But the president of the garden club appealed to the florists to split their profits with the fund, and they did.

The campaign culminated with a benefit exhibition game, between the high school's girls' basketball team and the boys' basketball team. That game is now an annual event, with proceeds going to the fund.

Fannie Munlin, a professional fund raiser for CARE, is a volunteer fund raiser for the youth center connected with her neighborhood church. "The voice teacher who taught music at the center on a volunteer basis had died, and I wanted to establish a fund in his memory," Miss Munlin says. "I wanted the money to be used for music lessons. Many students wanted music lessons, and we just didn't have the money for them. We had arts and crafts, remedial reading, sewing, cooking, but no music other than the volunteer efforts from the voice teacher who died.

"The voice teacher was very well-known in the community, so I thought it would be fitting to have a memorial concert in his memory to establish the fund. I found local people in the church who had talent—this was not to be a professional show, although I was surprised at the number of professional and talented people who turned out.

"I began planning the concert in January, and it was held in April.

"We ended up with a fantastic show. Standing Room Only in the packed church."

6. Special Events. The fund-raising event has long been the mainstay of most local organizations for both annual and capital campaigns. Special fund-raising events—including bake sales, rummage sales, dances, house tours, fairs, and numerous other activities—can be a part of any other kind of campaign, or they can be conducted on their own.

Chances are you know a lot about this kind of fund raising, but we're willing to bet you're also looking for new ways to raise money, to capture the enthusiasm of the community, to raise your group's spirit, and to have fun.

Fund-raising events, in addition to raising money, bring your group into the public eye. "The UNICEF greeting card program and Halloween program weren't initially started to bring in a lot of cash, although they've done beautifully," says Lloyd Bailey, executive director of the U.S. Committee. "They were started because those were ways we could involve the American people in the work of UNICEF."

"With a special event, you try to sell the organization. You want to let people know what the organization is doing," says Fannie Munlin of CARE. "And you also want people to come away with the good feeling of having enjoyed themselves—and the feeling that they've done something for the charity."

If you're raising money for something you don't think you can sell directly, either because the constituency won't support the case by itself or because the constituency can't afford a donation without getting some needed product or entertainment in return, then the special fund-raising event is exactly what you need.

Fund-raising events also serve to stimulate the spirit of your members, to bring them together for a common cause, to get them involved and enthusiastic. Events also bring your case and your organization into the public eye. They allow that segment of the constituency that isn't able or likely to give you direct support to participate in the fund-raising process.

Professional fund raisers contend that fund-raising events— which take time, planning, and hard work to bring off—are not the most efficient way to raise money. But they do fulfill a variety of other needs, in addition to money, and therefore they're a very important aspect of fund raising.

In other words, all other things being equal, the best way to raise the most money is to ask for it. But all other things are rarely equal. You'll be reading a lot more about fund-raising events in part three of this book.

The principles of fund raising apply to special events as well as to all other types of fund raising. The major difference is in the case, which in special events is mostly the event itself rather than your cause, or organization.

But, in order to sell your fund-raising event or affair, you must do everything you'd do if you were selling your case directly.

You must set a monetary goal, have a budget, and do something that fills a need.

You must have a good leader who can organize the whole affair and who can influence other people to support it.

You must have volunteers to take over various areas of responsibility and do the work.

You must have a constituency—people who will want to attend whatever it is you are having, who are financially able to come, and who are available and ready to come.

And, you must have a campaign, or a plan, because successful events just don't happen.

There you have the six basic ways organizations raise money: (1) the annual appeal; (2) the capital campaign; (3) the deferred giving plan; (4) special gifts; (5) memorial gifts; and (6) special events. They can be used singly or in any imaginable combination.

In the following chapters, we'll give you more how-to-do-it details.

Different as these campaigns are, they share a number of common elements. And they're worth description, before we go into the specifics of direct and indirect solicitation.

1. Quotas. Every campaign needs quotas—many kinds of quotas, in fact, all making it clear who's responsible for how much. Sometimes, quotas are expressed in dollar amounts, sometimes in percents, sometimes in percentage increases over last year's figures.

How do you determine quotas for your campaign? Well, let's say that your constituency is geographic—you're raising money for a project that will benefit the whole town: refurbishing the community theatre. You need $8,000.

The first thing you might do is to divide up your constituency into reasonable segments—north, east, south, and west, for instance. Then you appoint a fund-raising leader for each side of town.

Next, you meet with your four fund-raising leaders to see who's responsible for what. You might be tempted to say that each should bring in $2,000, but that doesn't really make sense, since the east side is rich and the south side is poor. Working together, the five of you divide your goal in some reasonable manner.

Let's say that you decide that the east side must come up with $3,000, the south side $1,000, the north side $1,500, and the west side $2,500. What now? Now it's time for further refinements. Each fund-raising leader should divide up her particular quota among members of her team. And the division shouldn't necessarily be equal. It depends on circumstances—who'll be visiting whom, who's a member of what peer group, who's new at fund raising, and who's a seasoned veteran, et cetera.

What does all this accomplish? Several things: It gives you a way to keep track of how things are going, so you can make adjustments at any time; it lets you put your strength where it will do the most good; it makes each person responsible for a reasonable amount—not the total goal; it makes the task seem less formidable.

Speaking of quotas and goals, there's one question every beginning fund raiser asks. And this is as good a place to answer it as any. The question: "Should I try to raise exactly what I need or should I aim for a little bit more?"

The answer, according to most professionals: Announce a public goal that's a little bit larger than the amount you actually need—enough larger to be a real challenge, but not so large that it seems impossible.

What's their explanation? Well, they say, you should always

add something to the budget for contingencies. You'll have them, you can count on it. No matter how carefully you plan, it always costs more than you estimate.

And, in the rare event that you come out with more than you need, everyone will be delighted—and full of suggestions about spending this unexpected surplus.

Let's say your overall goal is $8,000. When you break down this total into, for example, four different quotas for the four sides of town, make sure you end up with a total goal of $9,000. That gives you a built-in cushion against inflation, or against an underestimate of what you can actually raise.

And, if you are successful, you can use that success to raise even more money. When you reach the $8,500 mark, for example, you can publicize that fact and put on a last push for more, by announcing, "Better than we'd dreamed of, and a good thing, too, because the costs have gone up since our original calculations, and now we need only $500 more."

If you don't earn more than $8,000, you can cheer about having reached the goal. Either way, a contingency cushion will protect you.

2. Deadlines. Deadlines can be associated with your money quotas, as well as with the time within which various jobs must be performed.

Let's say you attach your deadlines to a quota. Take the chairperson who must raise $3,000 from the east side. By what date does that money need to be raised? Or, if you are working on a pledge system, when do the pledges have to be in? How many people are you going to contact between now and then? Do you have a month? Then you will contact a certain number the first week, and more the second week, and so on. By what date do you need one-quarter of it committed? By what date do you want to have half of the money committed?

Having deadlines, and deadlines within deadlines, helps break up the job into manageable parts. Setting deadlines also gives you a system that you can use to see if the job is getting done. If it's not, then you can make adjustments.

If one section of town isn't going to reach its quota, then perhaps another section of town, which is doing well, can help. If another section is doing better, then its volunteers can come to the rescue if some other part is doing badly. People who are not doing their jobs can be replaced, and others who may need a helper can be assigned one.

Even if you've never raised funds before, you know about deadlines, and deadlines within deadlines, and you know you can make adjustments if you have a schedule to guide you.

Let's say you're having a dinner party. You may have a schedule worked out. You know when you are going shopping, and what things you can prepare a day ahead of time, and when to set the table. If you don't do any of the jobs on time, you can change the menu to something that requires less of your time, or you can ask someone to help you, or you can get up an hour earlier to make time. You know that if you have to prepare dinner for six people on an hour's notice, the job can seem overwhelming, but if you have two days, you can break it up into smaller tasks and accomplish it easily.

If you're planning to serve your dinner at 8 P.M., you know that you work backward from there to establish your interim deadlines. The same holds true with fund raising. Your deadline may be the day the money is due, or it may be 8 P.M. on the night of January 23, when the curtain goes up for your talent show, or when the auction doors open.

You begin by making a list of everything that needs to be done and who is going to do it. Then you put the list of tasks in order. Obviously, you cannot put the chicken in the oven until you have bought it. You cannot hold your auction unless you have a place and an auctioneer and goods to auction. You cannot have a raffle unless you have a prize, and tickets, people to sell them, and people to buy them.

You'll have to estimate the amount of time needed to accomplish everything. And this can be tricky even for an experienced fund raiser. "Underestimating the amount of work involved is the most common mistake a beginner makes," says

Linda Abromson of UJA. "And it's very common for people with lots of experience to do it, too. You almost never *overestimate* the amount of work.

"When you underestimate, one of two things happens. Either you do a sloppy job, or you do a good job, but you resent it. Really, you just have to resign yourself to the fact that you underestimated, and then decide you're going to do a good job anyway," Mrs. Abromson says.

"The best way I know to estimate is to get a mental picture of what you're about to tackle and think about everything that's involved, then double that estimate and hope that you'll be pleasantly surprised at the end."

Of course, many things will have to be worked on simultaneously. The campaign chairperson's job is to work out the overall schedule with the committee chairpersons' help. And, within the areas of separate responsibility, the committee chairpersons help work out committee members' specific time schedules.

What should you know about deadlines? Too much time means nothing gets done. Everyone procrastinates because there's no feeling of urgency. Too little time and the result is the same. Everyone feels so overwhelmed that they don't know where to start.

If you are working six months in advance, work out a monthly schedule, so you will know what is to be accomplished within each month. Number the months backward. If this is November, and your event is to be held in April, then November is Month 6. Then assign each task to a month.

Some tasks may go on for several months—soliciting goods for an auction, for example. Others must be done right away. Finding the place to hold the auction, getting the auctioneer and setting an exact date will be among the most crucial tasks.

If they are your tasks, then your personal calendar for Month 6 might look something like this. The first number is the month, and the second is the week in that month.

6.1. —List all possible places for auction to be held, in order of preference; list all auctioneers in area. Get addresses, phone numbers, and the name of the right person to contact in each place. List three dates in order of choice.

6.2 —Visit, telephone, or write to top half of list. Give people choice of dates. Keep records of responses.

6.3 —Visit, telephone, or write to bottom half of list. Follow up on all contacts made last week.

6.4 —Follow up on all contacts made last week and repeat follow ups not accomplished from week 2 contacts. Select place, auctioneer, and date from what is available, and inform auctioneer and owner of local meeting hall. (Or, if you're not empowered to make this decision yourself, bring your recommendations to a meeting of your group for vote.)

You can refine your weekly schedule further into days, so that you're not caught short. For instance, in 6.2, you may decide on three phone calls Monday, two visits Tuesday, etc.

3. *Meetings*. Meetings are very important. They not only allow for planning, but also are in themselves interim deadlines. Suppose you have to go to a meeting and give a progress report at the end of week 6.4. You may be able to stall until week 6.2, but, knowing you've got a meeting coming up will help get you moving and stop sitting around.

If you're working on a six-month schedule, you might want to plan monthly meetings for the first three months, twice-monthly meetings for the next two months, and weekly meetings for the last month.

Whatever length of time between now and your final deadline, set up a schedule of meetings and be sure that the agenda includes progress reports. Jobs that have been accomplished can be checked off, and others begun.

Those jobs that have not been accomplished in time can be

carried over. Problems can be discussed and resolved. Areas of responsibility may need to be re-delegated, or some other adjustment may need to be made.

Meetings are not only a way to check on progress. They are a useful device for getting something started or for handling emergencies. Every leader needs to know when and how to call a meeting, how to run a meeting, and how to make the best use of them.

Philip Sheridan, author of *Fundraising for the Small Organization*, offers these tips for holding a good meeting:

i. "Hold the meeting at the place where your group regularly meets." Sheridan advises that if you can't do this, at least *don't* have it at your own house, where your family might interfere.

ii. "When setting up a meeting, contact the members and give them a choice of dates. Then select the date when the most members can attend.

iii. "When setting up the meeting, explain fully what it is for.

iv. "Start on time and keep it short. Other people value their time, too.

v. "Adopt a positive attitude." According to Sheridan, "Your enthusiasm will carry the Calamity Janes along. . . . Just be sure when you are tackling a problem that *you* are thoroughly sold on the project as a whole."

4. Publicity. Every campaign, no matter what kind, needs publicity or promotion or both. We will discuss publicity and promotion at length later in the book.

But, for now, you should realize that publicity alone does not make a successful campaign. Without it, however, most campaigns will fail.

This job—crucial in all campaigns—is probably second in importance and responsibility only to the overall chairperson's job. The person in charge of publicity should be selected early. He or she should be involved in scheduling deadlines, because very often his or her ability to do the job will depend on someone else's meeting a deadline. If places, dates, guest speakers, et cetera, are not established, then no publicity can be released. If items to be auctioned are not solicited early, then no auction catalog can be written and printed in time.

But more about this later.

5. Designated assignments. Along with quotas and deadlines, each job in your campaign should be assigned to someone specific. No job should be left open in the dim hope that someone will spot it and start working on it.

You don't need a rigid superstructure, but rather a flexible framework—something to lessen confusion and encourage open communication. No one should be confused about what he or she is supposed to do, and everyone should know whom to get in touch with if there are problems so help can be provided. Having a framework also avoids duplication of effort.

It also works the other way. That is, everyone who wants to work on the campaign should be assigned to some job. There is nothing worse than a ready and willing volunteer with nothing to do.

6. Committees. Hopefully, you'll have enough volunteers to have committees, rather than just one person to work on each area of responsibility. The committee system is a good way to get more people involved, especially those who don't function well with the entire load on their shoulders. The overall chairperson often appoints various committee chairpersons, and may suggest potential committee members to them. Ideally chairpersons can choose their own committees. "I always draw from my friends whom I've helped," says CARE's Fannie Munlin.

The committee system is a good training ground for future leaders of your organization and is a fine way to get new people involved. Within the context of the organization as a whole, they may feel unimportant. As chairpersons, they may feel overwhelmed, unless they have a lot of previous experience. But, working on a committee will give them a chance to make friends and to put their skills and talents to good use.

7. Budgets. If you're involved in a voluntary organization, you may be dealing with at least three budgets. The first is the annual budget of the organization itself. Second is the budget you prepare for the case, that is, what it will cost to accomplish whatever it is you're trying to do. And third is the campaign budget, or how much you can spend in order to raise the funds you need.

Naturally, you want to keep all costs as low as possible. If your annual budget has a fund-raising allowance in it, then you will have some idea of the amount of money you can spend. If you have no money to spend on fund raising, then you will need a campaign plan that costs almost nothing.

Much has been said about the high cost of raising funds these days. People resent giving money to an organization that is not going to put the great bulk of every dollar directly into its program. If a donor thinks that you've spent half of his dollar to get that dollar in the first place, he'll probably be reluctant to give it to you. If he knows that ninety cents is going to the cause he's supporting, he'll be delighted.

Experts have varying opinions on what is a reasonable amount to spend raising funds. Some say that if your costs run under 10 percent of your goal, you're doing extremely well. Others think that anything under 25 percent is reasonable, while others feel that 50 percent is sometimes appropriate, especially if large amounts are being raised and could not otherwise be raised.

Whatever campaign you select, you should know that you must *add* your fund-raising *costs* to your goal. If you need $750 to send three inner-city children to summer camp, then you're going to have to raise *more* than $750. How much more depends on how much you must spend on your campaign. Let's say that your organization's financial situation allows you $60 for fund raising. Now you must increase your goal to $810. Otherwise, you'll end up with only $690, after costs, and that will not get the kids to camp.

Some kinds of campaigns are cheaper than others. Generally speaking, person-to-person solicitation is the cheapest way to raise money. But mail solicitation can be very costly, especially the first time around, when you may be mailing to an unproven list. Later on, if you're mailing to people who have responded to previous mailings, it can be a very cost-effective method.

Indirect fund-raising activities run the gamut. A simple bake sale or rummage sale need not be very expensive if all the goods for sale and the location are free. Really, all you need to buy is posterboard and magic markers, and chances are that your organization has these things lying around, can borrow them, or get them donated along with your merchandise for sale.

CARE's Fannie Munlin and two other volunteers raised a fast $400 (all profit) for the neighborhood youth center with an unusual bake sale. How did they manage a bake sale with just three people? Easy. The three volunteers were solicitors, not bakers. If you live in a densely-populated area, with plenty of retail shops, a similar idea might work well for you.

"We went to all the bakeries and grocery stores in our neighborhood (in New York City), which is about two miles square. We asked each bakery and each store to give us one cake—just one. So much for the merchandise. As for publicity, the children in the arts and crafts classes made flyers, and we asked the local merchants to put the flyers in their windows. Two weeks before the sale, we had announcements going on the radio. And we sent a press release to the neighborhood newspaper."

What if you don't have enough merchants to carry out this idea? Well, you could have lots of volunteers lined up to do the baking, or you could try collecting donations without any cakes at all. This is what one group did when it sponsored a "bakeless" bake sale. They figured that since the costs of ingredients had risen so much, and since people really had very little time to bake, it would be more efficient for members to donate what a cake would have cost to make, plus the bit of profit that would have been made on it at the sale. They raised nearly twice as much as the amount raised in the previous year's bake sale.

Some experienced fund raisers say they don't even do a budget for any event that has a goal of $500 or less. "Just do the work yourself and get everything donated," one woman suggested to us.

More elaborate fund raising affairs must have a budget. They can cost a great deal, when you consider food, liquor, hotel ballroom, ticket printing, table decorations, et cetera.

But there may be no comparison between what you can make on an inexpensive bake sale and what you can make on a more costly dinner-dance. If you have a high-money goal, you may need to spend money to make enough.

Of course, you'll want to spend as sensibly as possible for any kind of fund raising. But don't cheat yourself by being penny-wise and pound-foolish. Just try to stick as closely to your budget as humanly possible.

And when someone tells you that fund raising can't be done on a shoestring, remember that Hadassah puts *96 cents* of every dollar raised into its *program,* and not into *fund raising* or administrative costs.

Then there was the local hospital campaign managed by George Martens of Camden, Maine. The total amount of money raised exceeded $420,000. The total cost was about $7,000, including advertising, mailing, a case brochure, and one paid secretary to keep the records.

Keeping your costs low requires: (1) willingness to do a lot of the work yourself; (2) creative investigation of all possible resources; and (3) shopping around for the best possible deal.

It's also a good idea to resist premature counting of chickens. Unless you have a proven fund-raising event, it's unwise to incur debts in fund raising. If you do and your fund-raising efforts fail, you end up raising funds to pay your campaign bills instead of for your cause.

8. *Good timing.* While writing this book, we got a letter from a Mississippi school girl who sold candy for her local elementary school. She had an intuitive understanding of good timing. She told us that she took her candy to all the fire and police departments in town. "Of course, I went right at the first of the month, just after payday. If I'd waited till the middle of the month, everyone would have been broke."

The way this young fund raiser saw it, she didn't have much choice. With so much fund raising going on these days, you may not have much of a choice either.

Let's say you're involved in a major capital campaign to add a new wing to the local hospital. Well, you wouldn't campaign at the same time the local university is about to raise money for the new library, or when the Y is planning to get its building drive underway.

Face it. There's only so much money around for things like these, and there's no point in competing directly with another worthy cause. Nor is it wise to hit donors who've just emptied their pockets for someone else. You'll do much better if you wait.

Annual appeals are a bit more flexible. Usually they connect somehow with your own organization's fiscal year or your cash flow needs, or whatever works best for you. A regular annual appeal is something your regular contributors will expect. Some groups find that people tend to give more during the Christmas season, so they do annual appeals toward the end of the year. Others do them in December because it gives donors a chance for a tax deduction before the year ends. And still others don't ask at Christmas time because they figure that everyone has overspent for the holidays as it is.

Most organizations choose fall or spring for annual drives, or fall and spring if the appeal is semi-annual. Mail appeals are most often sent in April and August (before vacations and right after), so that people will be at home to receive the mail. But stay away from April 15. That's tax time.

The date you choose should depend on a careful analysis of the financial condition of your constituency, and on who or what else is clamoring for their money. Just remember that many a good case has died on the drawing boards because someone else asked first.

It's also important to time special events properly. There's not much point in holding your rummage sale two days after someone else's, unless, of course, your group has the reputation to trounce the competition. And your civic club shouldn't hold its dinner-dance on the same night as the Little League championship game, if members are also parents of Little Leaguers and will be involved in the team's victory celebrations.

School calendars, church calendars, civic group calendars, et cetera, should all be checked before you finalize the date of your fund-raising event, especially if you're depending on good attendance for success.

In this chapter on campaigns, we've given you an introduction to the six major types. But, let's run through them again, quickly:

1. Annual appeals. Ideal for bread-and-butter money or continuing obligations.
2. Capital campaigns. Terrific for special projects. Be sure to have one at least once in every five years.
3. Deferred giving programs. Great for permanent organizations—and a genuine service to members.
4. Special gifts programs. They're what you have when you need a lot of money and you know some people who might be able to give it to you.
5. Memorial gift programs. Emphasize the purpose, not the tribute.
6. Special events. There's nothing better if you want to raise money and build spirit within your organization, or bring it into public view, or if your constituents can't afford to give without receiving something in return.

We've also reviewed those things every campaign has in common—quotas, deadlines, meetings, publicity, designated assignments, committees, good timing—and a budget.

What's next? Now it's time to learn some specifics.

8
PUBLICITY

WHAT IS PUBLICITY?

Trying to raise funds without publicity is like trying to sail without wind. If people don't know you're trying to raise funds—or if they've never heard of your organization—you're operating under a tremendous handicap.

If you expect anyone to support you, then you must tell them who you are, what you have to offer, what you're doing, what you've done, what you hope to do in the future.

How do you tell them? With publicity. With stories in newspapers and magazines, with news broadcasts on radio and television, with posters and flyers, with newsletters distributed directly to potential donors, with "hard" news stories and with feature stories.

Publicity alone won't convince anyone to support a case he or she doesn't believe in. It is only a vehicle—a vehicle you can use to carry your story and your sales pitch to everyone within your community. Nonetheless, it is hard to overestimate its value.

Whatever the size of your organization—and regardless of the amount you want to raise—it's essential that one of your members master the basics of publicity and put them to work in a systematic campaign designed to achieve the maximum possible exposure.

Unfortunately, many organizations, especially the smaller ones, feel that a few news articles in the local paper during fund-raising time are all that's needed—and all they can expect to get. They don't realize the value of a year-round publicity campaign. And they also don't realize how hungry the media are for news and how ready they are to print items from nonprofit organizations.

Why does the media feel this way? Professional publicist Richard O'Brien, author of the book *Publicity: How To Get It*, explains it this way: "Publicity is the art of furnishing or even creating news. People don't charge you when you give them news. They're eager for it, and quite willing, at their own expense, to disseminate it."

The key word, then, for publicity is "news." Sometimes, what is news is quite obvious. When and where and why your rummage sale will be held is news. It's news when the chairperson for the sale is chosen. It's news when somebody gives you an unusual item for the sale. It's news if a local celebrity buys something at the sale. It's news if you have a pickup committee that drives from house to house to get goods for the sale. It's news if you provide a baby-sitting service while parents shop at the sale. It's news when your husband donates his old ski sweater and your son buys it back.

Almost anything that your organization does can be news. If your day-care center is beginning its third year in operation, then your anniversary celebration is news. If your hospital adds a doctor to its staff, that's news. If your local symphony is beginning its concert season with a guest artist, or with a piece of music never performed live in your town before, that's news.

If what you are doing seems old hat to you, then tie a ribbon on it and call it a new hat. To create news, keep its name in the public eye, and raise funds, the United Cerebral Palsy of Nassau County, Long Island, created "Today's

Woman" awards to be given to outstanding women in the New York area. Since awards were given to metropolitan area celebrities, the awards luncheons drew good crowds—paying constituents as well as the press.

The publicity chairperson's job is to find the news angle in what her organization is doing or to create one, if possible. Then she must find outlets or markets for the story—newspapers or radio or television stations willing to carry the news.

Many organizations make the mistake of seeking publicity only when fund-raising time comes. Of course, special efforts are in order then, but publicity should really be a year-round activity.

Why? Because continuing notice in the media raises public awareness of your group, because it shows that independent sources consider your group's activities newsworthy, because it gives your group credibility.

As a result of this publicity, your past contributors will take pride in having supported you and will be inclined to do it again. And, when you approach potential contributors, your job will be half done. The public will know who you are and what you do. They'll understand the importance of your work.

According to publicist Richard O'Brien, there are two basic forms of publicity:

1. *"For-the-moment" publicity*—what is going on right now, what is about to happen in the very near future, or what has just taken place. This is "hard" news. Some examples:

- The fund-raising drive is in full swing and three-quarters of the monetary goal was reached with the hundredth check received in the mail on June 30.
- The rummage sale will be held in the church on May 2.
- The committee met last night and John Dear was named as campaign chairperson.

"For-the-moment" publicity stories must be released by a certain date, or the news will be too old to be meaningful.

You can think of "for-the-moment" publicity as a news story. The most important things in it are who, what, where, when, why, and how.

2. *"Institutional" publicity*—features or background stories. Background or feature stories often appear in newspapers in conjunction with hard news stories. The *New York Times,* for example, will run a biographical feature on a person in the news, while the hard news story tells about the person's appointment to an important post and the circumstances surrounding the appointment.

Your "institutional" publicity may or may not be connected to "for-the-moment" stories as they appear throughout the year. But it's a good idea to try to find an "institutional" publicity connection with your "for-the-moment" fund-raising publicity.

Let's say that you release a "for-the-moment" story about the fact that you've reached 75 percent of your monetary goal with the receipt of the hundredth donation. How can you back this up with more publicity? Well, what does this milestone mean? Maybe your day-care center can now make a down payment on playground equipment that will be built by Jim Jungle, a local woodworker. If so, take the day-care center children on a trip to his workshop and have Jim Jungle help them hammer in the first nails. Let them play on the jungle gym that Jim built for his own kids and get a taste of what's coming to their day-care center playground.

Or, suppose the wedding dress of the great-grandmother of the chief of staff of the hospital is going to be sold at the rummage sale. That's an opportunity for a story on the great-grandmother. Maybe she was an important person in her day. If so, there's a story. Maybe she was a teacher with students who still remember her. That's a story, too. Maybe her wedding was an extraordinary town event and photos of her wearing the dress are in the family album. That could also be a story.

Back to John Dear, the campaign chairperson. Anything

about him that's of interest to the community? Is he a new-comer to town? Or a citizen with an outstanding record of community service? Is he raising funds for the animal shelter? Maybe his dog came from the shelter. Anything unusual or interesting about his pet? Maybe John lives in the town's first solar house. Or he has some particular field of interest about which he could be interviewed. Any one of these things could make a story. And any story on him should mention his current post as your campaign director.

"Institutional" publicity that isn't specifically concerned with immediate fund-raising efforts should let people know your organization exists, who it serves, and how.

Any civic, cultural, social, or health need or problem and its solution can be news, and you can often tie in with national attention being given to these problems. What connections can you make between the work of your organization and, for example, Education Week, Secretary's Week, Mental Health Week, Year of the Child, or whatever else is going on in the rest of the world? These happenings can provide you with a timely news peg for your own story.

Media publicity is crucial because it gives your organization credibility. But, it's not the only publicity outlet available to you. You can also create your own publicity, without newspapers or radio or television. You can put up posters in store windows or bank windows or restaurants or in other places where the public is likely to see them. You can create displays in stores or demonstrations which will bring attention to the work your organization does. You can put flyers on car windshields. You can organize a word-of-mouth campaign.

In addition to publicity aimed at the general public, there is also publicity for your organization's members, constituents, or potential contributors—newsletters, organizational literature, annual reports, fund-raising literature.

Pamphlets and brochures about your organization's work, or its history, or the services it offers can be included with fund-raising mailings, for example, to explain further what you're doing. You can also use this literature in membership drives.

One of the most valuable promotional tools you can use year-round is a newsletter that goes to members, donors, your constituency—whomever you want to keep informed of your activities. Some larger organizations have special newsletters or magazines for their special gifts donors and a different one for smaller contributors.

If your promotional literature can provide an actual service to your constituents, so much the better. The Eagle Valley Mini-Park Committee in Sloatsburg, New York, has a publication that does triple duty. First, it provides area residents with a directory of names and numbers of all people living in the area (including baby-sitters). Second, the directory carries advertising, so it raises money for the Committee to apply to the growth and development of the park. And, third, it keeps the name of the Committee in the public eye.

The annual report is another valuable fund-raising promotional tool. It needn't be a sixty-page volume on slick paper with dozens of photographs. A one-page letter to all your contributors at the end of the fiscal year is fine for a small group. It can be informal, informative, encouraging, and thankful for past support. When you begin your fund raising, your prospects will remember this little annual report.

Remember, any kind of fund raising is news, but publicity for your organization should *not* be limited to fund-raising publicity.

PUBLICITY VS PUBLIC RELATIONS VS PROMOTION

Many people think publicity and public relations and promotion are different names for the same thing. Actually, they're separate—but related.

Promotion is a certain kind of publicity. Some people call what we've termed "institutional" publicity "promotion," and leave the word "publicity" to apply only to "for-the-moment" publicity or news items.

But promotion may also refer to the literature that is produced and marketed by your organization itself, because its purpose is to promote your organization to members and constituents or to potential members and constituents, rather than to publicize the organization or some specific event it is sponsoring.

Public relations, on the other hand, is a function of your organization. Public relations activities may be planned to create productive, cooperative, and friendly relationships among the people in your organization and the community or constituency. These activities may result in publicity, but they also provide a service of some kind to someone else.

Public relations activities can help to create a good fund-raising climate or to expand your constituency, but they are not fund-raising activities per se.

For example, one hospital we know of has established a series of "Medical Awareness Seminars," on various health topics of interest to the community at large. They are free to the public.

Each month, at the hospital auditorium, doctors, nurses, technicians on the hospital staff, experts in their fields, participate. There are speeches, panel discussions, and an opportunity for the audience to ask questions. Light refreshments are served afterward and those who have participated in the seminar mingle informally with the audience.

Each month a different medical subject is discussed: hypertension, heart disease, allergies in children, et cetera. This is an opportunity for the public to become better informed about health problems they feel most concerned about.

The program provides a real service to the community, and it is also a public relations activity—in this case, one which also gets publicity. The program itself was conceived and is administered by the public relations director and his or her staff.

The publicity chairperson, who might or might not be the same person, takes these seminars and gives the "hard" news to the press, which carries a "for-the-moment" news story containing the date, place, topic, and speaker or panelists. He or she might also arrange for a picture of the speaker to appear in the paper, or for the speaker to be interviewed on a radio or television show a day or two before the seminar.

The chairperson might also place an "institutional" publicity piece on how the hospital is equipped to handle this particular medical problem, or how it successfully conducted a search for a specialist in the field to join the hospital staff, or how the series of seminars is contributing to a healthier population at large, or anything else that seems relevant.

The chairperson might also handle or supervise the distribution of posters announcing the series and giving all the pertinent information that the public needs to be able to attend.

When fund-raising time rolls around, people who have attended these seminars and who have benefitted from them will remember that this is one of the services, besides patient care, of course, that the hospital provides to the community.

The seminars are not held to raise funds for the hospital, but they do contribute to the fund-raising climate within the constituency.

WHO DOES WHAT?

Since publicity, promotion, and public relations are not the same, they might be handled by different people. Large institutions and organizations, especially, may have a director of public relations and a staff to handle public relations activities. Publicity and promotional literature may also originate from the public relations arm of the organization. Small organizations more than likely have one person doing everything, and, unfortunately, this is very often a person who has other administrative tasks as well.

Fund-raising projects require someone to handle publicity (get the news out) and someone to handle promotion (writing, designing, and producing case statements and other fund-raising literature). Of course, one person can do both jobs if need be. But, if there are two different people handling publicity and promotion, each should know what the other is doing.

The promotion chairperson, for example, can and should make use of any publicity that has been obtained. But the publicity chairperson should not give out information that is contrary to, or inconsistent with, information contained in the organization's promotional literature.

PUBLICITY CHAIRPERSON

It should be clear by now why publicity is important and why your organization needs someone to handle publicity on a year-round basis.

You can capitalize on nonfund-raising publicity during fund-raising time using your valuable contacts in the press or broadcasting media reminding the public of the role your organization plays in the community—and giving your organization the credibility it needs.

If a publicity program is not already an important part of your organizational structure, then fund-raising time is as good a time as any to begin one, since fund-raising activities are news.

What qualities should a publicity chairperson have? Well, there are eight key characteristics:

1. *Well-informed.* He or she must have thorough *knowledge and understanding* of the organization's policies, purpose, goals, programs, activities, and resources.

2. *Articulate.* The publicity chairperson must be able to *think and speak* clearly.

3. *Write clearly.* He or she must be capable of *selecting and organizing information* and putting it on paper. The publicity chairperson doesn't have to be a creative writing genius. But he or she must be able to grasp what is *most* newsworthy, *most* important, *most* interesting, or *most* unusual and report it straightforwardly.

4. *Meet deadlines.* The publicity chairperson has to know

when the newspapers and radio and television stations require information if they are to use it in time to be meaningful to the organization, and he or she has to set deadlines accordingly.

5. *Belief in and commitment to the organization.* The publicity chairperson has to enjoy talking about the organization. Selling it should come naturally because he or she is already sold.

6. *Persistence.* The publicity chairperson can't get discouraged with a no answer. He or she must feel that if one paper doesn't want the story, another will and that if one paper refuses to print this story, it will print another one, another time.

7. *Access to typewriter and telephone.* These are the publicity chairperson's tools. To get publicity in newspapers, or magazines, or on radio or television, your chairperson must have them.

8. *Ability to deal with other people.* Like fund raising itself, publicity is a person-to-person art. Your chairperson should like other people and enjoy being around them. He or she should treat them with respect and have some awareness of their situations and their needs. A chairperson should also have respect for what he or she is doing. A chairperson should realize that he or she has something of value to offer and shouldn't think he or she is trying to get something for nothing.

If you find a publicity chairperson with these qualities, you're halfway home. But only halfway. To get that valuable publicity so essential to your organization and its fund-raising efforts, your publicity chairperson must follow a few logical procedures:

HOW TO GET PUBLICITY

1. *Know what you want to publicize.* If your organization doesn't have any "for-the-moment" news, then what is going on that can serve as "institutional" publicity?

Take a look at your organization's constituency and beneficiaries, leaders and volunteers. What about them sparks *your*
interest? You can make a story out of almost anything. What
did your organization do six months or a year ago? Any kind of
progress report, or beneficial effects of programs instituted
previously can provide the basis for a story.

Is your organization offering some service that people in
the community need to know more about? What does your
organization need? Volunteers? How about a "day in the life"
story about one of your current volunteers?

2. Study the markets. Just as fund raising will be more successful if you analyze the constituency, publicity stands a better chance if you identify and analyze the markets. If you
know the requirements and needs of the media available to
you, there is a good likelihood that you'll be able to give them
news they'll want to use.

i. *Newspapers.* Study all the newspapers in your area, if
your news is primarily of local interest. Other papers around
your county and state are also possibilities if your news is
pertinent outside your community.

If you live in a major city, it may be more difficult to get
coverage in a major paper than in a neighborhood paper. If
your organization has not previously received publicity in major newspapers, then you can consider starting out small and
using coverage in neighborhood or weekly papers to get attention from the major daily papers.

Take a good look at all the newspapers and see what departments they have. Look for the names of the editors of the
various departments. On a small weekly paper, there may be
only one editor and a couple of staff writers. Daily papers—
which carry international, national, state, county, and local
news—will have many editors. See where your news seems to
fit best.

Of course, for events that your organization may be holding, either fund-raising or otherwise, don't forget the community calendar section of your own local newspaper and those
in surrounding areas as well.

Don't underestimate the power of publicity in your weekly hometown newspapers. A creative publicist can keep a case constantly before the public, with appeals designed specifically for local constituents.

This is exactly what Albert Karsch, campaign manager and publicity agent for the Farmington (Missouri) Community Hospital, did in 1967, when he started a drive for more than half-a-million-dollars to help finance the hospital, which recently celebrated its tenth birthday.

Part of the fund-raising campaign included the sale of debentures available for ten- or twenty-year terms. Series "A" debentures, for ten years, were available in multiples of $100 to $1,000 at an interest rate of 5¾ percent. Series "B" debentures for twenty years in multiples of $50 to $10,000 at an interest rate of 6¼ percent were also available.

"The success of the campaign was primarily a result of constant newspaper articles in area newspapers," says Karsch. "These articles were accompanied by pictures of the hospital site, information on its size, names of the doctors who would practice at the hospital, and reminders of how easily the hospital could be reached in case of emergency, day and night, and in spite of inclement weather or poor driving conditions.

"Newspaper releases gave the hours the fund-raising office was open, the amount of money raised each week from debenture sales, the names of families contributing memorials and making donations as well as the names of civic groups who aided in any way," Karsch says.

"All kinds of details and information were worked into free newspaper publicity to quote individuals and doctors stressing the importance of early debenture sales and donations."

According to Karsch one means to attract attention was to stress February 29, 1968, as "Leap Year Day": a day for those born on February 29 to participate in the campaign. The results included a $3,000 undesignated gift that allowed the hospital board to use it wherever it was most needed at the time.

"Scores of details were worked into the flow of newspaper releases," says Karsch. "For example, 'Each room will be thermostatically controlled, giving patients the comfort of air conditioning or heating at any time. Private rooms will have a full bath. Semi-private rooms will have a half bath.'

"We also used lots of news such as statements like, 'A rural route couple purchased a $100 debenture for their first grandchild and another couple bought a $100 debenture which will include the names of three grandchildren, all of whom were born this year and are still looking forward to their first birthday.' "

Ten years later, the hospital is still getting tremendous publicity. For the birthday celebration, the *Farmington Evening Press* published a special "Happy Birthday" issue, putting the hospital into the limelight once again.

ii. *Magazines.* Getting national magazine coverage is difficult, but not impossible—if your organization is doing something unique that is pertinent and interesting to everyone.

Again, unless your group has already had important local publicity, it's probably wiser to attack the local markets first. Community coverage is often the best lever for national coverage.

Magazines you might consider include women's magazines, city or state magazines, newspaper supplements, trade or professional journals, and others of this sort.

iii. *Radio and television.* Although radio and television are two different media and should be studied and approached in different ways, they are both broadcasting media and offer similar publicity opportunities as a public service.

Practically every local radio station has a community bulletin board that will give the particulars of coming events. But to limit your use of the broadcast media to this outlet is to underuse it.

According to the National Association of Broadcasters, there are six different kinds of public service exposures you can get on the air:

—*Spot.* These are brief (30–60 second) announcements that may go out over the air at various times. You may have noticed these yourself. They may seem like commercials, but they don't sell a particular product—and they are broadcast for nothing. At the end of a public service spot, you may see or hear the words, "This message brought to you as a public service."

—*Personality spots.* These are messages delivered over the air by personalities at the station, "such as disc jockeys, farm directors, or directors of women's features," according to the NAB.

—*News items.* A short statement of the who, when, where, what, and why of a newsworthy event which can be part of a regular news broadcast.

—*Editorials.* Opinions prepared and offered by the stations stating the station's official viewpoint about local projects or programs.

—*Special programs.* These can be one-shot features or a series of programs. People from your organization can participate in interviews or discussions on shows that are relevant to the work your organization does.

—*Segments of programs.* The NAB describes these as "similar but shorter presentations inserted as 'participating' features of other programs."

In order to figure out which programs may be of value, and how to make good use of them, the publicity chairperson needs to know what's on the air. If he or she can't listen to the radio or watch the television during the day, then ask members who are at home to volunteer. A report on local radio and television programming can be very valuable to a publicity chairperson searching for outlets.

iv. *Neighborhood outlets.* If your publicity chairperson is concentrating his or her efforts on the press and broadcast media, it's a good idea to have a committee to take care of things like posters in windows, signs or banners, displays or demonstrations. Even tee shirts can get the name of your organization or event out in public (and, of course, you can sell them to raise money).

You may think posters are effective only as "for-the-moment" publicity announcing a particular event, but they are also good for spreading the "institutional" message, letting the public know that you do exist and that you offer services that may be of value to them.

Day-care centers, alcohol and drug abuse treatment centers, libraries, college counseling services, and many other nonprofit organizations can benefit from having well-designed and intelligently placed posters throughout the community.

If there is an artist in your organization or in the community who will volunteer to design a poster for you, then the offer of a design, the unveiling, et cetera, are good for publicity. If there is no celebrity artist available to you, then the local art teacher, or a high school student might volunteer. You could even sponsor a contest for a poster design. Again, more publicity, as you announce the contest, the judges, choose the winner, present an award.

If you do posters, design them with a clear, simple layout and no extraneous information in the text. Your local library or high school art department has books on poster design if you need them.

Request space for your posters where the people you most want to reach are likely to see them. This will put people from your organization into contact with others in the community. Even if their requests for space are turned down, volunteers will have a chance to talk about their organization and find out how much business people know about it and what their impression is.

Window displays—bank windows are often good for these—also create a public awareness of your organization or an event that's coming up. And the displays can be of practically anything interesting. For instance, the Portsmouth (Ohio) Area Mothers Milk Bank Club put a dollhouse on display in a local store window and designed a raffle around it. Store employees alone sold seven hundred raffle tickets. Why was the store owner willing to go to such trouble? Because the dollhouse—and the raffle—brought people into his store. If you can think of a display that will do that, chances are you'll be able to find a store owner who'll cooperate.

Of course, you don't always need a store window for your display. The Farmington (Missouri) Community Hospital managed quite nicely with a vacant building. The owner allowed the hospital to use it as a campaign headquarters. The hospital then not only spruced up the inside, but also installed a hospital bed in the window, together with other hospital equipment. That way, potential donors could see exactly how their funds would be used.

You don't have to be an organization the size of a hospital to do something similar. Suppose you're holding a crafts fair to raise money. You can design a display consisting of sample merchandise and posters giving the particulars of the event. Quilts, if you have any, are great, not only for window displays but as temporary wall hangings. And you can put such a display in almost any store window in town.

Your display needn't be static, either. It can include a demonstration, if you like. You can even sell goods or services. At a street fair in Chapel Hill, North Carolina, for example, the Kidney Foundation offered haircuts at $10 each. Proceeds were used to buy a portable display unit to use to educate the public about kidney disease and organ donation.

Says development director Veryl Barry, "Eighteen of Chapel Hill's finest haircutters volunteered to cut hair onstage out in the open air. A volunteer band performed on a platform adjacent to the stage and helped bring crowds to the location." Profits at this street event totaled $400.

One women's club makes and raffles off a quilt every year. One year they held a quilting bee and demonstration in a mall lobby during lunch hour and sold more than one hundred booklets of six chances for $5.00 each. Hanging on the mall walls were the quilts that had been raffled off the five previous years (borrowed from their owners), and the work-in-progress at the demonstration was actually the quilt for this year's raffle.

3. Use your typewriter. Once you know what news you want to publicize and where you want to publicize it, your next step is to write it.

It may surprise you to know that almost all news announcements concerning nonprofit organizations that appear in papers and magazines, and almost all public service spots you hear on the radio or see on television are actually written by people from within the organization and *not* by staff people of the paper or the station.

If you'll recall, we said earlier that the typewriter and telephone are the publicity chairperson's tools. The typewriter should almost always be used first. (You will probably be using the telephone before you *mail* what you've written, but you should write it before making your call.)

Why? First of all, you have to speak intelligently to whomever you get on the phone. You've got to be able to describe what you want to send, to have any hope at all of getting your material to the right person. And the best way to be clear about what you're sending is to have it in front of you.

We'll talk more about telephone techniques later, but whatever the purpose of your call is, you'll do better if you've got something written in front of you while you're on the phone.

Secondly, once you say you're going to send something, you should send it the same day. Having it written and ready before you call prevents delays. Even if your phone call tells you that what you've got isn't right and needs some changes, you're better off if you start with something instead of nothing.

Now, what do you write with your typewriter? There are four different things, depending on what kind of news you want to publicize and where.

i. *Press releases.* These are really news stories (sometimes called news releases). Most newspaper editors will use them verbatim, if they use them at all. Some will edit them and make them shorter. A few might want more information for a longer story. They'll call you.

Richard O'Brien, a professional publicist, says that in writing a press release you simply follow the rules of basic composition, which you probably learned in high school. Releases need an opening, which tells everything of real importance; a middle, which gives a fuller picture; and a closing. O'Brien urges you to keep releases short—three paragraphs for most releases, no more.

If you remember your high school journalism, you may also recall that newspaper editors should be able to cut a news story paragraph by paragraph from the bottom up, so that if there is only room for the first paragraph, all the essential news is still there.

"The five W's of journalism are helpful to keep in mind when you're writing a release," says O'Brien. "They stand for 'Who,' 'What,' 'Where,' 'When,' and 'Why.' The latter is not always stated but is at least implied."

What, besides the body (three paragraphs), goes into a release?

First, your name, your address, and your *telephone number*—usually at the upper left.

Next, comes your release dateline, below and to the right of your name, address, and phone number. O'Brien says to put this in caps also, underline it, and use the word "please" at the end, which might make a hassled editor feel a bit more friendly.

Your release date merely tells when you want this news to be published. If you want it printed right away, your release line would say "FOR IMMEDIATE RELEASE, PLEASE." If you want the publication to hold the release until a certain date, because you don't want the news to get out too early for your needs, your release dateline would read, "FOR RELEASE ON OR AFTER JUNE 30, PLEASE." If you say something like "FOR RELEASE ON JUNE 30, PLEASE," you might miss getting it published, because the editor may not be able to use it on June 30, but could use it on July 1. So don't limit your release date to one specific day unless you really mean it.

Below your release dateline, also capitalized and underlined, is the headline of your news story. Again, brevity is the key. "A good headline succinctly states what the story that follows is about," says O'Brien.

"And I mean succinct. One line is the ideal, and any more than two or three lines is asking for trouble."

After the headline comes your body—the two or three paragraphs that tell the news in more detail. Always double-space the body of the press release. And make sure your typewriter ribbon is well-inked and that the type can be read easily. Leave plenty of margin space on both sides (editors can use this space for additions and corrections), and make sure the release is clean and neat, without typographical errors.

Sample Release

Hedda Gobbler
76 Park Street
Smithtown, Maine
207-555-1212

FOR IMMEDIATE RELEASE, PLEASE

Smithtown Historical Society Antique Auction To Be Held February 8 in Museum Annex

The Smithtown Historical Society will hold its first Antique Auction in the Museum Annex on Sunday, February 8, beginning at 10:30 A.M.

More than 200 authentic antiques, many of which are unique and valuable treasures uncovered in the attics of Smithtown's gracious Victorian mansions, can be previewed at the Annex prior to the Auction. Preview hours are Saturday, February 7, from 2-5 P.M., and Sunday morning, from 8-10:30 A.M. Admission to the Auction is free. An illustrated catalog of the items for auction will be available for $3.50.

Bill Barker, a professional auctioneer for the Brownstone Galleries, will conduct the Auction. Proceeds will go towards the Smithtown Harbor & Dockyard Restoration Project, which was initiated last year by the Society.

For more information contact Auction Chairman, Mrs. Elsie Jones, at 555-2323.

ii. *Letters.* If you're looking for publicity other than hard news coverage pertaining to a specific event, then you'll probably have to write a letter suggesting what you have in mind— a feature or background story about your organization or one of its leaders, an interview given by some member of the organization, or a guest appearance on a radio or television show.

The letter is not just an inquiry, but rather a sales tool. You may be able to make this sales pitch over the telephone first, but even so, you may need a follow-up letter. And, as we said earlier, your telephone pitch will sound better if you've got your information on paper in front of you. So, take the time to do a rough draft of the letter even if you're going to try to do your selling over the phone.

The most important thing about a letter—especially one that's being sent cold (without a prior phone pitch)—is that it gets read. A busy editor or person who books people for broadcast guest appearances gets a flood of mail every day. So, keep it short. Long letters are likely to end up at the bottom of the stack.

Writing a good sales letter takes a little more imagination than writing a press release. Again, if you know what you want to publicize and you have an angle, you're halfway there.

Like a news release, a letter should be about three paragraphs long, advises Richard O'Brien. The first paragraph is a teaser, designed to get attention and whet the appetite. The second paragraph answers the tease. The third tells what you've got in mind.

Suppose you want some more publicity on your upcoming auction. You think the chairperson, Mrs. Jones, would make a good guest on the local morning talk show, "Good Morning, Smithtown." You've found out that the person who books guests is Miss Booker F. Show, so you write to her.

Sample Letter

76 Park Street
Smithtown, Maine
555-1212
January 15, 1980

Miss Booker F. Show
Good Morning, Smithtown
WSMT
99 Little Lawn Drive
Smithtown, Maine

Dear Miss Show:

Who knows what secrets lie buried in Smithtown's Victorian attics? What hidden treasure was discovered in Grandma Watson's dust-covered hope chest? What was stashed in Parson Brown's yellowed, nineteenth-century Bible?

Elsie Jones, chairperson of the Smithtown Historical Society Auction Committee, has wangled an invitation to browse in the attic of each and every one of Smithtown's thirty-seven true Victorian homes in search of treasures and heirlooms that haven't seen the light of day for seventy-five years or more. Among her finds: Grandma Watson's silk, embroidered ivory wedding gown and a letter written to Parson Brown's granddad by the old rough rider himself, Teddy Roosevelt.

The Historical Society's auction will take place on February 8, and we would like to publicize the event. Mrs. Jones has unearthed more than two hundred valuable antique treasures and would be delighted to bring half a dozen or so of the most unusual pieces to share with "Good Morning, Smithtown." She's traced the history of many of the items and can talk about the families who owned them, and what the items were used for one hundred years ago. Mrs. Jones is an attractive, bright, and energetic woman, and I think she could provide you with an entertaining ten minutes.

Enclosed is some material on the auction and about Mrs. Jones. I'll call you in a few days, if I may.

Sincerely,

Hedda Gobbler

The closing paragraph of your letter will vary according to the situation. In this case, we mentioned additional material because it is appropriate to send it. The press release on your auction, a photograph of Mrs. Jones with one of the unusual items, and photocopies of articles that may have appeared in newspapers or magazines about Mrs. Jones or any of the auction items would be fine.

Now, what other letters might you write, in addition to the sales pitch? Let's say you've already spoken to Miss Show and she hasn't given you a "yes" or a "no" but wants you to put the information in a letter. Easy—you've already got the letter. All you need to do is add a line at the beginning saying, "I enjoyed our conversation earlier today. To review briefly, . . ." and then go straight to paragraph 2. You don't need the teaser.

If Miss Show has said, "Yes, send me some materials," then you simply write her a note saying, again, that you enjoyed speaking with her earlier and here's the information on Elsie Jones and the auction, as she requested. No, you haven't wasted time writing the letter you're not going to send. Taking the time to think it out before hand helped you sell Miss Show.

If Miss Show books Elsie Jones, then you'll also have to send a letter to Elsie, and you should do this even if you give her the information by phone or in person. The letter should tell her what day and time to show up, where to go, whom to ask for, what to wear.

iii. *Photo captions*. Whenever you submit a photograph,

whether it goes with a release or a letter or just on its own, there must be a caption. The caption should be typed on a clean sheet of paper and attached with scotch tape or rubber cement to the back of the photograph. Or, the photo should be attached at the top of the page the caption is typed on, with the caption itself hanging below the photograph. You can then fold the lower part of the page up over the bottom of the photograph.

Photographs, ideally, should be 8 x 10-inch glossy prints, black and white, for newspapers. In the above examples, you might have a picture of Elsie and three or four of the items, with a caption that reads, "Elsie Jones, Chairman of the Smithtown Historical Society Auction, with some of her prize items: Grandma Watson's wedding dress, a letter written in the hand of Teddy Roosevelt, an 18-carat gold chain."

If possible, always send a photo, especially with news releases. Newspapers will very often use a photo even if they don't have space for anything else. The information in your headline can be slipped into the photo caption, so that the essence of your news can be told without an article. If you don't have a really good volunteer photographer, think about paying one to get decent publicity shots. It may be worth the expense.

iv. *Public service announcements.* Broadcasters, like newspaper editors, are most likely to use material that requires little preparation time and effort on their part.

You should send news releases concerning events to radio and television stations' news departments. But if you want to promote your town's or state's Library Week, or Little League Week, or Adopt-A-Pet Week, et cetera, then a public service spot is a good way to do it. Television spots, of course, require pictures as well as words. But a single photograph or slide often will be enough for a brief spot.

When you write a spot, you are providing copy for the announcer to read. Radio spots should strive to give the listener a visual image so that he can form a picture in his mind.

If you're writing copy for a television spot, your copy must fit your visual aids—one or more photos, slides, or videotape or film (should you have the facilities, skills, and resources for such things available to you). NAB says that slides are preferable to photos, and photos, if used, should have a matte or dull finish (the opposite of what newspapers require).

Copy must be timed, and television announcements are read more slowly than radio announcements, which means fewer words. According to the NAB, standard spot announcement times are ten seconds (approximately 25 words for radio, 20 for television); twenty seconds (50 words for radio, 40 for television); and sixty seconds (150 words for radio, 125 for television).

The NAB advises submitting several copies of your material (all clearly typed). Also, don't use onion skin for copy to be read on the air. It rattles. Public service announcements must also have your name, address, and telephone number, and the dates during which announcements can be carried on the air.

If you want to know more about using the broadcast media for publicity for your organization, send for the free booklet, *If You Want Air Time,* listed in the Appendix.

4. Use your telephone. Many people seem to freeze on the phone, especially if the person on the other end seems busy, or curt, or just downright unfriendly. But, if you're doing publicity with any regularity, and you're constantly looking for new outlets, you're bound to come across a cold fish at least once in your life.

Most newspaper editors, magazine editors, radio and television programmers are not unfriendly grouches, but they are all working against deadlines and their telephone lines, like their mail boxes, are always occupied. Some of them don't even like to take phone calls, and you may not know it until they're telling you, and not very nicely, that this is the case.

We're not telling you this to frighten you. Most of the time, something like this will *not* happen. But it should relieve you to know that even experienced professional publicists have had similar things happen to them.

Even a receptive editor will not be long on patience if you don't know what you're talking about. So you should know what it is you want to say. No beating around the bush. If your mind goes blank, you've got your release or your letter right in front of you to jog your memory.

Never underestimate the importance or the position of the person who answers the phone. Sometimes it will be Mr. or Mrs. Big. More often, it will be the secretary. And secretaries often have a great deal of influence with their bosses. If you show them respect, they can be tremendously helpful.

But talking to the right person—the person who actually has the power to decide "yes"—is important. (*Anyone* can tell you no.) In some cases, the "right person" doesn't take phone calls. Or you leave messages, but he doesn't return your call.

When this happens, keep trying–and send the letter you should have already written.

You should also use the telephone to follow up on a release or letter you've sent. If you send a release and it isn't printed, you might want to find out why. Maybe, in spite of your efforts to find out whom to send it to, it landed in the wrong place. Or, maybe it was simply misplaced and you'll need to send another one. Or maybe the angle wasn't quite right and you need to revise it.

If you've sent a sales letter cold (no previous telephone conversations with the recipient), then you'll also have to follow it up with a phone call. Never assume that there is no interest in your story just because the person doesn't call you back. Make a note on your calendar about four days after you mail a letter (sooner if your deadline for getting your story published is pressing) to call the person if he doesn't call you by then.

For everything you need to know about publicity, see our Appendix, which tells you where to order *Publicity: How to Get It,* by Richard O'Brien.

To sum it all up, briefly:

Whatever the size of your organization, however large or small your fund-raising goal, publicity is vital to your success.

And you should not only publicize your event or campaign, you should maintain an on-going, year-round publicity effort. The two work hand in hand.

You can use "for-the-moment" publicity to make sure the public knows about your fund-raising activities. And you can use "institutional" publicity to keep your organization in the public eye whether or not you're raising funds.

To get publicity, you must find something newsworthy about your organization or its activities—or you must create news.

You can place this news in newspapers and magazines of every description. Or you can see that it is broadcast on radio or television. Or you can create your own media—posters, newsletters, flyers, and the like—and distribute it yourself.

To reach the public media, your main tools are press releases, letters, photographs, and the telephone.

But you need not use the public media. You can also send promotional literature to your donors, members, or constituents, directly.

Your publicity chairperson—the person who handles all of this—must be well-informed, able to write and speak clearly, and deal well with people, since in many ways he or she is the chief spokesperson and salesperson for your organization, its leaders, and its programs.

What we've said here about publicity applies both to indirect solicitation—sales and other events in which donors get something in addition to the satisfaction of contributing—and to direct solicitation, in which donors give cash to the cause directly.

But, now it's time to take a look at these two major types of fund raising, to help you choose between them—and to show you what to do once you've made your choice.

$

$

$

PART THREE

*Indirect
Solicitation*

9
INDIRECT FUND RAISING

THERE are two main types of fund raising: indirect solicitation and direct solicitation. We've mentioned them before, but, as the saying goes, once is not enough. Let's do some defining:

Indirect solicitation (or indirect fund raising): That's when you *don't* go to your potential donor and say, "We need money to send a disadvantaged child to camp." Instead, you say, "How would you like to buy a ticket to a dinner-dance." Then you use the proceeds to send the disadvantaged kids to camp.

Indirect solicitation is when you sell something—anything —other than your cause: cookies, car washes, raffle tickets, rummage, social events, dinners, shows, "a-thons," auctions, parties, house tours, services, publications, tournaments.

Direct solicitation is—well, the opposite. It's when you ask for money directly, selling nothing other than your cause. Direct solicitation (or fund raising) can be done face-to-face, by telephone, or by letter.

According to professionals, indirect solicitation is distinguished from direct solicitation by the fact that it involves a "give-back"—something in return for the money in addition to the satisfaction of giving.

In indirect fund raising, give-backs become an important part of the case. In fact, in many instances, they're a substitute case. Give-backs are a marketing device, to stimulate interest, draw a response, and build a lasting connection between the donor and the organization that is satisfying to both.

This chapter and the two that follow it are devoted to indirect solicitation, probably the most popular of the two types, at least among small- and medium-sized groups. We intend to give you an idea of its advantages and disadvantages, when to use it (and when not to), how to compute its cost efficiency, how to combine it with direct fund raising, and what its basic aspects are.

Let's start with the advantages and disadvantages.

THE ADVANTAGES OF INDIRECT FUND RAISING

In its *Special Events Chairman's Handbook*, the American Cancer Society—which uses both direct solicitation and special events for fund raising—says that indirect fund raising has these advantages:

1. Versatility. Events can be large or small, fancy or simple, geared to different interests or age groups.

2. Broad reach. Can involve people who usually don't respond to direct approaches. Involves both those who promote the event and those who participate.

3. New sources of funds. Introduces new people to your organization and increases the likelihood that they will respond to a direct approach in the future.

4. Education. Assembles captive audiences and puts them in a receptive frame of mind.

5. Long-range benefits. Focuses attention on the work of the organization. In the case of the American Cancer Society, special events encourage people involved in the event to become regularly active volunteers.

6. Newsworthy. Publicized events keep people informed about the organization's activities (and in the case of the American Cancer Society, about cancer control in general).

THE DISADVANTAGES OF INDIRECT FUND RAISING

Unfortunately, indirect fund raising has some disadvantages, too. The most serious of these is inefficiency. Most professional fund raisers believe that it usually costs more to raise money via indirect fund raising than via direct fund raising—more money, or more volunteer hours, or both.

In fact, in some circumstances, indirect fund raising can cost so much in expenses and in volunteer time that you wind up in the red. And those are circumstances worth avoiding.

How can you tell if you're headed toward that kind of disaster? There's only one way: to analyze the event you're planning—and well before you're committed to it. This analysis can be broken down into two parts: the "costs" of the volunteer services and the monetary costs of the event itself.

"Hold on a moment," you say. "The 'costs' of volunteer services? They're free, aren't they? Isn't that what volunteer means?"

Well, yes. Volunteers do give their time freely. In a way, it's one way of contributing to the cause. But if you plan an event that squanders this gift, you're being just as irresponsible as if you were squandering cash donations.

The Chicago Chapter of NOW, concerned with exactly this issue, has come up with a formula to determine if planned fund-raising events are cost-efficient, from the standpoint of the amount of volunteer time expended. Their formula:

1. Estimate the amount of money you can reasonably expect to raise with your event;
2. Estimate the number of person-hours it will take to carry it off, from planning to wrap-up;
3. Divide the money goal by the person-hours;

4. Take a look at the figure you come up with. How does it compare with the minimum wage? How does it compare with the hourly wage of people who are paid to do the kind of work your volunteers are doing for nothing?

Of course, there's one thing we've left out of this formula: the side benefits of fund-raising events, such as public relations, membership recruitment, or leadership development. These side benefits should be factored in. Try not to over or underestimate their worth. But add it in and check the hourly "wage" again.

Now comes the question: Will your event make enough money to "pay" for your volunteers' time? Or will they be working for a pittance?

If you're aware that your time—and that of your volunteers—is valuable, you'll be less inclined to take on projects that "earn" little money.You'll also tend to make your money goals more reasonable—which, in many cases, means aiming higher.

All too often, fund raisers don't aim high enough. Why? Because they tend to think that the time they and their volunteers put in—being without cost—is without value. But it isn't so. Or shouldn't be.

All right. That's part one of the analysis—time-efficiency. What's the second part? An analysis of cost-efficiency. Since your costs must be deducted from the total amount you raise, you can end up in the hole if you don't figure them out first and add them to your money goal.

COMPUTING COST EFFICIENCY

Joan Flanagan, author of the *Grass Roots Fundraising Book*, has devised a formula for estimating cost efficiency. First, she says, make a list of everything you'll have to buy or rent—tickets, invitations, posters, programs, postage, insurance, advertising, band, speakers, sound system, rental hall, chairs or other equipment or supplies, food, drinks, paper goods, punch bowl, extension cords, bags, Scotch tape, receipt books, pencils—everything you can't borrow or get free. Then get the *current* price of everything and total it all up.

Now, take your money goal—the specific dollar amount you need to raise—and add your costs to it. If you need to raise $350 and you estimate costs at $50, then you really need to raise $400. The total you must raise is called your gross figure, and the profit you'll have left over after costs is called the net figure.

To find your percentage of profit, divide the net by the gross amount. In this case, that would be $350 divided by $400, or 87.5 percent profit.

Some people feel that any profit of 50 percent or more is okay, especially when the amounts involved are large. But more and more professional and amateur fund raisers (as well as the government) are frowning on such high fund-raising costs. Many say that fund-raising costs exceeding 25 percent are unreasonably high.

Groups with state or national affiliations with parent organizations often have guidelines set by the parent organization.

Some states also have regulations as to the percentage of allowable fund-raising costs. Your organization's attorney or accountant can advise you.

Despite the costs and high number of person-hours involved in indirect fund raising, nearly every organization and institution finds this the method of choice at one time or another.

Think of direct solicitation as the straight line between two points—the fastest, easiest, and least expensive way to get from here to there, if nothing's in your way.

But, what if something is in your way? If there are obstacles, then there are also reasons for turning to the less direct route. Here are some examples of such barriers or circumstances:

WHEN TO USE INDIRECT FUND RAISING

1. When your case can't be sold directly. If it's not popular enough, or substantial enough, to attract donations without a give-back, or when the number of people directly concerned are too few to contribute all that's needed, then you have no choice but to sell something else.

Of course, we're not encouraging you to raise money for cases that benefit no one but you or your members, or to fool people into giving money to someone they don't want to support, for something they really don't want to buy.

Remember, a good case serves a need beyond the organization itself. And the more people who can relate to the need, the more likely you can raise money directly. There are certainly times, though, when you need money from outside the organization, when your own membership has dug into the pocketbook beyond the call of duty. And there are times when your case may not meet with the prevailing mood of the community, and people who will not contribute outright will buy a needed product or other give-back.

"Sometimes an organization that needs to raise money can provide a real service to outsiders who won't normally give," says Linda Abromson of Portland, Maine. "Once I was having a big meeting at my house, with one hundred people coming, and the Greek Orthodox Church was having a bake sale.

"I saw the sign, so I went. Now, I don't normally buy at bake sales, but I knew some of the women involved and I knew the stuff would be good. They performed a mammoth service. Now, I'm not going to be a contributor to that church ordinarily, but in this case, they made a contribution to me and I made one to them."

2. When you want to involve low-range givers and you're not going to campaign door-to-door. Up to this point, we've talked a lot about raising most of your money from a small number of people, of soliciting large gifts that will speed your

fund raising and give more assurance of reaching your financial goal.

However, in almost every significant case, it is very important to involve lower-level givers in some way, to give them a sense of participation. This is especially true if your case serves the whole community. *Everyone* should feel a personal connection with it. The low-range givers need an opportunity to give. Their gifts are very important (and you should be aware of that, and communicate that awareness to them), even though, collectively, they don't always amount to as much as the large gifts.

3. When the constituency can't afford to give substantial gifts directly, but can afford to give if they are getting a needed product or entertainment in return. In low-income communities, people will put aside money for food, clothing, and entertainment, but they'd enjoy being able to get what they want *and* support a good cause at the same time.

4. When a community's philanthropic giving is centered elsewhere. If people in your town are more likely to support a national charity than a cause closer to home, or if their long-time allegiance is to some other organization, you'll have trouble switching them. You might begin a long-range promotion program to create more awareness of what your organization does, but meanwhile you can raise funds with give-backs.

5. When your organization has too low a profile and needs to get into the limelight. If low visibility is your problem, an event that will result in publicity and public awareness of your good works is important, and it can open up the way to direct fund raising the next time around.

6. When your members or volunteers don't have much social interaction, when they need to become better acquainted, or when you need speedy new-member involvement. A fund-raising event brings people together and helps them feel good about themselves, the organization, and others in it. Events also can be good pick-me-ups for the apathy that nearly every organization suffers from time to time.

7. When you've got too many volunteers or members who aren't busy or involved enough. Usually nonprofit organizations have too few people and too much work. But, if you find yourself in the opposite situation, don't just sit there. Get your people involved in an exciting fund raiser before they go looking for excitement elsewhere.

8. When no one in the inner family is willing to solicit funds directly. "One of the purposes of board members is to help raise money," says Linda Lese, a partner in Project Specialists, Inc., a New York City fund-raising consulting firm. "But they don't have to go out and ask for it. They can create and push an event to raise money."

9. When you're doing another kind of campaign, and you need to capture attention and build constituency enthusiasm with a splashy kick-off.

10. When a long, direct campaign is sagging in the middle and needs a pick-me-up.

11. When you've fallen short of your money goal in a direct campaign and need something with extra "oomph" to put you over the top.

COMBINING INDIRECT FUND RAISING WITH DIRECT FUND RAISING

Most of you are probably telling yourselves that, whatever the assets and liabilities, you're more comfortable with the notion of indirect fund raising than with that of direct fund raising. You've probably had more experience with it. You probably like the idea of not having to ask for cash directly.

But . . . as you shall see later in this book, direct fund raising has some undeniable advantages. It's a tool that every organization should master. And the ideal time to start is when you're launching an *indirect* fund-raising event.

For example, if you're planning a raffle or a party with a door prize, don't purchase the prize. Solicit it directly from a local merchant. Remember—you have something to offer in return: good publicity, in the form of a newspaper article or in your program itself, or on posters.

If you're already soliciting small door prizes or raffle items, you might try for something larger—a color television set, maybe even a car. Whatever you can do to hone your ability to solicit directly will stand you in good stead in your fund-raising activities.

Eventually, you might think of combining an indirect fund-raising event with direct solicitation. There's no reason why you have to keep them separate. And the combination could help you raise more money and accomplish bigger things than you ever dreamed possible.

How can you combine indirect and direct fund-raising techniques? Well, here's an example—the best one we know of. It involves a group that wanted to raise money to buy band uniforms for the high school in Bel Air, Maryland (population about 7,000).

It didn't take much figuring to come up with a money goal. The band uniform committee wanted to buy twenty new uniforms—deluxe ones. Total cost: $3,000. It seemed like a lot of money, and the group didn't want to risk failure. So it pulled out all the stops. It planned a full week of activities—a band concert, a spaghetti dinner, a bake sale, a roller skating evening, an auction day, a square dance, a car wash, a concert at the mall, and a raffle. They called it all "Band Bash Week."

And to all this, the uniform committee added one other fund-raising technique: direct solicitation for special gifts. The chairperson of this committee personally contacted (face-to-face, by letter, or by telephone) banks, selected large businesses, and social and fraternal organizations.

The direct fund-raising effort brought in $4,876—all by itself. That was $1,800 more than the total original goal. The other activities brought in another $6,590. Grand total for the week: $11,466.

Band Bash Week was a success. In fact, it was a greater success than anyone had hoped or dreamed. And the uniform committee was not only able to buy the twenty uniforms they wanted, but uniforms for the majorettes and the pom-pom girls, new flag poles, and everything else needed to bring all the older uniforms up to snuff.

Of course, Band Bash Week would have been a success even without the direct fund-raising effort. But the combination was dynamite. And it's something you should keep in mind when you need to combine high-level giving with the active participation of the entire community.

ASPECTS OF INDIRECT FUND RAISING

Fund-raising affairs, or events, or projects (everyone calls them by a different name) have four different aspects:

1. Who attends or participates
2. How often events are done
3. What they do (other than to raise money)
4. The types of fund-raising events

In this chapter, we'll talk about the first three aspects—the contexts of the event. In the next chapter, we'll go into the specific types of indirect fund-raising events.

1. *Who attends?* Fund-raising events can be public or private. "The difference is really masses of people and how invitations are issued," says Alice Davidson, who is Chairperson of the Women's Division of United Cerebral Palsy and a partner in Project Specialists, Inc., a New York City fund-raising consulting firm. "Even an event that is open to the public and that receives mass publicity can be private. That is, tickets can be sold privately, and most of the people who come have been personally approached. The people who've bought tickets through public channels are in the minority."

The public event, on the other hand, *relies* on attendance or participation by the general public. "If there's a charge for admission to a public event, it's usually less than for a private one," says Alice Davidson. "And even then, you might have some special tickets and invitations at higher prices for important people who can be patrons, or sponsors."

You can also hold a small private event built around a public event. "For example," says Davidson, "you may be holding a big craft fair, and the night before the public opening, you have a dinner and a preview, and this could cost people $50 or $100, maybe. And then you're open to the public for the next three or four days, and there's a gate admission, maybe $3 or $5. Of course the exact price would be scaled to your community, both for the private and the public events."

Another illustration of the difference between public and private is the pre-follies dinner that each trustee of a southwestern hospital held before the annual talent follies to raise money for the hospital. Eight people were invited to each trustee's home for dinner. The cost of the dinner was a $50 donation which included the price of the follies ticket. Follies tickets were also sold to the general public for $5 and $7 and $10.

Private events are usually aimed at prestigious, influential, and more capable donors. Benefit dinners, which honor an outstanding member of the community, are often private affairs, with invitations issued to the honoree's friends and business associates. Movie premiere benefits, too, are usually private affairs, although the advertisements for them may sometimes mention that a limited number of tickets are still available and may give you a phone number to call.

2. How often? Fund-raising events can be held at four different frequencies:

i. *Annually.* As your only fund raiser, or one of many that you do throughout the year. Events that are held annually generally increase in net profits each year and cost less in time and money.

Why? First, if the event has a good reputation, more and more people will spend their money on it. Second, as you gain experience, you can put on an event more efficiently each time you repeat it. In addition, any initial financial investment—like a sound system, a tote board, or clothing racks— won't have to be repeated.

With this in mind, whenever you do a new event, you might want to consider repeating it annually.

ii. *Occasionally or irregularly.* Some fund-raising events are so large, elaborate, and costly that they can't be done regularly (though what is an occasional event for one organization might be an annual event for another).

A theatrical production, for example, might be occasional or annual, depending on the available talent and other resources. A gala dinner-dance might bring people out every two or three years, but they won't pay a high admission price every year for that event. Or maybe the audience would be willing, but your members wouldn't have the time or energy to do something so big each year.

Of course, if the event is truly unique, a once-in-a-lifetime creation, like the inventive Maryland Band Bash Week, chances are that it would never be repeated.

iii. *Continually.* This is a money-maker that goes on throughout the year, a thrift shop or gift shop, for example. Or a cookbook that sells continually once it's been published and provides you with ongoing income.

iv. *In combination.* If you can, try to use all three, especially if all your fund raising is done indirectly. Chances are you may already have one or more annual fund-raising projects. Does one of them lend itself to a year-round venture? If you have a good rummage sale that's the talk of the town, you might consider starting a thrift shop to bring in dollars all year-round.

The St. Anne's Circle of St. Theresa's Church in Three Lakes, Wisconsin, did just that. It turned an annual rummage sale into an all-summer thrift shop that earns upward of

$4,000 a year. Over the years, the income has refurbished the parish house, carpeted the church, renovated the church kitchen.

If your group regularly holds bake sales or dinners as fund raisers—you have plenty of good cooks and recipes—a cookbook might be your thing. Or a frozen homemade food service, so that people can buy main courses and baked goods prepared by your members. Other services that can provide ongoing income include errand services, taxi services, babysitting, ticket sales (in small communities where there is no Ticketron outlet), food catering.

The larger-than-usual occasional event can be a vehicle for building public awareness of your organization, or for boosting club spirits, or for making more money when circumstances require extra income.

v. *How many events to do in a year?* Should you try to raise all the money you need with one event, or should you plan a series of affairs at different intervals through the calendar year?

You may feel that you have no choice. Your money needs may be too great for any single event. In that case, try offering the constituency a variety of give-backs at different times.

Here's an example: In Clay, New York, the Pop Warner football league needed $3,000 for uniforms and equipment. They used a combination approach. A public auction brought in $1,000. In addition, the players sold pens at $1.00 for a box of five pens. That gave them a profit of 50¢ a box—and raised a total of $500. The group also operated the concession stand at home football games. Average net profit: $100 a game. This combination enabled the thirty players and fifteen cheerleaders to get their league onto the field. Incidentally, they plan to continue their fund raising because they hope to double the number of players soon.

Here are some more examples: In Chehalis, Washington, the Christian Women's Fellowship needed $3,000 to sponsor a young woman who was invited to tour the United States and

Europe for three months with the Continental Singers, a non-denominational Christian young people's choir. They conducted a mail campaign to other churches in the community and also held a lunch/bake sale, quilt block sale, and an Easter service collection.

In Washington, Pennsylvania, a group starting a fund for a child's kidney transplant needed to raise $40,000. It used the many-event approach. A grocery raffle brought in $800. A Pittsburgh Steeler benefit game netted $3,000. A "money raffle" brought in $1,000 (1,000 tickets were sold at $2.00 each, winner takes half and fund takes half).

Within six weeks, this group had raised $10,000. Coming events include dances, a car wash, flea market, luncheon, and fashion show, and a local college plans to hold a carnival—with proceeds going to the fund.

There's nothing wrong in going to your constituents over and over again for funds, especially if you have a "give-back" each time. But if you're going to combine direct and indirect fund raising among the same constituents, you should use the direct method first.

UJA's Linda Abromson puts it this way: "You can hold a pot luck supper, and then a bit later you can have a bake sale. Or you can go door-to-door and ask for a donation, and then you can have a pot luck supper next month.

"What you can't do is have the pot luck supper and then go door-to-door, because they'll say they've already given at the pot luck supper. However, once having given a direct donation, the donor may well be willing to spend money on a give-back."

If there's no emergency, and you're not forced to use every method available as fast as possible, your one-event-vs.-many decision may well rest upon your members' willingness to commit themselves to a battery of fund-raising projects.

Some people are happy to work on a project if they know it is the only one. Others don't mind being continuously involved. And sometimes groups are large enough that several projects can take place during the year with different people working on all of them.

But, Mary Webber, of the Maine National Bank, who counsels nonprofit organizations on community fund raising, has a warning for groups that plan many fund raisers each year.

"It is absolutely vital that the projects *for the year* be coordinated to avoid confusing the public ('Didn't someone at that church just have a supper?'), to avoid a poor image ('Are they asking for money AGAIN?'), and to be sure you don't overload those few people in every organization who work on everything."

Some fund raisers who believe in fund raising projects spaced throughout the year say that method is better than placing all their eggs in one basket. "If one thing flops, you're not completely lost," one woman told us. "But if it's the only thing you do, what happens if you lose money or don't make what you need?"

Then there are those people who prefer one, or at the most two, annual events. "By selecting just one thing to do," a woman in Georgia who organizes an annual bazaar told us, "your efforts and energies don't get spread too thin."

There are a few distinct advantages to holding one annual event, and these have to do with how the event can boost your image in the community.

Mary Webber says, "When you think of certain church fairs or other community group fund-raising efforts, an immediate picture springs to mind, right? You expect a certain standard from a certain group. . . . Although it may be foolish to blindly follow tradition, your group would do well to establish an event and a time that are identified with your group and can be expected.

"Everything your group does should be well done so that people will respond to your group as much as your event. They'll know that you did such a good job on your auction that your film festival or exhibition dance program will be good, too."

3. *What they do (other than to raise money).* Why have a fund-raising event? The answer seems obvious enough: to raise money. But fund-raising events can (and should) have more purposes than that.

They can be used to make your organization more visible. If your nonfinancial need is more visibility in the community, then you should plan an event that will capture the imagination of the general public. The emphasis should not be on the prestige of the event, but on the good bargains you might find or the good time you can have if you go. Plan something that people will find interesting and entertaining, like an antique show, an enormous rummage sale, a haunted house, or a sporting event they can either participate in or watch.

A fund-raising event can also be held to raise your organization's prestige. If this is your nonfinancial purpose, then you will have to get people with influence involved in the event. A humanitarian awards dinner to honor a distinguished person in the community, a ball or dinner-dance, a costume gala, to which tickets are pre-sold by invitation only to a selected group (the friends, business associates, and family of the honoree, for example). Prestige can be a factor in influencing more and bigger contributions. Plan an event that people with prestige will attend—the mayor, the president of the university, the chief of staff at the hospital, the town benefactress, or whoever else in your community has influence and prestige. You can make these people an integral part of your event by honoring them, or asking them to give a speech, or by inviting their personal mailing lists in their behalf to the event.

The people with prestige are actually lending their prestige to your organization. Others will contribute because the people with prestige and influence are behind you and think that your organization deserves their support. At a prestige function, the people who must be in attendance are the most influential in the community, while if public visibility is your purpose, then the general public must turn out for your event.

You can also engage in fund-raising activities for the purpose of strengthening the organization to rouse your members to vigorous and frequent participation. A strong organization has active volunteers, so if you need to get people more deeply committed and involved, you'll need something that keeps them busy working for your organization on a regular basis. An ongoing project, such as a thrift shop, serves this need. And it provides a service to the community-at-large, providing good-quality used clothing at a price they can afford.

Our point here: There's more to consider than money when you're choosing a fund-raising event. Your nonfinancial needs may, in the end, be even more important. That's why you should spend some time identifying them—with the help of your organization's inner circle (those core members who seem to be in on everything)—and keep them in mind when you make your choice. If you do, your fund-raising event will have a long-term payoff that goes far beyond your immediate money goal itself.

Now, let's take a closer look at some of the many ways to raise funds via indirect solicitation.

10

WAYS TO RAISE MONEY

THE single most asked question about fund raising is, "What's the best way to raise x number of dollars?"

Of course, there's no universal answer. The number of ways to raise money is endless—and the best way varies, according to circumstance.

Many *Woman's Day* readers have told us about their favorite fund raisers. And their stories show that with imagination, creativity, determination, enthusiasm, and commitment, the "impossible dream" can come true.

We wish we could give you a magic formula for choosing the best way to raise money, but no such formula exists. That's one of the reasons fund raising is exciting—and fun.

There's always the chance that you'll succeed beyond your wildest dreams—as the Band Uniform Committee of the Bel Air, Maryland, High School did when it raised $11,466 with a week-long Band Bash Week—and it had a goal of only $3,000.

"How do you decide which way to raise money? You can't punch it out on a computer," says Betty Forhman, Director of Women's Activities at United Cerebral Palsy. "Each case is special. Each group is special. Each community is special. There are so many things to consider."

In the preceding chapter, we tried to show you the *context* in which your group should raise money, that is, how your fund-raising affair can best serve your organization's needs.

In this chapter, we'll talk about the various kinds of "give-backs" you can choose from. We'll provide you with a list of ways in which people spend money and give you some examples of how various groups have used these ways to earn money.

How much money your organization can earn with any indirect fund-raising method depends on the amount of wealth within the constituency, on the skill and energy with which your organization produces the event, and on the willingness of the constituency to turn out for the event.

As you read through these various fund-raising ideas, keep your organization's needs and your constituent's desires in mind.

Ask yourself these questions:

- Can this type of project meet the organization's needs?
- Am I excited about doing this project?
- Are other people in the organization also enthusiastic about it?
- Do members have the time, skills, and special talents needed to carry it off?
- Does the organization have the resources needed for such a project?

If you've answered "yes," to all of these questions, then go on to consider your audience—and whether it will buy the give-back you have in mind.

In indirect fund raising, you promote your cause, of course, but you promote the give-back even more. If you're having a bake sale, for example, the first emphasis is on the merchandise—its quality, its uniqueness, its price, its freshness. Your secondary emphasis is on your cause, on the fact that the bake sale proceeds will buy new books for the school library, for instance.

Your cause may draw people to your bake sale, but the main reason they'll come is to buy baked goods.

A fund-raising affair or event, then, should be something special, something that can stand on its own, something people want, in addition to helping a worthy cause. And since the event must be tailored to the audience, you've got to take stock of who that audience will be.

To whom are you marketing your function, event, project, service, or product? How many people are there who will come? Or must you go to them? What is the median income of this group? How much can they afford to spend? How much are they likely to spend? What do they like to do? What are their interests? How do they like to spend their time? Their money?

It is nearly impossible to tell you how much money you can earn with any given fund-raising affair or event, because there is so much variation from place to place. "Two communities of the same size may have entirely different interests," says Betty Fohrman of United Cerebral Palsy. "There are all kinds of peripheral factors in deciding what kind of event to have."

Your money goal is just one factor. Others are income level, geography, climate, age range of the constituency, social interests, job interests, cultural and ethnic backgrounds. All these play a part in selecting the best fund raiser.

"The key thing is to give people something they want," says Linda Lese, a partner in Project Specialists, a firm which consults with nonprofit organizations on their fund-raising needs. "In some cases, this is easy, because the people's interests tie in with the interests of the organization.

"Take a museum," Linda Lese says. "People are interested in art. So we have a museum membership for $1,000, which entitles the member to a free trip to visit a private art collection in some distant city. The trip costs the museum about $250, so it clears $750 from each membership.

"Now these members could afford to take a trip on their own, but our trip gives them something they can't get by themselves—a visit to a *private* art collection. That's priceless.

And the only way they can go is by buying a museum membership," she says.

But what if the interests of the audience are less apparent. You either have to figure them out, or create the interest. You might have to do a little feasibility study. Go through last year's issues of your local newspaper. See which fund-raising events pulled big crowds or earned high profits. See what's "in" with the young people, the young adults, the older crowd.

Above all, think about what will be fun for you. "Very often, something that does not appear workable will work because of the commitment and energy of the people involved," says Betty Fohrman of UCP.

If you're enthusiastic enough to organize, plan and promote a super event, you can create public interest. And you're better off doing that than trying something that doesn't interest you much.

To help you find what you're looking for, we've divided fund-raising events into thirteen different categories, including practically every type of give-back that's ever been invented. You can choose just one event, or you can combine several, in different categories.

You can pick any category of fund raiser that appeals to you as long as it also appeals to your audience. You're not limited, necessarily, by the size and experience of your membership, since nearly every category contains something for nearly every type and size organization.

And no one category is necessarily better than any other. The amount of money that can be raised in any one of them is enormous, as you'll see. It depends not only on the cause, but also on the constituency.

All right, then. Here are the thirteen ways to raise money via indirect fund raising: 1. Sales; 2. Tournaments; 3. "A-thons;" 4. Tours; 5. Eating Activities; 6. Games of Chance; 7. Shows/Entertainments; 8. Auctions; 9. Parties; 10. Radio/TV Marathons; 11. Individual Initiative Programs; 12. Services; 13. Publications.

In this chapter we'll talk specifically about each method. We'll also give you some examples of how groups all over the country have used them to raise money. And we'll tell you how much they've raised.

But don't look at these dollar amounts and tell yourself you'll do at least as well. Remember—please—it all depends on your constituency, its affluence, its interests, the talents and energy of your membership, publicity opportunities, even luck, to a degree.

In chapter 14, we'll discuss how you can figure out whether an event is likely to meet your financial needs. But, for now, on to the thirteen categories. . . .

1. SALES

People spend money on merchandise. They buy everything from art to zeppelins, new or used. And if you can give someone an opportunity to buy some wanted item, you can make money. You can also provide entertainment, since shopping is also a form of amusement.

You can sell a single category of merchandise or a variety. You can offer new merchandise or used. You can get people to come to your sale or you can take your merchandise to them.

Homebaked goods, handmade items, books and clothing are today's top charity sales items, with antiques and works of art also strong. Here's a sampling of some favorite sales that have proved to be winners for *Woman's Day* readers:

Children's Christmas Fairs

Christmas sales still top the list. People need to buy presents and many would rather have something unique, possibly handmade, than something mass-produced. Inexpensive items, priced for children, turn a handsome profit for many groups.

Children's Christmas Fairs, held in schools, with classes being brought to the sale one by one, usually offer handmade items worked on throughout the year by volunteers within the sponsoring organization. Candy and items donated by area merchants may also be featured. Items are usually priced at $1 or less, so that a young child can go home with Christmas presents for the entire family. The organization sets up the sale and helps at tables. School gyms or cafeterias are the best locations.

The Women's Guild of St. Thomas More Catholic Church, Brooklyn, Ohio, (pop. approx. 14,000) made $1200 on this kind of sale, which they called the St. Nick's Fair. All craftspeople working on items got their materials through the chairperson, who had access to craft materials at a discount.

In Walingford, Connecticut (pop. approx. 36,000), the PTA of Yalesville Grammar School earned $800 with a Christmas Children's Fair. Members met once a week throughout the year to work on handmade goods—hats, mittens, scarfs, bean bags, bookmarks, napkin rings, handmade flowers, stuffed animals, ornaments, personalized stockings, et cetera. School families saved and donated yarn, fabric, lace, buttons, empty cans, wood, et cetera, from which they were made. This particular fair is in its eighth year, with profits climbing every Christmas.

Garage and Rummage Sales

Garage and rummage sales are generally good money-makers, especially if you live in an area where money is tight or where people get a kick out of looking for bargains.

There are customers galore at the Blair Memorial Community Hospital Auxiliary annual rummage sale in the Blair, Nebraska (pop. approx. 7,000), high school bus barn. This sale, which has been repeated annually for twenty years, has cornered the market on rummage sales in this area.

About 1,000 members of the Auxiliary work on the sale, and people in every community in the area take part. Doctors, housewives, nurses, factory workers, secretaries, salespeople all donate time—and rummage. The bus barn is literally turned into a department store. Electricians donate their time to light it, lumberyards donate boards for shelves, Boy Scouts load and unload trucks of merchandise, which includes everything from knick-knacks to furniture, clothing, and antiques.

During the sale, selling departments engage in friendly competitions. Wares are attractively displayed, and clothing departments have volunteers modeling the merchandise.

Profits from the most recent rummage sale were nearly $13,000. But the first time the event ran, it earned $600.

Repeated sales usually do earn bigger profits year after year, because the expertise of the organizers and the reputation of the sale grow together.

If you're thinking about doing a rummage sale, here are some *musts:* Clean merchandise; size labels; electrical appliances in good working order and outlets so buyers can test them; attractive displays; jewelry in boxes; china and silver sparkling; furniture polished and repaired. In fact, whatever you're selling and no matter who you're selling it to, you'll raise your profits if it's displayed and packaged attractively, with prices clearly marked.

If you're dealing with high quality used clothing, too good to be called rummage, then make a point of that. Thrift shops which specialize in designer label clothing, and furs are thriving in larger cities where wealthy women discard their expensive clothes after a season of wear.

The National Council of Jewish Women in Akron, Ohio, earned more than $8,000 on a three-day sale called Designer Dress Days. It featured designer clothes at a fraction of their original price. This, too, has become an annual event, and it is well publicized and well attended by women in Akron.

A few days before the sale, the organization holds a luncheon/fashion show (featuring merchandise that will be sold, plus some new fashions which will also be on sale). This is basically a private event, with limited reservations, but open to all women who are members of the group.

If you belong to a small group which can't stage an event as elaborate as the Blair rummage sale, you can try something more modest. That's what the North Hudson B&P Hadassah of West New York, New Jersey (pop. approx. 40,627), did. To make sure its first rummage sale was a success, it obtained permits to hold a "Sidewalk Sale" in the center of town.

A group from St. Paul's United Church of Christ in Lakewood, Colorado (pop. approx. 93,000), used a similar idea to help pay the enormous hospital bills incurred by a couple who had premature twins, one of whom died after nearly a year of hospitalization.

St. Paul's held its sale in the church parking lot, with booths for clothing, books, greeting cards, toys and games, shoes, purses, furniture, small appliances, et cetera. An orchestra and bluegrass band were on hand, and they sold "requests" for a donation to the cause. To make sure the event was well-attended, St. Paul's put up a banner on the church grounds, publicized the sale in the church newsletter and in newspapers and on the radio. The human interest story on the twins helped. In all, more than $4,000 was raised.

In Camden, Maine (pop. approx. 5,000), a group raising money for a sheltered workshop holds a used clothing sale twice a year and raises about $3,500 each season. The whole community looks forward to the annual spring and fall events (the tenth sale is coming up as of this writing), and Cash for Clothes is known as *the* place to shop.

Emphasis is on high-quality clothes at low prices. One of the unique features of this sale is that the clothing donor can get a refund of half the selling price. Most constituents do want the refund. If you live in an area where you haven't had much luck in soliciting good used merchandise for resale, try offering merchandise donors a percentage of the selling price and see if your luck improves.

As an ongoing fund raiser, there's nothing that can beat a thrift shop or second-hand shop. Really, this is a permanent, somewhat upgraded rummage sale with a continual turnover of merchandise.

What you need for this, besides merchandise, is a permanent location and a staff of volunteers willing to sort, price, display, sell, and do the bookkeeping. A thrift shop does not need to be open full time. A few days a week, or half a day all week long, or even weekends only, will do. Some groups, unable to afford shop rental, have begun thrift shops in corners of their own headquarters or in church parsonages or garages. Once they become established as money-making operations, they can move to a larger location and pay rent if necessary.

Of all the organizations which raise money with thrift shops, the Junior Leagues are perhaps the most adept and knowledgeable. According to the Association of Junior Leagues, they had 103 thrift shops in business in 1975–1976, which made a total net profit of more than $2 million.

"The most successful . . . are located in densely populated low-to-medium income urban areas . . . stock good-quality donated and consigned clothing geared to the needs of blue collar families who appreciate good values and are willing to pay a fair price," writes Ena C. Swayze, former Director, Division of Area and League Services, Association of Junior Leagues, Inc., in *Junior League Review*.

Whether you've got a thrift shop in mind, or just a rummage sale, you can benefit from the Junior League's experience. They've found that children's clothes are the best-sellers, with women's clothing (especially larger sizes) next best. Men's clothing is usually not much in demand, and may not be worth the time and space needed to sort, mark, and display it.

Boutique bazaars, which often sell both used and new merchandise, are also big money raisers. Again, booths for every category of merchandise make the boutique bazaar a shopper's paradise. The St. Anne's Ladies Society in Cincinnati, Ohio (pop. approx. 435,000), netted $18,000 on a Harvest Boutique, which also included a flea market and auction with services donated by a professional auctioneer. (More on auctions later.)

Door prizes of $5 were given away in hourly drawings, and each booth raffled off one of its better items. (More on raffles later, too.)

Incidentally, if you set up your bazaar so that it is an attractive, amusing, and fun place to go, you might as well charge admission. This particular group charged $1. Others charge more for admission, and some charge as little as a quarter. It depends on what your audience can afford.

We like children to be admitted for free, when accompanied by an adult. Otherwise, people with children might have to stay home, or spend on a sitter money you'd rather they spent at your sale.

Some people think that only large communities can support a big bazaar, but this is not true. Even in a tiny town, a bazaar can bring in a good profit. In Byronville, Georgia (pop. approx. 500), over $4,000 was raised with two fall bazaars by the Edith Elrod Circle of the United Methodist Women. The money raised paid for renovation of the kitchen and landscaping of church grounds.

What to do with Leftover Sale Merchandise

The most common way to dispose of unsold merchandise is to give it to another charity. However, you can add to your profits by having another sale with the stuff that didn't move the first time around.

The Camden, Maine, Cash for Clothes committee has a bag sale, held on the day after the original sale ends. Bargain-hunters come to the location and have the opportunity to fill up a paper bag with remaining clothing and buy it for a buck a bag. Women's groups in town often send representatives to the bag sale—it's a cheap way for them to pick up extra items for their own fund-raising rummage sales.

You can keep your leftover merchandise for a follow-up sale the next week or month. The Cincinnati St. Anne's Ladies Society held a special Sunday Sale ten days after the Harvest Boutique and turned another handsome profit.

Door-to-Door Sales

Many groups that don't have the staffpower to stage a major sale prefer to go to the customer instead of having the customer come to them. Basically, this means door-to-door, although you can vary this approach by renting a truck, or decorating your car, playing music, ringing bells, and in general doing something to bring people out of their houses to satisfy their curiosity.

Advance publicity will tell people that your mobile sale will be in the neighborhood on a certain day. In the car you can have a driver and from 2–5 other volunteers who can hop out and ring doorbells and cover a block at a time. (Be sure to get permits if your town requires them.) Fresh baked goods, eggs, produce (if you have access to a discount supplier), and books go well in sales like this.

So does ice cream on a hot day, as any ice cream truck man will tell you. If someone in your group has access to a camper or trailer or van with refrigeration, you can try a Beat-the-Heat Super Sunday Sundae Sale, and provide some welcome relief to Sunday gardeners and folks doing their weekly lawn mowing, as well as to those sweltering inside.

You can also sell new merchandise—pens, flowers, candy, cookies, greeting cards, et cetera—which you purchase at a discount or take on consignment. The profit margin on these items is rarely more than 50 percent. But the group's investment is very low, or nothing at all if you take merchandise on consignment. And it does give people, especially young people, good sales and business experience. A list of firms that offer merchandise for resale to nonprofit organizations is included in the Appendix.

We still feel that unique merchandise or things otherwise unavailable in stores are good bets for door-to-door volunteers, and homebaked goods still head the list, as the senior girls of Mt. Pulaski, Illinois (pop. approx. 1,700), High School recently found out.

They held a "slumberless" slumber party, during which they stayed up all night baking yeast bread, tea rings, and breakfast rolls. The next morning, they took their still-warm baked goods around town and sold out within two hours, earning the money needed for the senior band trip.

Every Christmas, a group of church women in Mishawaka,

Indiana (pop. approx. 36,000), earns money selling homemade peanut brittle. Every weekend from Thanksgiving to shortly before Christmas, the women get together to make the candy and the husbands join in, weighing and boxing the product. This project has been going on for several years. Church members enjoy the convivial atmosphere and the product has a reputation which makes it easy to sell.

If you have a unique food item that your members can make and package, you can offer it for sale in bank lobbies and other high traffic locations. In smaller towns, the company which agrees to accept the merchandise and display it will often allow an employee to sell it for you (a bank teller, for example, if your goods are displayed on a table in the bank lobby). This can be very helpful if your own members are unable to man the table full time. Cookies in tins, fruit cakes, boxed candies, and similar items go over well. By the way, your price on such items should be an even dollar amount, say $1 or $2, so that the employee can easily take the money without having the hassle of making change.

Sponsored Sales and Shows

If you live in an area where there are many potential customers, but your own group is really too small to make or accumulate enough merchandise to hold a full-scale bazaar, you can raise money by sponsoring a bazaar or show where *other* organizations or merchants rent booths or tables from your group and supply their own merchandise.

In Atlanta, Georgia (pop. approx. 500,000), a group of only thirteen women has run the largest bazaar in the Atlanta area for twelve years. Known as the Christmas Charity Bazaar, it is held the last weekend in October and organized by the XI Gamma Sorority, Alpha Chapter of Beta Sigma Phi.

The sorority makes money on table rentals (last year 222 tables were rented for $8 each to 75 different charitable organizations.) This particular group makes space available *only* to other organizations, and it stipulates that the organizations donate 15 percent of their profits to charity or civic causes.

Last year, this bazaar contributed approximately $13,000 to various Atlanta charities, and the sorority itself earned enough to support its own chapter plus eight service projects.

If you decide to sponsor such a bazaar, your organization can make money in one or more of the following ways: table or booth rental, admission, food and concessions, and your own tables or booths.

Profits from merchandise sales usually go to the merchant or organization that rents the space, although, as in Atlanta, the sponsoring group can sometimes make sure charities get a percentage of the profits. Of course, this requires additional bookkeeping—and profit statements from each booth or table.

Shows

Sales which feature similar merchandise from many participating merchants or dealers are called "shows." An antique show, for example, features antiques, and many antique dealers come to the show to display and sell their wares. Sometimes a dealer will travel quite a distance to come to a good show.

The charity sponsoring such a show can make money from space (booth or table) rental, general admission, and food concession. If you decide to sponsor such a show, make sure that your merchandise and dealers can draw a crowd. Your publicity plan is important, because show publicity draws buyers, and that's what your dealers need to make their trip profitable.

Now, what draws customers to a show? One thing is the chance to see a lot of merchandise under one roof. This makes shopping easier. The antique buyer, for example, doesn't have to go from store to store. On a given day, he or she can see hundreds of dealers at your show. Also, according to Joan Flanagan, author of the *Grass Roots Fund-Raising Book*, such shows are appealing to shoppers "because they can browse with no commitment to buy and they can do comparison shopping."

The show's big advantage is that a small number of people

can pull it off. Since you don't have to worry about the merchandise, you can concentrate your efforts on finding a location, contacting dealers and merchants, publicizing the show, and arranging for food.

What kind of show you will do depends on the interest of the audience and what type of merchandise goes well in your community. Antique shows of course are very popular almost everywhere.

Boat shows are popular in areas where boating is a main form of livelihood or recreation. In the coastal city of Rockland, Maine, the Lion's Club holds one annually.

A boat show sponsor should invite all retail boat dealers, marinas, marine hardware companies, cruise clothing retailers, sporting goods stores, et cetera, in the area. Many of these companies deal in large items and can't bring many of them to the show, but they can usually bring something for display, plenty of brochures, and a salesperson to take orders.

Another type of show you can sponsor is a farm show, to which you would invite farm equipment manufacturers, grain suppliers, seed distributors, and individual farmers who market their own goods. Home shows are also becoming popular, gathering builders, furniture and appliance dealers, hardware stores, kitchen remodelers, roofers, plumbers, carpet/tile dealers, interior decorators, and any other type of merchant whose products or services would be needed by people building, remodeling, or buying a home. Model rooms can be constructed if time and space permit.

Art shows and craft shows are also good money-makers. Local museums, artists or crafts associations can supply you with names of potential exhibitors. So can a little legwork. You can attend craft shows in other areas, visit bazaars, flea markets and shops to compile your own list of names. Of course, any type of show that depends on handmade items must be planned well in advance so dealers or craftspeople will have time to make up an inventory large enough to exhibit.

One of the longest-running antique shows (twenty-five

years) takes place in Cedarburg, Wisconsin (pop. approx. 7,800). This city is very history-minded, so the antique show fits the awareness and needs of the community. The sponsoring group is the Cedarburg Women's Club, and it's their only fund raiser every year. All the money raised ($6,200 last time around) is poured back into the community with donations to other organizations, schools, and scholarship funds.

Private Sales

Sales can be public or private or both. For instance, you can have a private sale prior to a public sale. The Damon Runyon-Walter Winchell Cancer Fund did this recently when it sold original cartoon art by famous cartoonists at its New York headquarters.

Before this art show/sale opened to the public, a private opening gala was held, with tickets at $15 per person (or $60 for a sponsor). Cocktails and hors d'oeuvres were served, and many of those who came bought artwork that was on display. Cartoons that had been sold were kept on display, along with those still for sale, for the following week, during which the show was open to the general public. At the private opening were the artists and art patrons, plus the press.

You can have a similar private opening to your sale if there's a special group among your constituents who would purchase tickets and feel honored to receive an invitation. Perhaps you could invite officers and their families and friends, or community leaders, especially if the money raised from your sale will benefit the community at large.

2. RAFFLES AND OTHER GAMES OF CHANCE

If you want to hold a raffle, plan a Las Vegas night, or run a Bingo game, start out by checking state regulations and making sure your plans conform. If you fail to check the law and disobey it, you could be in for serious trouble. But if the law says OK, it's full speed ahead. This is not a time to make assumptions or do as others have done. Find out for yourself.

The simplest game of chance is a raffle, and in raffles there are two keys to making a good profit: a good prize and a battery of ticket sellers.

First let's talk about prizes. Sad but true, the fact is that a desirable prize sells more tickets than a worthy cause. In a raffle, the *prize* is the case. Make sure people want it, know about it, and have the opportunity to buy a chance at it dumped in their laps.

Sometimes the opportunity to sell chances can come through another event. Sometimes you must create the opportunity.

Of course, you have to analyze your audience and your prize resources and try to make a match. Author Joan Flanagan says cash is a favorite prize. She also points out that in many cases, the winner of cash will donate a portion of the prize money back to the organization.

Some of the best raffle items are still the traditional things. *Quilts* always do well, and why shouldn't they? Most quilts we know of have a minimum value of $300 and have the added value of being unique works of art.

A quiltmaker who is a member of the Unitarian-Universalist Society in Manchester, Connecticut (pop. approx. 49,000), taught other members of the church how to quilt. A dozen women working for seven evenings made a queen-sized quilt with an estimated value of $350. Raffle tickets were sold for $1 each during a four-week sales period and the group netted $850.

Autographed quilts are also popular raffle items. Quilt blocks are sold to individuals, who autograph them. Then quilt workers embroider the autographed names in various colors and types of stitches.

The Ladies Auxiliary to the Swedish Club in Edmonds, Washington (pop. approx. 25,000), did just that. It sold autograph spaces to club members and their families at 25 cents each. (But you can charge whatever seems reasonable in your community.) The club logo was embroidered in the center square. The finished quilt was displayed—and raffled off—at the club's annual bazaar. This particular quilt (queen-sized) cost only $38 to make, and it netted the group more than $300.

A variation of the autograph quilt is the celebrity autograph quilt, which is particularly appropriate if your organization serves the entire community. You can directly solicit signatures from local celebrities—business leaders, politicians, radio and TV personalities, or any nationally known people who happen to live in your area. You can charge from $5 to $100 or even more, depending upon the ability of the people to give, and their interest in supporting your cause. (If you have a baseball, basketball, football, or hockey team in your area, you can sell the whole quilt to a team for individual autographs.)

The money paid by the signators goes to your case, of course, as does the money you earn from selling chances on this prized and unique item. A celebrity autograph quilt also provides numerous publicity opportunities, and the public support of those who've autographed it will influence others to support your case with outright donations or by buying raffle tickets.

Another type of autograph quilt is the advertising quilt. In this version, spaces are sold to local businesses. Their names are embroidered on the squares. Again, this involves direct solicitation of the merchants, and indirect fund raising through the selling of raffle tickets.

Other handmade items which go over well as raffle prizes include *afghans* (the Lakewood, Colorado, group mentioned above raffled off a rainbow afghan at their sidewalk sale for a profit of $500), and *hooked rugs*. Every year a church in Orange, Texas (pop. approx. 25,000), raffles off an all-wool hooked rug made from a kit. The rug kit is donated by the church and the labor is donated by a member's son who is retarded. The last rug he made netted $578 for the church. Donating his time in this way is very rewarding to the young man, who has been making rugs for a number of years. The group sells chances on the rug at 3 for $1, and it is a very popular raffle.

Dollhouses are another craft item which do well in raffles. The Porthsmouth, Ohio (pop. approx. 28,000), Mothers Milk Bank Club raffled off a six-room dollhouse, complete with redwood shingles, windows, and lights, made by one of its members. Lumberyards and hardware stores donated some materials, and club members furnished and decorated the interior, which had fireplace, crystal chandelier, canopy bed with quilt, and petit point rug. The raffle brought in a profit of $992.

The dollhouse itself was unveiled at a fund-raising dinner and bazaar, which itself netted $590. Subsequently, the dollhouse went on display in a downtown shop, where employees alone sold 700 raffle tickets.

Food items are the second most popular type of raffle prize, and we don't just mean turkeys or hams. For example, the members of Epsilon Sigma Alpha Women International, Alpha Beta Chapter, Chattanooga, Tennessee (pop. approx. 120,000), raised $5,000 for the Chattanooga Birth Defects Center when they raffled off a shopping spree—a 3-minute fling in a local food chain.

But hams and turkeys do make good raffle items, as do food baskets. A Maryland Catholic school parents club made a fast $250 with a Christmas food basket, which included a full breakfast and complete Christmas dinner, with all the trimmings, plus fruit, snacks, and candy. The turkey for this food basket was donated by the parish priest, with each family club member donating an item or two.

The Roadrunner Junior Women's Club of Tucson, Arizona (pop. approx. 263,000), decided to raise funds with a raffle—but they wanted to do something unusual. So they held a "bottle of booze" raffle, with each member donating a bottle of liquor or wine. The raffle netted $296 in support of service projects, needy families in the area, and donations to other community nonprofit organizations.

Raffle prizes like bikes, tennis rackets, furniture, even cars, are always popular, even though they are less original than one-of-a-kind handmade things. If you're in a constituency where people can afford to buy a raffle ticket at $50 or more, then you should consider having an expensive and highly desired item like a car, especially if you can buy it at a substantial discount or, better yet, have the dealer donate it.

Civic-minded merchants may be inclined to help out with big prizes because of the public relations benefits—good image, lots of publicity and, of course, good feelings about participating in a worthwhile endeavor. Of course, this involves skillful direct solicitation.

You can also get good items if all your members donate their trading stamps to the prize kitty. You can run a monthly trading stamp competition among your own members. Do this for a year and you'll probably be able to pick up a choice item to raffle off (maybe a color TV), either in conjunction with another event (a bazaar, maybe) or as a separate fund raiser.

As we mentioned earlier, getting the best possible prize for your audience solves but half the raffle problem. The other half is getting those tickets sold. How many tickets must you sell to reach your money goal? That depends on the price of the tickets. How much can your audience afford, and how much will they be willing to pay for a chance at the prize?

If you need to raise $700, and your prize has cost you $100, then you must actually sell $800 in tickets. Can your members sell 800 tickets at $1 each? 400 at $2? Will people pay $2 for one chance at a $100 prize? Only by analyzing your constituency can you answer these questions.

If you have a very expensive prize, like a car, with a constituency that can afford a costly ticket, then it may be to your benefit to limit the number of chances available and set a high price. If you ask someone to spend $50 on a ticket, and he knows there will be only 200 chances sold, he may be more likely to take a chance than if 500 tickets will be sold.

In most raffles, however, the idea is not to limit the number of tickets, but to sell as many as you have to in order to reach your money goal.

"Whenever you're selling tickets, you've got to look at the size of your sales force," says Betty Forhman. "How many people do you want to reach? How many sales people will you need to reach them?

"If you have a small group of volunteers, or you've got lots of members but members who will not get out and push, push, push those tickets, then you might have to go through the schools and get the teenagers to do it for you. Sponsor a contest, give a prize to the person who sells the most, train them, organize the collection of money. These things are important with a raffle—or any other kind of event which requires the selling of tickets."

Our point: You can't assume that people will beat down your doors for tickets, even if you're offering the world's greatest prize. You'll need a willing, aggressive sales force. If you don't have one, think about going outside your own organization (to students, or members of other organizations) if necessary *and* if your case justifies it.

Raffles are only one of the games of chance that can be put to charitable purposes. But most of the others are better suited to fund-raising fairs, carnivals, and bazaars, rather than to single events based on the particular game.

Among these are game booths of various kinds—ring toss, penny toss, shooting gallery, guess-your-weight, jelly bean count—all very popular with kids and other young-at-hearts, who will willingly buy chances at a dime each or three for a quarter, to test their skill or luck.

Gala Evenings of Chance
Some fund-raising groups actually stage entire affairs based on games of chance—casino nights, or Monte Carlo nights, or Las Vegas nights, they may be called. These types of fund raisers can be very costly and time-consuming to stage, but they can bring in sizeable sums if presented to the right au-

dience. Before you start planning one, however, make sure they're legal. Check state and local laws. If you're on solid legal ground, start planning. If not, think up another fund raiser.

Church groups, service clubs, fraternal organizations and others have found that such evenings can provide enjoyable social contact and entertainment, while raising healthy amounts of money.

In such an event, your costs might include room or hall rental, food, decorations, play money and game tables and equipment (if you can't borrow what you need). Experts advise renting this equipment, if possible, rather than buying it. Rental houses usually show you how to run the games. Of course, simple casino nights can be run with homemade gaming equipment.

It's usually a good idea to charge admission to the event itself, but that's up to you. If you do, you can set a higher admission price if you include a buffet supper. If food, cooking, and service is handled by members, rather than by paid outside help, your profits will be that much greater.

The actual gambling should be done with play money, which can be sold at a teller's booth in a couple of different packages, perhaps $15,000 of play money for $6 and $30,000 for $10. But these prices are arbitrary. Yours should be based on your total money goal (costs plus what you need) and what your audience is willing and able to pay. Your teller's booth can also sell tokens or beads for beverages and snacks. That eliminates the need for any other cash transactions.

Lynnette Teich, President of Oram Group Events division of Oram Group, Inc., fund-raising consultants, suggests that a raffle be held at the close of your casino night. "Sell tickets during the early part of the evening. Anyone who's winning at the tables will buy like crazy, if you've got a good prize."

You might cap the evening by awarding a grand prize (hopefully one that's been donated) to the big winner. According to Philip G. Sheridan, author of *Fund Raising for the*

Small Organization, a grand prize can stimulate people to spend their play money more eagerly, in hope of winning it.

Sheridan also suggests holding an auction at the end of an evening of gambling, so that people can bid with their play money winnings, walking home with something other than a fistful of play money.

Having this opportunity also gives players incentive to gamble heavily with their play money because they will be able to use their winnings at the end. (Again, get auction items donated if possible.) The auction can take place after the game tables close, while the supper is being set up, if you've planned a midnight feast.

3. EATING EVENTS

Many big fund-raising events do involve food in one way or another, as you know. But there are also fund raisers where food is the *main* attraction, where the event is built around the meal.

And even when the meal itself isn't the main attraction, it can be the basis of an event. One example of this is the benefit dinner to honor an outstanding citizen. People who attend pay "by the plate—" not for the meal, so much, but to pay tribute to the honoree.

Pancake breakfasts, spaghetti suppers, box lunches, pot luck dinners and other informal events are not very complicated to do, and are quite profitable if your members are willing to donate food and do the cooking. If your constituency likes such events, you can have them frequently. They work very well in communities where people like to socialize, but can't really afford to eat out a lot.

With fast food chains getting more and more expensive, you can draw a good crowd by pricing your meal competitively. We can hardly count the times we've chosen a fund-raising breakfast or supper over a fast food place because it's better and cheaper, and a lot more fun.

Ethnic meals are quite popular in some places, particularly where there aren't a wide variety of restaurants offering a lot of food choices. One school we know of has a big fund-raising supper each year, featuring cooking from the country of that year's foreign exchange student.

The exchange student usually supervises the menu and cooking, teaching fellow students and teachers how to prepare the dishes. The meal is served buffet style in the high school cafeteria, and a good part of the community turns out to experience new taste treats and visit with neighbors, teachers, and students.

"Progressive suppers," in which each course is served in a different place, are still popular. If you can find a place with several different rooms, you don't have to progress from one house to another with each successive course, but from one room to another. The room-to-room supper allows for progressive meals to be held in bad weather, when people may be willing to travel to one place, but not to many places in a single evening.

Adults or teenagers can raise funds with progressive suppers, and don't have to put in much time planning, since most arrangements can be done over the phone. The actual set-up can be done just a few hours before the event. This is how the B'nai B'rith Girls of Flossmore, Illinois (pop. approx. 8,000), raised $500 for their Israeli Service Fund. They charged $3 for adults and $2 for children. Food and cooking were donated, as was a raffle prize which brought in $75.

Any change-of-pace food event will probably be supported by the community. For example, in Cape May, New Jersey (pop. approx. 4,400), the Ladies for Deborah Heart Hospital decided to sell submarine sandwiches to working people. Two women in the group put notices in banks, city offices, beauty shops, office buildings, and stores a week before sandwich tickets were to go on sale. The notices said that the subs would be available and that orders would be taken the following week. When the women returned to take orders, they got seventy-seven in one building alone.

The night before the sale, two people spent five hours slic-
ing meat. On the sale day, six women prepared the sandwiches in a central location convenient to all the buildings
where orders had been taken. Extras were available for those
who didn't order in advance. Sandwiches were priced at
$1.35. In all, $385 was raised.

It's a well-known fact that people will pay money to
eat, but will they pay not to eat? Sure, if they're going to
trim down at the fat farm. But what about *not* eating as a
way of raising funds? That sounds peculiar, but that's just the
method St. Paul's Lutheran Church of Craigs Meadow, in East
Stroudsburg, Pennsylvania (pop. approx. 8,000), used to raise
money for the World Hunger Fund of the Lutheran Church.
It cleverly linked event and cause by sponsoring a "hunger
dinner" at $100 a plate. The dinner consisted of broth, rice,
and tea, and was attended by 30 people who were deeply
concerned about the world's hunger problem. (One boy even
gave up his Christmas bicycle to attend this dinner and make
a contribution.)

When an event and cause are linked this way, you're most
likely to attract those who are most concerned about the
cause—those most likely to make a large donation. In the
above example, $3,000 was raised at practically no expense.

Food fund raisers lend themselves especially well to themes
—global, or specific cooking styles all make for fun eating and
preparation.

When looking for a theme, don't forget to look in your own
back yard. If you live in an area that's known for some specialty food or cooking method, capitalize on that—especially if
you get a lot of tourists in the area who want authentic regional food. In Maine, they'll practically run each other over
at the height of the summer for a good buy on a lobster or
bowl of chowder. If you have access to a discount for some
indigenous, highly prized food item, you can build a public
fund-raising event around it during tourist season.

Food fund raisers can be public or private events. Private
events may be private in that only your group's members are

invited, or they may be private in that invitations are issued to those people able to give larger-than-average gifts.

4. LIVE SHOWS/ENTERTAINMENTS/AMUSEMENTS

Theatrical performances, talent shows, talent contests, fashion shows, beauty contests, concerts, lectures, slide shows, demonstrations (crafts, cooking, make-up, et cetera), sports exhibitions—anything that people will pay money to watch for amusement or education purposes can also be used as a fund raiser.

You can produce a show yourself, using talent within your organization and community, or you can use shows (or movies) that are produced by professionals and rent a theatre for a benefit night, or make a deal for a percentage of the house.

If you want to have a demonstration (say of make-up or Chinese cooking), you can often get free services from a commercial firm. In that case, you either charge admission or, if there's a product being sold by the demonstrator, you get a percentage of the gross sales receipts.

Any kind of entertainment can be turned into a public or private event. If public, consider holding some private event beforehand to boost profits. Give the people who come to the private event something special—a chance to meet the guest of honor, the speaker, or whoever has a major role in the event if outside talent has been imported. Entrance to the main event should be included in the price of the pre-event ticket.

If you're producing your own show, whatever it is, you're giving people the opportunity to use their talents, fulfill long-time dreams of stardom, or discover themselves.

Fashion Shows

In Rivera, Arizona, the Desert Daisies Homemakers Club decided on a style show/luncheon fund raiser to earn money for a new Resucci Anne (a doll used for practicing lifesaving techniques), which the town fire department badly needed for firemen's training courses.

This was a well-chosen event for this group, since one of the members was owner of a dress shop. She coordinated the style show. The group had a good case for soliciting donations of goods and services, since the cause was something that affected the entire town.

And the town responded. Merchants donated hams for the luncheon. A local woman radio announcer volunteered to be emcee of the fashion show. Club members made and/or donated doorprizes. The event cost only $20, and it netted more than $500.

Pre-show publicity brought good attendance, and post-show publicity brought in additional donations. Within a week, all the money needed to buy the Resucci Anne was raised. Next year, the group plans to repeat this fund raiser, with proceeds going toward a new youth center for the town.

Thematic fashion shows are also popular events, and the fashion theme that seems to top all others is weddings. In Chico, California (pop. approx. 20,000), the Butte Glenn Chapter of the American Heart Association held a bridal fashion show. It also featured display booths by merchants in the bridal and related fields. Tickets to the event were sold by participating merchants and at the door. Again, the talent and resources of a member were used in planning this particular fund raiser. The organizer is manager of a bridal shop.

The fashion show itself lasted about an hour, and then people had a chance to visit the display booths set up by twenty merchants—cake decorators, caterers, photographers, tuxedo rental shops, gift shops, travel agents, bridal wear shops, florists, et cetera. Two of each kind of shop participated, paying a space rental fee of $50 each. The merchants were able to answer questions for prospective brides and grooms and their families. At the end of the day, a drawing was held for a grand prize (weekend trip).

The St. Victor Altar and Rosary Society of Richfield, Ohio (pop. approx. 4,000), also used a wedding theme for its fashion-show fund raiser. Its goal was to raise money for a home for mentally retarded children.

The Society called its show "Weddings of Yesterday." The event chairperson scoured the town for old wedding clothes. She located thirty-eight wedding dresses dating as far back as 1819. She also worked up a space-age wedding dress for the show's finale, the wedding of the future.

This show was held in the church, all 250 seats of which were sold well in advance at $3 each. The wedding theme was carried out in tickets, which looked like wedding invitations; in the atmosphere (church bells were ringing); in decorations.

In Bloomingdale, New York (pop. approx. 8,000), a combination fashion show and dinner brought in a whopping $6,376 for the St. Anthony's Home School Association. This event was attended by 500 people, who filled to capacity the parish hall where it was held.

You can have a fashion show with all antique clothes, or all nearly-new clothes, or even a show of handmade fashions if your members have that talent. Or you can have fashion shows featuring one type of clothing—sleepwear, or children's wear, or sportswear, for example.

The most popular fashion events usually show a variety of the latest fashions. They are often done in conjunction with a store. The store's fashion coordinator can stage the show for you, or at the very least supervise the production to give it a professional look. "Try to get the store to supply the commentary," says Lynnette Teich of Oram Group Events. "They do it best." Teich also suggests always including a meal or tea as part of a fashion-show fund raiser.

Why should a store help you do a show? Because you bring them an audience full of potential customers. That's why Saks Fifth Avenue agreed to stage a fashion show for Hadassah in 1977, when 3,000 women from all over the country were attending the organization's convention in New York City.

Hadassah had discovered that its members almost always did some shopping when traveling. The planners of the convention gathered this information and presented it to Saks, which was convinced that doing the fashion show would give the store an edge over other New York stores.

If you decide to do your fashion show with one particular store, Aline Kaplan, Hadassah executive director, has some suggestions: "Make sure you choose a top notch store. Anything sleazy is no good. First, try the president of the store. If you get nowhere, try the fashion coordinator. If you have a choice, you're better off going to an up-and-coming store than to an established store, because they'll want the publicity and the business."

If you can't get a store to provide the merchandise and stage the show, then you'll need a volunteer with a flair for fashion, showmanship, and plenty of organizational skill. You can probably get merchandise from several different stores on a loan basis. They'll probably be more willing to lend you merchandise than personnel.

Of course, you can offer publicity in return, listing the store's name on the program at the very least. And your audience members are potential customers.

Beauty Contests

Beauty contests are another profitable form of entertainment. The Rural Retreat, Virginia (pop. approx. 800), Women's Club added a new twist to the beauty contest idea when they held a *men's* beauty contest, to raise money for a child with Cystic Fibrosis.

The chairperson made phone calls to men in the community (doctors, mayor, attorneys, businessmen, laborers, et cetera) and found 34 men willing to participate. The club also found a business sponsor for each man, at a sponsorship fee of $10 per person. The show was held in the high school auditorium—capacity 400—and it was a sellout.

A jazz band from the school and a talented club member provided live music. The contest was judged by the mayor and two college professors. As you might guess, the event got a great deal of publicity, including a newspaper picture of each contestant that might take them a lifetime to live down.

Live Entertainment

Theatrical shows also make good fund raisers. If you don't have people who are able and willing to produce and direct, you can hire a professional (budget permitting), who will use local talent and provide all other production elements, including the script. (See Appendix for how to find a professional director.) This is one kind of event where the cost to you might result in a big profit that makes it worthwhile. The average profit on an event like this is $10,000, but much higher amounts are common. The Junior League of Shreveport, Louisiana, for example, netted $96,000 with a 1974 follies production called "Happy Birthday, Uncle Sam."

If something on a smaller scale is suitable to your organization's resources and talents, you might try something similar to an event staged by the United Methodist Women of First United Methodist Church, Fullerton, California (pop. approx. 86,000), which earned $1600 for the church's mission work at home and abroad. They staged a dinner show, entitled "Magic Moments." The event was held at the church, in the room where wedding receptions are usually held. Tickets were pre-sold at $25 a couple.

The show portion consisted of performances by a talented church couple who sang a medley of Broadway show tunes, and a sleight-of-hand magician.

The dinner was elegantly prepared and served by club members themselves. This event ran for two nights, and seventeen club members served as hostess/waitresses (eight on each night). There were sixteen tables, each seating six people. Every night, each hostess was responsible for two tables. Hostesses provided their own silver and china and serving pieces. Food was cooked at home and brought in prior to serving. The first night's hostesses took home the dirty dishes, washed them, and gave them back for the second night. The hostesses were guests at the show on the night when they weren't serving the meal.

Exhibition Games

Sports exhibitions can also be effective fund raisers. Professionals have found that people will pay to see almost any team sport, not only at the professional level, but also at the college or high school level.

For example, in Menomonee Falls, Wisconsin (pop. approx. 32,000), the Village Workers Union, Local 31, challenges a local women's softball team to a benefit exhibition game every July.

Last year, in the eighth annual game, they raised more than $5,000 for the Waukesha County Association for Retarded Adults.

The chairpeople of this event are local tavern owners, Al and Dorothy Vait, who organize the whole affair and hold a post-game party in their place of business, provide beer and soda free.

Dancing, doorprizes, and high community spirit make this family fund raiser a summer highlight. But planning and publicity begin in late spring.

And how is the money raised? First, game tickets are sold for $1 each. Second, donated doorprizes—including a $100 savings bond—are given out at the post game party. Over the years, the money raised has been used for such things as scholarships, a hydraulic wheelchair lift, and the Special Olympics.

Another way to raise money with a sports exhibition is to buy out a stadium for one night and sell game tickets yourselves, at a profit. Of course, something like this requires a good sales force if the stadium is large. Your organization may also have to put up money in advance to stadium management.

The Epsilon Sigma Alpha Women's International Sorority, Alpha Beta Chapter, raised $5,000 this way for the Chattanooga, Tennessee (pop. approx. 120,000), Birth Defects Center. It bought out an evening at the local baseball stadium and sold tickets to a class "C" league game.

This same group has sponsored a number of other fund raisers in this category with good results, including a horse show, which raised $2,000. For that event, profits came from ad sales in a program book, tickets to the event, and concessions.

This group's most profitable fund-raising sporting event is one which has audience participation. It has been held for thirteen consecutive years to benefit the Orange Grove Center for Retarded Children. If there's a small airport in your area, you might consider this one.

Known as the "Fly-In," it consists of airplane rides. The local airport agrees to hold the event, pilots donate their time and planes, fixed base operators on the field donate the fuel. The group sells airplane rides for 3 cents a pound and also sells concessions. Last year this event netted $5,000.

5. A-THONS

No, don't try to look this word up in a dictionary. It's a term peculiar to fund raising. It refers to a kind of sponsored activity contest in which participants and nonparticipants join in the fund raising. The participants walk (walk-a-thon), run (marathon or run-a-thon), swim (swim-a-thon), ride a bicycle (bike-a-thon), et cetera. The nonparticipants join in by pledging money to "sponsor" the participants—so many pennies or dimes or dollars per mile walked, or laps swum, et cetera.

The event itself may attract a large crowd of both doers and watchers. If it's unusual—and you've publicized it well—you may even be able to sell admission tickets to spectators. After the event is over, the participants return to the "sponsors" to collect the money pledged, and they turn it in to a designated person from your organization. Sometimes prizes are given to the participants who win in various categories of the "a-thon"—first to cross the finish line, most laps swum, most "sponsors" obtained, most money collected, et cetera.

A-thons have become more and more popular during the last few years. College students skate, dance, and sing for their favorite charities. High school students shoot free throws, bat at bat-a-ways, play instruments, march, and twirl batons. People have dieted for a cause (winning so much per pound lost), read books for a cause, rocked in rocking chairs, exercised, skied, and even slept in water beds (at so much money per hour). No doubt you can think of something new to do. If you live near the water, for example, where fishing is a popular pastime, you could hold a fish-a-thon.

Whatever kind of A-thon you have, you'll need some basic tools. First, a registration form for participants. If you're holding some kind of public event where people other than your own members will be participating, you can consider charging an entry fee. (Some bike and running marathons do have a registration fee.)

Registration can be by mail or in person at a public location a week or two prior to the event. The time between registration and event is used to obtain sponsors. You can also have late registration on the day of the event, if you're charging a fee. This gives your organization the money from the registration fee, even though the entrant may have no sponsors. (There are some A-thons—running, for example—which may earn money exclusively on entry fees, and not have sponsors pledging at all.)

If school children are the main participants and the school cooperates, you can distribute information and hold registration at the schools.

Every A-thon entrant should receive a kit. The kit should contain:

i. Rules of the event, including date (rain date if there is one), time, and place.

ii. How to get sponsors and how to collect money after the event. Give participants a deadline of one to two weeks after the event to collect and turn in their money (or a week or two before the event, if you're following that plan). Tell them who to give the money to—name, address, and phone number. Make clear whether money is to be handed over in person or mailed. If it is to be mailed, include pre-addressed, pre-stamped envelope. Give instructions for what to do with cash (as opposed to checks) collected from sponsors. For example, you may want to advise participants to purchase a money order or cashier's check with all cash collected to avoid mailing cash.

iii. A card or sheet of paper on which participants will list names, addresses, and phone numbers of sponsors. There should also be a column by each sponsor's name for amount pledged ($1 per mile, for example), amount owed (which participant calculates after the event, such as 5 miles walked × $1 per mile = $5 owed), and date collected. *This sponsor list should be returned with the money.* With the list, you can double check to see if the correct amount has been turned in. And, even more important, you've got a list of contributors to use some other time.

iv. Winner's prizes and conditions for winning. Figure out what prizes you're going to give and be sure to let entrants know. You may decide to hand out a lot of prizes, maybe something to everyone who turns in more than $15 or $25 or $50 or whatever seems reasonable.

This kit needn't be elaborate or expensive. A mimeographed page of instructions, plus the page for sponsors' names to be filled in, and perhaps a collection envelope should do it.

Here are some examples of recently held A-thons. Perhaps you'll be inspired by some of them.

Diet-A-Thon. Among other groups, a League of Women Voters chapter in Highland Park, Illinois, dieted "Pounds away for ERA." Members paid, as did sponsors, $1 for each pound lost within a certain time period. The group raised $1,000 for passage of the Equal Rights Amendment.

Slim-A-Thon. United Cerebral Palsy of Greater Boston held this event in conjunction with health clubs in the area, which underwrote the program. Health club members got sponsors to pledge a certain amount for each sit-up done. The theme of this event was "Let's Do Sit-Ups For Those Who Can't."

Rock-A-Thon. A church youth group in Hingham, Massachusetts, held a twenty-four-hour event (rocking in rocking chairs) on the church porch and raised $1400. Money was used to make the church "barrier free" for handicapped and elderly people by installing ramps, expanding restroom facilities, and purchasing a chairlift.

While the youngsters rocked, church women prepared food for them. The church choir director was on hand at the church to lead musical entertainment and singing.

Sleep-A-Thon. Fund raisers for the March of Dimes, in Longmont, Colorado (pop. approx. 24,000), held a forty-two-hour marathon in a waterbed store and raised $900. The contestants were the local Jaycee president and a radio disc jockey who remained on the waterbed (on display in store window), for forty-two hours straight. This marathon stirred the curiosity of the town, and many people attended, watching from outside the store or inside.

Other events held at the store in conjunction with the sleep-a-thon were a volleyball game played on a waterbed, a stop the music sale, a midnight madness sale, disco dancing, and appearances by special guests. Five percent of all sales made during the forty-two hours were donated to March of Dimes by the store. The success of the event was largely due to plenty of publicity, cooperation of local celebrities, and enthusiasm of the store manager.

Read-A-Thon. Friends of Richards Memorial Library in North Attleboro, Massachusetts (pop. approx. 19,000) recently held a read-a-thon to raise money for a new circulation desk. You can do something similar and have children, teenagers, and/or adults obtain sponsors for every library book read during a certain month. (This particular read-a-thon was for adults. Minimum pledge per book was 25 cents. With only 5 participating readers, $240 was raised.) The potential for raising money with a read-a-thon is enormous if you can get many library users to participate.

The winner (most books/most money collected) of this event was awarded a $25 gift certificate donated by a new bookstore in the town, which was eager for the publicity.

Skate-A-Thon. In Carmel, Indiana (pop. approx. 7,000), a skate-a-thon raised a whopping $5,828 for the American Diabetes Association. Part of this money was used to send diabetic children from the area to a special summer camp. This particular event was managed by only *four* volunteers, plus the owners of the skating rink, who gave unselfishly of their time and facilities.

The event organizer started by contacting the rink owner and arranging for event date and follow-up awards ceremony. She then began (with a friend and two other volunteers) to distribute registration forms. She first started distributing at all fast food places in the county and then saturated all county schools.

Two weeks later 150 skaters turned up at the rink with their entry forms and sponsor pledge lists, so much per hour of continuous skating. The collection date and awards ceremony was a week later. Eighty-three percent of the skaters returned with their pledge money. And all who collected $10 or more were allowed to skate free that day. Prizes were given to the first three winners, and others qualified for tee shirts, frisbees, and Gatorade. (The first place winner turned in $702 and the second place winner raised $657.)

Run-A-Thon. The League of Women Voters of San Francisco held "A Race Against Time" to raise money for ERA passage. It earned $4300. This is the kind of event for which you need a race advisor or running expert, since it involves many technical details. Because few League members were runners, pre-planning centered around getting runners involved.

League members worked at the event in nontechnical

jobs—manning registration tables, selling food and tee shirts, distributing flyers, and arranging for traffic control.

So that runners of all abilities could enter, three different races were held—a six-mile race, a three-mile race, and a one-mile race.

Announcement/registration forms were mailed to all running groups, women's groups, universities, law schools, YWCAs. Letters were also sent to all women doctors and dentists in the city. Notices were placed in newspapers. Flyers were distributed at other races.

One element of the event's success was the inclusion of a raffle ticket along with the registration fee. The raffle was a big hit with the runners, who felt they were getting a bonus just for entering. The raffle also provided a way for nonrunners to support the cause, because they could buy a ticket without registering.

The organizers of this race feel that without the raffle, the percentage of return in relation to planning time would have been small.

In an event like this, prizes should be secured far enough in advance to publicize them. That's an excellent way to boost participation.

Running for charity is also popular with student groups. A fraternity in Arkansas ran a 200 mile relay and raised $2,000 for the American Cancer Society.

Businesspeople also have taken up running for charity. In Houston, Texas, employees of an ad agency ran for charity when the agency president offered $1 a mile to the charity of their choice. The twenty-one employees who participated— they called themselves the Joggernuts—logged 426 miles in a designated three-week period. They voted to give the money to the American Cancer Society.

The organizer of this event hopes to make a bigger fund raiser out of it in the future, by inviting client companies, public relations firms, and other ad agencies to join.

And in Boston, local physicians each ran five miles for the benefit of the American Heart Association. More than 100 doctors participated in the event and raised more than $30,000.

Ski-A-Thon. Charity ski marathons began in the U.S. on the Western slopes and made their way to the Northeast. In a recent ski marathon for the Maine Easter Seal Society, held at a popular ski resort in Maine, skiers obtained sponsors for each 1,000 feet of vertical feet skied. The ski resort was packed with participants and spectators. Each entrant who brought in $50 or more in pledges got free skiing. Other awards and prizes added to the fun and drama of the area's first ski marathon.

6. AUCTIONS

Some people feel that auctions belong in the sale category. But we think they're a separate category, because they're as much entertainment as they are sale.

Just what makes auctions so entertaining? Well, it's a combination of things—the auctioneer, the crowd, the items up for auction, the drama, and the tension. You don't even have to be a buyer to enjoy them.

It all starts with a good auctioneer. Someone really well known can draw a crowd from miles away. If your group decides to hold an auction, consider getting a professional— especially if he or she is willing to donate the time (and many professionals do, for charity).

If a pro is out of the question, consider using local celebrities or your own members. They can work in hour-long shifts, if they don't have enough experience to conduct the entire auction. Wouldn't you love to see your police chief, or high school principal, or mayor, step out of his daily role and have a go at auctioning off Aunt Tillie's blue vase?

Auctions can be held by themselves or they can be part of

some other fund-raising event. They can be open to the public, or for invited guests only. And you can offer any kind of merchandise you think your audience will buy.

In rural or farm areas, auctions of livestock and farm equipment do well. Antique auctions are popular almost everywhere. Auctions of new goods or services donated by local people also go over very well in most places. In short, the list is endless.

If you can't get a professional auctioneer, another way to draw a crowd is to offer some unusual and/or expensive items—well publicized in advance, of course. In fact, unique items are excellent ways to *get* publicity. They also usually cause excitement at the auction—and heavy bidding.

The Girl Scouts of Ogden, Utah, held an auction with *all* one-of-a-kind items—cakes, which were baked and decorated by each individual troop. The cakes were auctioned off at a box supper/picnic for the girls and their parents. Tickets to the picnic supper were sold at $1.50 each, and cakes were auctioned, bringing prices of $5 and more. Naturally, each parent was eager to get the cake created by his or her daughter.

Auctions don't need to be sponsored by a large number of volunteers to be profitable. In Leeds, North Dakota (pop. under 1,000), the Homemakers Club (twelve members) held an auction to raise funds for the town swimming pool. Members teamed up in pairs and went around the town and surrounding countryside to solicit merchandise. An auctioneer donated his services. They raised $1200.

Another successful auction was sponsored by the Committee to Combat Huntington's Disease, Puget Sound Chapter, Renton, Washington (pop. approx. 26,000). Though this group has only 10 active members, it raised $10,000 at its second annual auction.

The women started by writing letters to businesses, friends, and associates—people they thought would contribute goods or services, and followed up with telephone calls. Donations were picked up, numbered and cataloged for the auction program, and then stored until auction time.

Printed invitations were sent to friends, relatives, and associates, each of whom paid $5 each the first year. The event was so successful that prices were raised to $10 a person and $15 a couple the second year. Since the auction hall held only 200 people, tickets were grabbed quickly.

The group had a wide variety of items on hand for auction, including expensive vacations, works of art, sets of radial tires, and even an evening with the Seattle Seahawks quarterback.

7. PARTIES

Parties can be formal or informal, public or private. You can give any kind of fund-raising party you want, use any kind of theme or excuse to celebrate, have entertainment, decorations, and incorporate other kinds of fund raisers (games, auctions) to increase fun and profits.

Charge an admission (whatever the traffic will bear) to cover your costs and make you a profit. Include food in the admission price. As for drinks, you can include them in ticket price, let guests purchase them, or have them bring their own.

Keep in mind that restaurants and hotels make their best profits on liquor. If you hold your party there, it will be nearly impossible for your organization to make money on beverages. Usually the establishment insists on keeping the bar to itself. You have to weigh this factor against the convenience of holding your party there. (If you use a grange hall or legion hall, you can make money from the bar, but you may sacrifice glamor and convenience.)

If you intend to have an open bar for your guests at no extra cost to them, you can keep your costs and complications down by limiting the types of drinks you offer. For example, you can offer a nonalcoholic fruit punch, vodka, and wine. Or you can offer beer, wine, and soft drinks. Try to arrange for your supplier to give a refund on unopened bottles.

Small private cocktail parties are an excellent way to raise funds for political candidates. If that's what you want to do, your first task is to find a host/hostess to hold the party. The host and hostess invite a personal guest list and the fundraising committee helps to establish the price of admission, which goes into the candidate's election fund.

The host and hostess donate and prepare all the food, and except for the presence of the candidate, who mixes with the guests, the party is just like any other the host and hostess might have. The one difference: the guests pay for the privilege of rubbing elbows with the candidate. Since the host and hostess are in effect asking guests for a contribution, it would be appropriate for them to make that contribution, in addition to having the party.

Incidentally, parties are also an excellent way to introduce potential new members to your organization. Ask current members to bring a nonmember guest. Be warm and friendly, but don't try to pressure anyone into joining. Have organizational literature on hand, as well as photos, scrapbooks, and press clippings.

Parties can not only raise funds, but also help group members get to know each other better. The St. Pius Altar Rosary Society in Urbandale, Iowa (pop. approx. 15,000), recently held a series of parties for exactly these two reasons. The parties helped pay off the church mortgage and they helped build friendships among the members, some of whom didn't know each other very well.

The group's officers started the ball rolling, each one planning a party for his own home. They included everything from sit-down dinners, to ethnic meals, to brunches, to football TV parties with beer and pretzels.

The church membership list was divided among the officers. Each officer invited five people (couples counted as one person) to whatever type of party he or she had planned.

The guests were charged a reasonable amount to attend the event, and all money was given to the church. The cost of the event was absorbed by the host/hostess.

Anyone who accepted the invitation had to agree not only to pay the donation required, but also to hold another party of his or her choosing and to invite four other people to attend, who in turn would pay a reasonable set price and invite three additional people to come to a party in their home.

Each host/hostess was urged to invite people they did not know well. The overall chairperson kept track of the various types of parties that were going on, and also coordinated invitation lists so that *all* members were eventually invited to one function and no one was invited twice.

Each person who agreed to host an event had an invitation list from which he or she could choose names. The chairperson was on hand to give any kind of assistance needed.

This particular group raised $2,500 with its series of parties, which it called a "Social Pyramid."

If your organization has recently added many new members, the Social Pyramid is a quick way to raise funds and get newcomers acquainted with old-timers.

Any party that has something unusual to offer can also be a successful fund raiser. If someone in your organization has an unusual home, for example, people will attend a party simply for the chance to visit the place. Homes with lovely gardens, exceptional architecture, et cetera, are almost always good drawing cards.

Pool parties in homes with swimming pools can also be used for fund raising. One of the women who founded ECHO (Every Christian Helping Others) in Weymouth, Massachusetts, has an annual pool party/barbecue and last time around raised $740. This is a private party limited to 100 invited guests. There's an open bar, complete barbecue with plenty of homemade clam chowder, and live musical entertainment. Invitations are sent to the organization's supporters and contributors, who also receive a line by line listing of the past year's expenditures, which lets people know how their money has helped others and encourages them to keep giving.

You can raise funds by taking any popular activity and building a party around it. The Jefferson County Association for Children with Learning Disabilities, Prospect, Kentucky, has found a way to raise funds by capitalizing on the current roller skating craze.

This group rents a skating rink for $90 and invites children from all over the county to attend a skating party for $1, plus 75 cents skate rental. Four schools are invited to each party (parties are held for individual age groups, with elementary schools attending one week, middle schools the next, et cetera). Doorprizes are given (skates, bikes, etc.) to individual skaters and a cash prize of $25 is given to one of the schools for its special education program.

This fund-raising project, which nets about $1,000 in a year, is currently managed by one person, who hopes eventually to have a fund-raising chairperson in every school district so that more children can skate and raise funds to help other children with learning disabilities.

By their nature, parties are fun. But when you join them to a good cause, they can be an excellent way to raise money.

8. TOURS

People love the chance to see something they don't ordinarily get the chance to see, and you can provide them with the opportunity by sponsoring a tour.

House tours, garden tours, romantic bedroom tours, back stage tours, private art collection tours, inner city tours, nightclub tours, private yacht tours, and dozens more can attract hordes of ticket buyers.

You don't have to limit your tours to private homes or establishments. But, if you go to public places, you should include sights unavailable to the general public. For example, if you're running a restaurant tour, visiting and eating at a number of restaurants over a period of weeks, you might have special visits to the kitchen, talks with the chefs, or trips to the wine cellars.

You can even have tours of houses where visitors see only a single room. The League of Women Voters of St. Louis recently held a "Great Kitchens" tour. Visitors got to see spectacular kitchens, which most people only glimpse in the pages of decorating or cooking magazines.

If you live where there are many examples of outstanding architecture—museums, restaurants, skyscrapers, et cetera, you can plan a tour accordingly. If you live in a port city, you might be able to arrange for a tour of an ocean liner when it docks. (Steamship companies often have free tours, but if you can arrange something special on your fund-raising tour, say lunch with the captain, then you can charge for admission and offer the line some valuable publicity.

Give your imagination free reign, see what unusual offerings might be available in your community, and don't assume anything's impossible before you investigate it thoroughly and ask for permission to visit.

Of course house tours are still one of America's favorite fund raisers. If all the older homes in your town have been done to death, get into the newer ones. If all the houses have been included on tours, concentrate on apartments. If you live in a lake or ocean area, try for waterfront properties. Or energy-efficient homes. Or guest houses. Or farmhouses. Remember, you don't need hundreds of places. Half a dozen or even five houses are plenty.

In Pompton Lakes, New Jersey (pop. approx. 12,000), the Suburban Junior Women's Club (fourteen members) recently raised $1177 with a house tour. Most of the preparatory work was done by just two people. The others in the group were on hand to help during the event.

Letters were sent to twenty homeowners in search of five or six suitable homes for the tour. Five homes were obtained. Club members visited each home to write a description of it to be printed on the tickets.

Maps and tickets were printed and donations from local business people were solicited to help defer printing costs.

Tickets were sold in advance for $4.50 each. Club members provided baby-sitting service at a convenient church and $1 was charged for the first two hours of baby-sitting, with 50 cents for each additional hour. (Pre-registration was required to take advantage of the baby-sitting offer.)

The tour was held from 10 A.M. to 2 P.M., with club members working two-hour shifts in the various homes. Five local florists donated floral decorations for the homes. Wine and cheese, coffee and danish were served to guests in a local furniture store.

Some people say that house tours need 300–500 guests. But how many you need depends on your goal, your costs, and the price of your tickets. In many small towns, house tour tickets have been $5 for years. But it may be time to raise the price to $7.50, particularly if you think what you're offering is worth it. Remember, in many communities, it costs $5 to go to the movies these days.

9. INDIVIDUAL INITIATIVE

One of the newest and most daring fund-raising methods is something called "individual initiative." These projects rely on a certain individual's specific ideas, talents, dedication, and willingness to do something special for the cause. How does this work? Well, here's an example.

In Westerly, Rhode Island, the priest at the Church of the Immaculate Conception gave out $2,000 in $5 bills to parishioners, so that they could "go forth and earn money for charity." The parishioners did just that. One family made and sold macramé plant hangers, turning its $5 into $425. Two women baked and sold pies and earned $185. In all, the original $2,000 was turned into $5,000, which went to help poor people and to repair the church building.

The United Methodist Church of Alexandria, Alabama, did something similar. Its pastor gave $5 each to fifty-one participants in what he called a "Use Your Talents" competition. Some competitors used their money to buy ingredients, then baked or cooked their specialities and sold them to friends, fellow employees, or relatives. Others invested in materials and made and sold craft items. A student beautician gave haircuts. This program began in October. By Christmas Eve it had made a profit of $2500.

The Lutheran Church Women of Holy Trinity Lutheran Church of Abington, Pennsylvania, did the same thing—but without giving out money. Instead, the organization sent members a dollar-sized piece of paper with the words "stretch-a-dollar" written on it. Each participant invested his or her own dollar. Participants provided a service or made and sold articles. As the program progressed, a chart was put up in the church showing what services or merchandise were available so that members could call on "stretch-a-dollar" participants to fill their needs. This group earned $1500, which went a long way toward refurbishing the interior of the forty-year-old church building.

The women of the First Covenant Church of Cleveland, Ohio, have devised another kind of individual initiative program, one designed to encourage people to save money for charity.

Every month, this group distributes a "savings calendar." Each day's square has a different payment instruction, such as "Pay 15 cents if you drove today and 5 cents if you took the bus," or "Pay 10 cents for each room of your house you did not clean today."

But the instructions in each square are covered up with a piece of paper which states the date. At the end of each day, the participant pulls off the date, revealing the instructions. At the end of the month everyone turns in the money saved—an average of $120, when all the participants' monthly contributions are added together. If this idea appeals to you and your members, you can set prices that are comfortable for you and the others.

10. SERVICES

Services—something you perform for someone else, for a fee—can also be used to raise funds. It's just a matter of turning over the fees earned to the organization or charity you're raising funds for.

Teenagers can make money for youth groups, Y's, and scouts, by holding car washes, offering baby-sitting services, and doing odd jobs. Adults can do the same by providing ticket sales to athletic and entertainment and cultural events, filling reservations by mail or phone and charging a small commission (which people are happy to pay if you've saved them a trip to the box office), or by offering catering services, or errand services, or by running food concessions at sporting events or entertainments, just to name a few possibilities.

If you're thinking of earning money by providing a service, make sure it's something people need and will use. Do a good job, promote yourself well, and you can have a good *ongoing* money-raiser.

One successful catering service we know of is managed by the Summit, New Jersey (pop. approx. 24,000), Jewish Community Center Sisterhood. It raises money (approximately $4500 annually) for the synagogue budget and for a scholarship fund for children of synagogue members. (Some of the profit is also put back into the catering operation to improve kitchen equipment and buy needed commercial equipment.)

This service started five years ago and has been growing steadily. It is heavily used by synagogue members for luncheons, weddings, bar mitzvahs, and parties. If your members have the time and talent for such an ongoing service, and if there is genuine need within your community, it's worth considering.

On the other hand, seasonal service projects can also be very successful. For example, the Junior Federated Woman's Club of Petersburg, Virginia (pop. approx. 37,000), decided to raise money by setting up a Christmas gift wrapping booth in a shopping mall.

This project began with a bow-making workshop, so that there would be a good supply of bows on hand when the wrapping booth opened on November 30. Posters advertising the service were set up around town and in the mall, and display boxes were arranged in the booth. The booth was open for business from 5-10 P.M. on weekday evenings, and all day on Saturdays through December 22. Net profit was $357.83.

This service was extremely popular, as many, many mall shoppers brought their Christmas presents to the wrapping booth. Event organizer Mrs. Glenn A. Dean says, "Since this was a new project for us, we were conservative on our purchase of paper. Two weeks before Christmas, we ran out, and had to purchase additional paper at a smaller discount. The demand for a service such as this was truly remarkable, and in the future, we plan to be better prepared."

If this kind of project appeals to your members and would fill a need in the community, see if you can get some local businesses to underwrite your supplies or ask stores to sell you large quantities of wrapping paper at a discount. Just think, if your organization wrapped 500 packages at $1.50 each, you'd make $750 (less costs).

11. PUBLICATIONS

Publishing is another favorite way to raise funds. It offers two money-earning possibilities: you can sell ad space in your publication, or you can sell the publication itself. Sometimes you can do both.

Take a high school yearbook, for example. Maybe you worked on yours. High school yearbooks make money both ways. Local businesses buy ad space. Students purchase the books.

If you are going to sell advertising space in anything, you will have to decide what your rates will be. Ads are priced according to the amount of space. Most charitable organizations publishing ad booklets sell whole pages, half pages, quarter pages, and possibly eighths of pages, depending on how large the page is.

Or you can charge by the line, if you're just having a one-page publication that will also contain ads.

If you are going to publish an ad booklet, you should know what your printing costs will be so that you can establish your advertising rates. At the very least, you'll want the advertisements to cover printing costs.

To get a printer's estimate, you'll need a pretty good idea of what it is you're planning to do. And it's not a bad idea if you know something about what's involved in printing so you can communicate intelligently with your printer. If you have no experience with printing anything, then reading a primer will help you. We've recommended one in the Appendix.

Before you begin selling ads, you might (in addition to settling on the rates) make up some sample ads for businesses that don't have their own ads ready for the printer. Many businesses, however, will use the same ad that runs in the local paper, and if this is the case, then nothing new has to be designed and written. A business card can also be reproduced for an ad, blown up to the proper size for ad space that's larger than card size.

What kind of publication should your organization consider? There are several possibilities.

Journals

A journal can be published and given away at a fund-raising event. Say you're having a dinner to raise money for your organization. Maybe you've decided to honor someone at this dinner—the pastor of your church, or a past president of your group, or anyone who has contributed a great deal of time and energy to the work your organization does.

You can publish a journal which includes a history of your organization, some photographs, a report on the future of the organization, a biography of the honoree.

You can sell advertising space in this journal. Who will buy the space? Local business people and friends and business associates of the honoree are good candidates. It is a way that people can use to express their best wishes or congratulations to the honoree on the occasion of this dinner. Or if the celebration is for some notable achievement or anniversary of your organization, then the ads purchased can congratulate your organization.

Such an ad message might read, "The Middletown Furniture Company congratulates the Middletown Garden Club on its Twenty-fifth Anniversary. Thanks for brightening up our town."

People who read the journal will see the name of Middletown Furniture and recognize that this business is community-minded and a supporter of the club.

The journals are given out to everyone who attends the dinner as a momento.

Programs

Is there a symphony or community theatre where you live? Or any other kind of cultural event, such as a lecture series? If so, you can make money by printing programs. Programs offer the opportunity for ad sales or for one-line listings of patrons or sponsors of the event.

You don't need an elaborate booklet, although a program can be several pages long. Any event your organization does to raise funds—a follies or variety show or concert, for example—is a good candidate for a program money-maker. Even if your program consists of a one-page flyer, you can use the back for ad copy.

Directories

Directories are also good bets for advertising. Chambers of Commerce and other civic groups publish all kinds of directories for townspeople and tourists—antique shop directories, church directories, gas station directories, motel/restaurant directories, small business directories, craft stores—you name it.

You can even print neighborhood directories, or directories with names, addresses, and phone numbers of all children in a given school. A Kentucky PTA group sold school directories to students for a quarter each and earned $200. The directory was mimeographed and typed by volunteers, and costs were quite low.

The Sloatsburg, New York, mini-park committee sold ads to business at $5 each for its directory and distributed the directory free to all households and advertisers. Extras were sold for 50 cents each.

Directories are often given away free, and they can be distributed to individual households, supermarket checkout counters, motels, restaurant cashier's booths, museums, hotel lobbies, real estate offices, or any place the public is likely to be. Municipal offices and Chambers of Commerce may also find them useful to have on hand.

Soliciting Ads

Remember to look at this expenditure from the buyer's point of view. How does buying ad space help him? How many people will receive this program or booklet you're publishing? What does it actually cost your prospect to reach each person who will see the ad? That's how the effectiveness of advertising is measured. And that's what may convince businesses to advertise in your publication.

After publication, make sure you send a copy (or a copy of the ad page) to each advertiser along with a thank you note.

Cookbooks

Cookbooks are among the best sellers in bookstores, and they're also terrific fund raisers for organizations. If you're a local organization, the local bookstore will certainly want to sell your book. You can also sell it in banks, gift shops, drug stores, and other local outlets. Of course your own members will also be able to sell the books, and you can sell by mail, too. At every event you have, be sure to have cookbooks available.

You can use a local printer or go to a commercial cookbook printer, who specializes in printing cookbooks for fund raising. (See Appendix.) The advantage of using one of these printers is that they can produce large quantities and reprint as necessary, sometimes at a very low cost. Most organizations usually begin with a local printer, then switch to a specialty printer for the second printing if sales have been good.

You can also sell your cookbook *before* it's printed, by taking orders for it. This will give you some idea of how many to have printed in the first run.

Besides being a wonderful ongoing fund raiser (once it's done, all you have to do is keep selling, handing in a print order, and counting the cash), publication of a cookbook is all by itself a reason for an event.

A group of church women in Massachusetts held a tasting party when their cookbook was published. Food was made from recipes in the book. Forks and teaspoons were passed out at the party, and guests paid a nickel a taste. Of course cookbooks for sale were on hand. Other groups which have held tasting parties to introduce their cookbooks charge admission fees up to $5, or even more if an elaborate meal is being served.

Women from the First Christian Church of Sidney, Ohio, not only published a cookbook but also sold ad space in it. Each member approached five local businesses. The total income from ads alone: $500.

The group took 260 orders for its cookbook before publication and 300 more soon after. This earned them another $700 in profit, and of course, money continues to come in, since the book is still selling at banks, grocery stores, and at this group's annual hobby show.

Cookbooks are super money-makers, but that doesn't mean you should think writing, producing, and marketing them is a snap. If you choose this fund-raising method, be prepared to work hard at it.

The Junior Leagues have found that cookbooks are their second most successful ongoing fund raiser (thrift shops are first). According to Ena C. Swayze, former director, Division of Area and League Services, Association of Junior Leagues, Inc., it can take "a minimum of two years to produce one publication. Recipes must be collected and tested before the book can be organized and written. Designs and illustrations must be planned and obtained from artists or a talented League volunteer. Printing must be arranged, sometimes paid for in advance or within thirty days after delivery, proofs corrected, and provision made for sales distribution."

Does the cookbook idea sound good to you? If so, we strongly suggest that you *study* both cookbooks and the cookbook market in your area. What other organizations have books for sale? Are the stores in your town saturated? Are there any types of cookbooks missing? Would a general cookbook or specialty cookbook go over best?

And most important of all—do you have good cooks in your organization? Are they willing to part with their recipes? Can others follow the recipe and actually duplicate the dish? (How many times have you made soup from Aunt Mary's recipe, but it doesn't taste like Aunt Mary's? This should not happen to people who cook from your cookbook recipes.) You must test all recipes and be sure that your book isn't filled with recipes clipped from newspapers or magazines. The big selling point of all cookbooks is that the recipes are original and delicious.

How-To Books

How-To books can also be good sellers and excellent fund raisers. If you or any members of your group have some special knowledge, you can write out step-by-step directions, print up a booklet, and sell it by mail via classified ads in newspapers and magazines.

If your organization has had a lot of experience in putting on one particular fund-raising event, for example, you can write step-by-step instructions (including event description, committees, number of people needed, job descriptions, equipment needed, schedule of deadlines, et cetera) and sell it to organizations elsewhere in the country.

Your booklet can be mimeographed or copied on a Xerox machine to start. Get twenty-five copies. Staple it or punch holes and bind it with three hole fasteners.

Then, choose a magazine your members regularly read and that you think people who belong to charitable groups in other parts of the country also read. Take out a small ad (classified if possible) and offer the booklet for a reasonable price, say $2 or $3. If your first few copies sell like hotcakes, you can produce more and take out more ads. Your booklet will cost you next to nothing. In fact, your only substantial expense will be the ad itself.

12. RADIO/TV MARATHONS

The radio marathon or telethon is different from other A-thons since it is done on the air. Listeners/viewers phone in pledges during the program. Pledge amounts are periodically announced, which stimulates more givers to phone in pledges. There is also an address repeated on the air, so people can simply send in donations. Callers should be sent a pledge reminder or bill. Much of the collection work is handled like a telephone campaign.

If you live in an area which has a "listener sponsored" radio station or public TV station, then you're probably familiar with telethons or radio marathons.

You may also have seen fund-raising telethons conducted by one or another national health agency. The Jerry Lewis Muscular Dystrophy telethons are legendary. United Cerebral Palsy, after having a great deal of success testing with local telethons in various parts of the country, has also gone national.

Producing a radio marathon or telethon is as intricate, time-consuming, and involving as producing any other kind of big show. It must be handled by someone who understands the media and knows how to use it. If a telethon is dull, repetitive, or poorly done, it won't entertain anyone, let alone inspire pledges. Anyone can turn you off by switching the dial. Almost every radio or TV marathon that is successful has an expert behind it, even though the expert may do it on a voluntary basis. If you're lucky enough to have a broadcasting or telethon professional in your ranks, then you might consider it, even if your organization is relatively small.

One small institution that's used radio marathons since 1975 is the Ashley County Sheltered Workshop in Crossett, Arkansas. The workshop provides work opportunities for physically and mentally handicapped adults.

This organization raised more than $23,000 in their most recent marathon, which required about 150 volunteers. (The first year around, they started with just five volunteers, which goes to show what can be done by people who are really dedicated and determined.)

The air time for this organization's marathon is bought and paid for by sponsors, who are solicited directly. Buying air time is important, say the organizers of this event, because people tend to listen more to sponsored air time than they do to donated time.

The person who originally conceived of this radio marathon is a broadcasting professional who made a personal commitment to helping this organization. He has since moved away from the area but returns each year to help with the marathon.

Having an expert on hand is one of the things that enabled the Chilton Memorial Hospital in Pompton Plains, New Jersey, to conduct a telethon fund raiser for the past five years.

This successful event got its start when the local cable TV station, looking for an opportunity to serve the community, teamed up with the hospital's development director, Jim La-Mont. LaMont had previously produced telethons for United Cerebral Palsy, so he knew how to do it. According to La-Mont, you don't need a large staff to put on a telethon, but you do need one or two full-time people for about eight months or so prior to the broadcast. LaMont himself has a 300-point telethon checklist, which gives you some idea of the size of the undertaking. And although a large staff may not be required, some 300-400 volunteers served in one capacity or another in Chilton Memorial's telethon.

If you think the telethon idea is for you and want to know more about how to do it, you should send for a cassette tape of a detailed interview with Jim LaMont, conducted by *Fund Raising Management Magazine*. (See the Appendix for ordering information.)

13. TOURNAMENTS

In olden days, knights in armor clashed on fields of battle in spectacular tournaments, attended by lords and ladies. Very often, these tournaments were staged to raise funds. Jousting may be out of style now, but there are still many contests that will draw big audiences—and bring in substantial funds.

A tournament can be a spectator sport (you sponsor the tournament and raise funds by charging admission to a contest everyone wants to watch), or something that a lot of your constituents can participate in themselves. In either case, people either pay for the privilege of watching something they want to see, or doing something they want to do.

Tournaments can involve a sport like golf, tennis, billiards, or bowling. Or they can center around a game of some sort—bridge, chess, Monopoly, dominoes, Scrabble, backgammon.

If there's a sport that's very popular in your community, then you can capitalize on it and use it for fund-raising purposes. Your money will come mostly from ticket sales (and food sales at the event). A program book with ads will add to your profit. So will registration fees for participants. If necessary, expenses can be underwritten by businesses in return for publicity.

Two of today's most popular athletic fund-raising tournaments involve golf and tennis. For example, the Junior League of Birmingham, Michigan, produces the well-known Virginia Slims women's professional tennis tournament.

Just to give you some idea of what's needed to put on this type of fund raiser, one recent tournament, according to Ena

C. Swayze of the Junior League, "involved 359 League members and 594 volunteers from the community, whose responsibilities included everything from ushering and lines-calling to manning the ticket office at League headquarters." This event netted over $100,000.

If a giant-sized tournament featuring celebrities or athletic superstars seems too large an undertaking for your organization, you might consider a smaller tournament of the home-spun variety to raise funds—a game tournament, perhaps. Although there are certainly world-champion players in bridge, chess, Scrabble, et cetera, you can center your tournament around home-grown stars or teams.

Be sure to encourage high school students to enter, as well as adults. You can even get businesses to underwrite the tournament or at the very least to sponsor teams or individuals. Get other organizations to sponsor players from their own membership.

With good publicity and a game that appeals to a lot of people, you can run a contest and end up with a home-town Scrabble champion, or whatever.

Sometimes the manufacturers of the various games will give you some guidance on sponsoring a tournament or provide you with special tournament rules.

The main idea is to involve the community as widely as possible. Find prizes that will draw an audience. In some places, $50 in cash will bring out hundreds of entrants. In other places, a Moped will do it, or a vacation, or a larger cash prize.

You can run the tournament for a week, or hold it over several weekends, eliminating the losers from each afternoon's or evening's games until you get down to semi-finals and then finals. All of this, of course, is a natural for newspaper, radio, and even TV publicity. The broadcast media may also want to cover the finals of your event. Spectators may also wish to attend, so arrange to hold the tournament in a suitable place and serve refreshments.

If the game lends itself to different categories of contestants, by all means set it up this way. A Scrabble tournament, for example, can have a junior high category, a high school category, and an adult category. You can, if you want, hold women's and men's competitions in almost any game, with playoffs for Grand Champion. If your game has partnerships of players (bridge, for example), you can also hold a mixed doubles class.

The entry fees you decide on will vary according to the willingness and ability of people to pay to participate in the tournament. You will want to have a lot of registrants, so make the fee reasonable. You can have a reduced fee for students. (See if you can find a local merchant or two willing to contribute refreshments in return for publicity. You can offer free snacks to the players and sell them to spectators.)

You might also want to offer a premium to everyone who enters. Tee shirts are great, if you can get them donated or underwritten by businesses. Give your tournament a name and have tee shirts printed accordingly. These can also be sold to nonplayers to increase profits and publicity. If tee shirts can't be obtained for nothing, consider buttons or bumper stickers.

THE THIRTEEN CATEGORIES

As you read through the thirteen categories, you probably found some that appealed to you and some that didn't. You found some that you thought your constituents would enjoy. You've probably already thought of many variations, variations that would make a particular activity just right for your organization and your audience.

It may sound strange to you, but different as these events are, the planning process for all events is similar. In the next chapter, we'll show you how to organize an event, and how to figure out whether the event you have in mind will get you to your money goal.

11
PLANNING A
SPECIAL EVENT

HERE's something we hope we've made clear: Every fund-raising event is unique. Even if the same people run exactly the same event in the same place twice in a row, it's bound to be different somehow.

That said, let's go on to the next point, the fact that makes this chapter possible: Nearly all fund-raising events have a great deal in common. All must have a case, leadership, volunteers, and a constituency. All have quotas, deadlines, meetings, publicity, volunteer assignments, committees, budgets, and timing.

But this chapter is going to talk about one other element all events have in common: execution—the thousand and one details that must be attended to if you're going to pull it off, if you're going to reach or surpass your monetary goal, if you're going to make it a positive experience for those who attend and those who do the work.

Whether or not you execute your event successfully depends, except for acts of God and other lucky elements, on *planning*. There's no substitute for it. Fortunately, if you start early enough, there's no reason why you can't plan your event to something at least resembling perfection. All it takes is logic—and a little bit of hard work.

STEPS IN PLANNING

1. Choosing the date.

Some people say there's nothing as important as picking the right date for your fund-raising event. And there is certainly some truth to that. Even if you do everything else right, if no one comes because the date is wrong, then what have you got? A flop.

There are several factors involved in picking a date—season, day of the week, and conflicting events, for instance. The amount of time you need to reach your money goal is another. And, of course, it's nearly impossible to put on a bazaar a month after you've decided to have one. That kind of event needs six months of planning, maybe even a year.

i. *Season.* Fund-raising experts have found that spring and fall are the best seasons for most events, at least in most of the United States. Winter means snow and uncertain weather. Summer means vacations. That leaves spring and fall. And the possibility of rain. But you can usually cope with that by arranging for a rain date (or alternate inside quarters).

Your theme choice can be influenced by the season or by seasonal holidays. Early fall gives you harvest time, Halloween, or Thanksgiving motifs, while late fall is perfect for Christmas-related events, especially sales and bazaars filled with all kinds of goodies for the coming holidays.

Early spring offers such theme possibilities as Ground Hog Day or Valentine's Day or Easter. In late spring you can build your event around May Day, apple blossoms, vacation time (summer's coming), wedding themes (June is coming), et cetera.

If you need to, use your chosen season to help name your event and suggest appropriate decorations, food, and games. Just think of what you can do with a Harvest Ball instead of the Middletown Club Dinner-Dance. The Woman's Guild of United Church, Stonington, Connecticut, did just this.

Looking for an original theme for an early fall (October) event, they came up with the Hiawatha Luncheon and Heap Big Sale, an Indian theme appropriate for the harvest/ Thanksgiving season. Baked goods and craft items were displayed and sold at the "Trading Post." Waitresses wore Indian costumes, with feathers in their hair. Small pumpkins, decorated like Indian faces, with small feathers sticking out of the top, were used as table centerpieces. And these centerpieces themselves were sold for use as Halloween decorations, adding to the total net profit.

Although spring is an excellent time for fund-raising events, avoid April 15. That's when income taxes are due.

Other times to avoid scheduling a fund-raising event, according to Joan Flanagan, are: important religious holidays; legal holiday weekends; state holidays; first and last weeks of school, and the week before and after a primary or general election.

ii. *Day of the week.* Since many people get paid at the end of the week, weekends are usually the best time to hold sales events with admission charges. On the other hand, events with pre-sold tickets aren't necessarily best on weekend nights, especially if you live in an area where you have to compete with parties, movies, theatres, restaurants, concerts, and many other nonfund-raising events. In that case, consider a week night, instead.

iii. *Other fund-raising affairs.* Be sure to check out your date with other local organizations to avoid conflicts. Remember, nonprofit organizations can share equipment (tables, chairs, sound systems, et cetera) with good will—and no conflict of dates. So, avoid not only direct conflicts, but even near conflicts.

One way to sidestep conflicts is to check Chambers of Commerce event calendars. Of course, in some places there are so many things going on that your event could never be the sole attraction. But, at least, then make sure it's listed on the community calendar, so other organizations will know what you've planned.

2. Organizing Chairpersonships, Committees, Deadlines, Quotas, Meeting Schedules.

Once you've settled on a date, you can begin to work out a schedule. Make a chart, giving every job a deadline. The person responsible for doing the job can check it off when it's finished. Committee chairpeople can refer to the chart and easily see where the problems are. Schedule meetings to organize the event, appoint chairpeople and committees, and hold additional meetings as needed to coordinate interdependent tasks and hear progress reports from chairpeople.

Experienced fund raisers agree that, when possible, committee chairpeople should select their own committee members. That way they can choose those they know are reliable and with whom they know they can work well. This also presents an opportunity to recruit people who might not otherwise be involved, and who, indeed, might not even be members of your organization.

But committee chairpeople shouldn't forget to include new people as well, especially if they're eager.

3. Arranging for Location.

It's also important where you hold your event and what you have to do to fix up the location to make it suitable. Some fund raisers hold their events in any suitable location that's free or that doesn't cost much. But some events need a specific location to go along with their theme. And, in others, the location is the main attraction.

Veteran fund raiser Helen K. Knowles, author of *How to Succeed in Fund Raising Today,* says, "The 'where' can become the major theme for publicity. . . . Eager opportunists will recognize that in almost every town or city there are buildings and spacious rooms used only some of the time by their owners—like museums, art galleries, and other cultural and historic shrines."

If you know of such a room or building, it might be the perfect place for your fund-raising event. As Helen Knowles says, "It so happens that you can really have a ball in a museum."

One of the most unusual fund-raising affair locations we've heard of was a subway train. The "Underground Bash," as it was called, was held by the Junior League of Brooklyn and it involved a New York City Transit Exhibition.

The party was a celebration of the history of New York's transit system. It took place en route from Manhattan to Brooklyn, aboard a special subway car. Live music, food, champagne, slide shows, and movies were provided. The 750 guests got off at an abandoned subway station in Brooklyn, where the exhibition was being held. Net profit from this unique event: $22,000.

Finding an unusual location may not be possible, or necessary, or even advisable for your event. But you should think about the possibilities, especially if you need a theme, and an unusual location can provide one. Of course, sometimes it's more important to get a rent-free location than to find an unusual location.

When choosing a location, be sure it's large enough. If you are having a sale, for instance, find a place large enough to permit comfortable shopping. If shoppers have to elbow their way to the merchandise, they aren't likely to stay around long enough to buy much.

Here are a couple of tips from the American Cancer Society to help you figure adequacy of space: if you're having a dinner or luncheon, figure 40 square feet per table of ten people. If you're holding a dance, space can be figured at 800–900 square feet for every fifty couples.

Here are some examples of possible fund-raising event locations: convention halls, old mansions, schools, farms, garages, sports clubs, restaurants, hotels, streets, churches, schools, race-tracks, theatres, bus depots or storage barns, art galleries, vacant lots, airports, libraries, museums, grange halls, municipal buildings, yacht clubs, excursion boats. Try to choose the location that best suits your needs.

Other things to consider when choosing a location: parking (Is there room? Can guests park their own cars, or will you need a car parker/attendant?); restrooms; coat-check facilities (Will you be liable for losses?); and kitchen facilities.

4. Making a Checklist.

Every event chairperson should make an all-inclusive checklist of everything necessary to bring the event to a successful conclusion:

i. *Personnel needed*—salespeople; cashiers; waiters and bartenders (one for every three tables of ten people, at least one bartender for every fifty people, advises the American Cancer Society); security personnel; ticket takers; go-fers (someone to run errands during event, to pick up anything forgotten, or any additional things needed at the last minute); cleanup people; scorekeepers, et cetera.

ii. *Items needed*—theatrical equipment, such as lighting, sound systems, decorations, costumes, stages, ramps; tables and chairs; dishes, silverware, tablecloths; cash boxes, receipt books; cash for making change; prizes.

From Joan Flanagan come these suggestions of things oft-forgotten: first aid kit, pens, tape, poster board, markers, watch, aspirin, comfortable shoes, phone numbers of key personnel, especially band leader, hosts, speakers, ice, name of doctor or nurse at event, emergency numbers for police and fire, fire extinguishers, coins for pay phone.

iii. *Insurance*—make sure your organization has an insurance policy that will protect it from claims that may come about as a result of the event—claims for property damage to the location and facilities; claims for injuries at the event, et cetera. Have your legal advisor study any contract you may be required to sign with the location's owner.

iv. *Printing requirements*—tickets, invitations, programs, menus, signs, posters.

v. *Publicity*—make sure you coordinate your publicity with your planning. Remember, good publicity doesn't start with the event. It's a year-round proposition (see the publicity chapter for further details).

Of course, the checklist for your event will be more specific and probably longer. The important thing is to make one and to see that everything is taken care of.

One way to help yourself prepare a checklist for the event itself is to run through the event in your mind. Visualize it from beginning to end. Put yourself into the location, see the decorations, the merchandise for sale or auction, eat the meal—do whatever you can to make the event, in all its details, real in your mind. This little exercise will help you see what you need to do to make the event run smoothly. The more thoroughly you can visualize it, the less likely you are to forget something important.

One thing you should realize—almost everyone forgets something, even experts. This is the reason for a *go-fer*. He or she can "go for" things at the last minute, allowing the chairperson to remain on the premises, in control.

5. Setting Prices.

Deciding how much to charge for admission to fund-raising events is almost always confusing to beginners, especially for a first-time event. The best pieces of advice on this come from Joan Flanagan, who says there are seven factors to consider when pricing tickets:

i. *How much do you need to raise?* Figure your costs, add that amount to the amount of money you actually need to get the gross income that you'll have to raise at the event.

For example, imagine you've got to raise $800 and your event costs are $200. That's $1,000 you need to earn at your event. Divide your $1,000 by all possible ticket prices to see how many tickets you would have to sell at each price, i.e.,

100 tickets at $10; 200 at $5.00, et cetera. Then have your committee discuss what *can* be done—how many tickets can realistically be sold at what price.

ii. *What do other, similar events cost?* "The price of every event in any town will start to escalate once one organization starts charging more than the usual amount," says Lynnette Teich of the Oram Group. "It's always hard to be first but it can be done." Chances are good that people will willingly pay the going rate, but if you want to charge more you "will have to do a super sales job, lower your profit goal, or add in other ways to make money besides the ticket price," says Flanagan.

iii. *What are the hidden costs in attending your event?* (Take into consideration baby-sitters, parking, money people will have to spend once they get to the event.) Can people afford it? If not, "it may be better, and more profitable, to have a day-time, free-parking, family event," says Flanagan.

iv. *What else will bring in money at your event?* A cash bar? Raffle chances? If you can count on 100 people buying drinks at $2.00 a drink, and you need $1,000 gross income, you can make $200 on drinks and $900 on ticket sales, for example.

v. *How about more than one ticket price?* Can you sell a small number of higher-priced tickets to patrons or sponsors? How many? Do you want some lower-priced tickets for students or senior citizens?

vi. *What is the price/image relationship?* Flanagan points out that lower prices make ticket sales easier. With a low price, you can get a big crowd and people at all income levels can attend. "On the other hand, you may decide you want to give the impression of prosperity and success by sponsoring a classy, high-priced, downtown event."

vii. *How many complimentary tickets will you hand out?* You may want to send complimentary tickets to your event to the press and possibly to some VIP's whose attendance would be an impressive coup for your organization.

You can also use free tickets as a public relations tool, according to Flanagan. You can give them to groups of people who might never be able to go to your event otherwise (handicapped people, inner-city kids, senior citizens, for example).

Be sure not to include complimentary tickets when you calculate income from ticket sales.

6. Stashing the Cash.

Any event at which you expect to bring in cash needs a "stash-the-cash" plan. Imagine how you'd feel if, after all your hard work and excitement, your money was lost or stolen.

Make arrangements to get the money into the bank as soon as possible after you receive it. Some organizations advise using night deposit facilities if they're available. At least two people should count, record, and take the money to the bank. Arrange for a security person—possibly a local policeman—to accompany your treasurer and assistant, if this seems advisable (especially if large sums are involved and lots of people know it). If you can't go directly to the bank, arrange to have the money kept in a safe overnight or through the weekend. Again, more than one person should put the money away and arrange for any necessary security. Be sure you have coin roll papers, envelopes for bills, deposit slips, and moneybags on hand.

7. Planning for Later.

Use this fund-raising event to build a list of potential new members and/or future donors. The single most important asset of any nonprofit organization is people power. Anyone who attends your fund-raising event is a potential resource, so be sure to get names of all who attend, if at all possible. The stranger at this year's rummage sale might well be the chairperson of next year's bazaar, for all you know. The person who cares enough to come to your summer fair might also care enough to make a donation when next year's campaign rolls around. But if you don't have a name, you're trusting to chance.

Here are some ways to use your event to build your list of potential donors and volunteers:

i. *Raffle or door-prizes.* Make sure you put the names of attendees on the ticket stubs—not just a number.

ii. *Attendance books and guest registers.* You can't force anyone to fill the pages, but people who are most interested probably will.

iii. *Organizational literature.* Have some handy and displayed attractively. Also make sure someone is on hand to answer questions and to meet strangers and make them feel personally welcomed to the event.

iv. *Ticket sales inventory.* Be sure every salesperson knows who buys every ticket she sells. Names of ticket buyers should go on your list.

v. *Donors of used merchandise.* If anyone contributes merchandise for a garage sale, auction, rummage sale, et cetera, be sure to get their names.

How else can you use this year's event to plan for the next one? Keep accurate *records.* Make sure that all suppliers, all costs, all equipment, all organizational charts, all workers, all quotas, all publicity outlets are on record. Then, when you're planning a repeat of an event, everything will be easier. You can check food costs next year against what you had to spend this year. You'll know just what each job entails. You'll have a list of things to buy, borrow, and rent, and you'll know where you got them.

Actually, winding up an event is so important that we've devoted a chapter to it. (See chapter 15.) But, what do you do once it's really over and every last button has been buttoned? Well, you start planning another, of course.

You can repeat your last success or you can put on a completely different event. Or, you can switch fund-raising methods entirely, from the indirect variety to the direct variety.

And, as it happens, that's the method we intend to discuss next.

$

$

$

PART FOUR

Direct Solicitation

12
DIRECT FUND RAISING

FOR THE last three chapters, we've discussed indirect fund raising at length. It offers many exciting possibilities and in many cases it will be exactly the right approach for your organization.

Now it's time to turn to direct fund raising (or direct solicitation). It is as large and varied a field as indirect fund raising. And, according to most experts, it is the fastest and cheapest way to raise money.

Ed Grefe, an experienced political fund-raising consultant— and himself a donor to numerous causes—puts it this way:

"It's a mistake to think you have to put on a big show to raise money. If I can afford to give you $100, then I can also buy my own fancy dinner if I want one. If I like your cause, I don't need a dinner to make me give. I want the money to go to the cause itself—*directly.*"

Direct solicitation is nothing new. People in search of money for universities, hospitals, museums, and many major charities have used this method of fund raising since the early days of philanthropy.

But we think it's time that *everyone* concerned with raising funds—not just big-time fund raisers who need hundreds of thousands of dollars—explore and consider direct solicitation.

If your organization's money needs are greater than ever before, if your traditional fund raisers are not bringing in enough to justify the time and money spent on them, if many of your volunteers have reentered the job market and are unable to give as much time as before to planning fund-raising events, or if the case for your idea, program, or project is very strong and serves a demonstrably great need, then direct solicitation may be the route for you to take.

Again, let's define direct solicitation. It is raising funds by selling an idea, rather than by selling a product or an event, then using the proceeds to support the idea.

By building a strong case around the idea, and by presenting the case directly to the potential donor, you increase your chances of getting a gift that is thoughtful and proportionate—and that can mean *substantial*—from people who care about or believe in your idea.

There are three kinds of direct solicitation: face-to-face, telephone, and direct mail. In this chapter, we'll talk about face-to-face solicitation. It's the most effective type, and should be used, if possible, if the constituents are within easy geographical reach.

FACE-TO-FACE SOLICITATION

Face-to-face (or personal) solicitation can be used for gifts in all ranges. At the lower range of gifts, it usually takes the form of a door-to-door canvass. At the middle or higher ranges, solicitation takes place by appointment at the potential donor's home or office. (Sometimes a special donor dinner, luncheon, brunch, or cocktail party may be planned for this purpose. Prospects attend and are solicited there as a group or one at a time.)

Most fund raisers feel that someone who is able to give you a thoughtful and proportionate gift deserves a personal visit. A personal visit is the best way to let someone know how important she is and how meaningful her gift can be.

A personal solicitation campaign at any level needs planning and volunteers. And there are some rules of thumb to follow which are as true for door-to-door as they are for big-gift solicitations made by appointment.

1. Make your own contribution first.
2. Work from a prospect list that isn't duplicated by another volunteer.
3. Solicit from your peers. Look for gifts within your own giving range.

LARGER-GIFTS SOLICITATION

You can best use direct solicitation in capital, special gifts, and memorial campaigns, and for goods and services in special events.

Professional fund raisers feel that you should personally approach anyone capable of giving $100 or more. You may want to set a lower figure, especially if the constituency is not wealthy or if your pace-setting gift can be lower than $100.

Decide what your upper-, middle-, and lower-range gifts will be. Remember, a gift of about 10 percent of your total goal (or two top gifts of about 5 percent each) will set the pace for other gifts.

The pace-setting gift usually comes from the "inner family" or board of directors. If there is no single person who is capable of making the necessary gift, then the entire board as a unit should raise the money among its members, with each person giving at her own individual giving level. The public doesn't need to know who on the board gave what, but the board commitment is important, as it influences those not as closely associated with the organization to make substantial gifts.

"If you cannot get a certain number of dollars from your board, how can you expect outsiders to give?" asks Ruth Logan of the Federation of Protestant Welfare Agencies. "This does not mean that all board members must be affluent to serve, but they do have a responsibility for fund raising, and the board as a board must be pace setters, and each person on the board is obligated to support the organization to the best of her ability."

So, what do you need to conduct a personal solicitation? A board or "inner family" which is committed financially and in spirit, and other committed people, some of whom *are willing to ask others to join them in this commitment.*

Five Steps to Larger Gifts

1. *Identify the prospects.* The campaign leader should start by sitting down with members of the organization's "inner family," people on the case committee, and anyone else within the organization who is interested in the fund-raising aspects.

Volunteer solicitors should be drawn from those who are already most informed about the case, most involved, and financially committed themselves. But even people who are not going to solicit should take part in prospect identification.

Then, brainstorm for names. Take plenty of time. *And,* at the same time, search for a connection between your prospects and your organization. This will be your solicitation route.

Regular contributors, of course, should be your first prospects. They're already interested, and they deserve a visit. If personal visits to them are not usual, they may be so flattered, delighted, and impressed that they'll give more than you expected.

You and everyone else on the fund-raising committee should begin listing friends and acquaintances, business associates—everyone you know who you think is capable of giving a thoughtful and proportionate gift. If you've done a feasibility study, you may have a list started already.

Ask all current leaders, officers, and board members for a list of their friends and acquaintances and professional associates. Ask past officers, board members, and leaders.

Make a list of every important and influential person in the community. Do not try to decide whether they'll support you at this point. Just make the list.

Rack your brains for the names of anyone who would be interested in your case, even peripherally.

Then start cross-checking and searching for connections. Do you want a contribution from the bank president? Who in your organization knows him or her? (Maybe he's a past trustee's brother-in-law or sister-in-law, who knows?)

If you or the people on the committee who are willing to solicit funds do not have personal access to the prospect, who in the organization does, and how can he or she help?

The idea is to match up each prospect with a volunteer solicitor from your organization. Ideally, prospect and volunteer should have something in common. They should be peers in at least one respect—socially, financially, or professionally.

The prospect will gauge the amount of his contribution partly by the amount contributed by the volunteer solicitor and partly by how he sees himself or herself in relation to the volunteer.

"You should have like people talking to like people, even when you're soliciting small gifts," says Linda Abromson, UJA volunteer. "Let's say I'm a working woman and so are you. I can then go to you and say, 'Listen, I'm working and you're working and neither of us has time to bake a couple of cakes. But this money has to be raised, and I'm going to give $5.00. How about joining me?'

"It's the 'join me' philosophy that's so important," Abromson continues. "You just can't use that approach unless the volunteer and the prospect are in similar situations."

"The volunteer and the prospect must be compatible," says Kurt Johnson of Campaign Associates. "If I'm running a little hardware store in my hometown, I'm not the one to go calling on the president of the utility company. In the first place, I'll be awed by his importance and I won't be able to do the job. And in the second place, I won't have any influence with him.

"Now, you want to line me up and have me call on a bunch of shops. Why then, I'll get into those stores and raise money like you wouldn't believe."

Says Aline Kaplan of Hadassah, "Peer pairing extends to income levels. You wouldn't pair a middle- or lower-income woman with a wealthy woman or man. They don't have the same understanding of money. A contribution of $100 means something different to all of them."

According to Victor Swanson of the American Cancer Society, "People can be matched up according to their interests, as well as other things. There are all kinds of tricks to matchmaking.

"A few years back, our church was raising some money and they wanted me to make a pledge. They sent a doctor and a nurse to call on me. They were both members of my church. They knew I worked for the Cancer Society, and they knew about our program, and we had this common interest, and they got a good pledge from me."

Are there any exceptions to the personal solicitation rule of like give to like?

"One," says Ed Grefe. "If you're the president or the director of the organization, and you're going to be in office a long time, and you're in charge of the program that the money's being raised for—in other words, you're the one who is going to be *spending* that money—then you can ask anyone for money, a higher giver, a lower giver, whoever you want."

What do you do when the prospect's peer is not your organization's best fund raiser, and you know the job is going to require a crackerjack salesperson? In that case, send in a team—one volunteer who has contributed in the prospect's gift range and who knows the prospect, and another who is chief salesperson. The team effort is also helpful when you've got a volunteer who doesn't want to work alone but will be willing to go with a partner.

"Don't send three people to a single prospect," says Ruth Logan. "That's a crowd. But two people are fine. When you've got a partner, you can do what's called a 'dog and pony show.' You put your act together, and each person has a role to play.

"The really nice thing about it is that if you've got a real tough prospect who turns you down, you can console each other."

Some organizations, including Y's and churches, often have husband-and-wife teams soliciting other couples. In this case, you should make the solicitation a social call and visit the prospect's home. And of course, keep careful records, with cross-indexing, so that neither the husband nor the wife will be approached at the office by another volunteer.

Each volunteer or team should end up with a *prospect list*. Maybe there will be five names, maybe ten, or maybe more, depending on how many volunteers you've got, how many prospects, how much you need to raise, how long you can take to raise it, and how big the constituency is.

You should aim to have volunteers visit about 10 percent of the constituency—the 10 percent most likely to donate up to 90 percent of the total money needed.

How to find the early success candidates. Remember that an early success is very important. This builds confidence and enthusiasm, which communicates itself to later prospects. It is also a powerful persuasive tool because everyone wants to know who else has given and how much.

Every volunteer, then, must have on her prospect list an early success candidate. Once prospects are identified, some judgments will have to be made about the likelihood of getting a donation from them.

The easiest prospects to make a judgment about are your regular contributors, if your organization has kept a card for every donor (if it hasn't, start now).

Study each donor's giving history. Try to find some correlation between the amount of a gift and the urgency of the need your organization had for money at the time of that contribution.

The United Jewish Appeal, for example, discovered that some contributors made a dramatic increase in 1973, the year of the Israeli-Egyptian war. Afterward, the contribution dropped back.

But other contributors increased their donations every year, no more in 1973 than in other years. Still others gave the same amount every year.

In matching prospect and volunteer, you want to identify which of your regular contributors is most likely to give *more,* since a fund raiser always tries to get the contributions upgraded.

Of the three donors in the above example, which is the *most likely* candidate for an early success? The one who automatically increases every year. That contributor will give you a donation no matter what. He or she is a good early success prospect for a volunteer solicitor with little or no experience but who, nonetheless, should be *trained.*

What about the person who always donates the same amount, even in times of urgent need? This is the person who is least likely to give *more,* so don't waste the talents of your best volunteer salesperson on him. Chances are his gift will stay the same no matter what. But he is also a good candidate for an early success, *as long as you don't attempt to get him to increase his donation.*

Now let's move on to the person who made the dramatic increase in time of the organization's greatest need.

This person is not an early success candidate. Yet he or she's worth the time and effort of your *best salesperson or solicitation team.*

Why? Because the potential is there for an increased gift. He or she has already shown his willingness and ability to give more.

Now, suppose you've got a contributor who gives your organization $10 every year, but three years ago gave $25. Try to figure out why that happened. If other contributors did something similar, you can figure that there was some need in the community they were responding to. (If no other contributor did it, maybe it was the result of a good Christmas bonus.)

By suggesting this kind of analysis, we're not implying that you should twist arms or try to force people to give. But we are saying that using your knowledge and awareness of where your money is most likely to come from is an intelligent way to raise funds.

Many amateur fund raisers shy away from direct solicitation because they think (wrongly) that it requires figuring out the prospect's income or net worth. They think that this is greedy, crass, and they don't wish to be associated with any such invasion of privacy.

This need not be a part of prospect research and identification. Most of the time you always know who is capable of giving more than a token gift. And if they've given to your organization before, then their giving history is no secret. The idea behind prospect research is to identify the people who will feel a deep satisfaction in making a substantial gift.

Prospects who have not contributed to your organization before will be a bit more difficult to analyze, because you can't be sure of their interest. They are "cold" prospects, but worth a try.

If your organization has kept good records, you will know who has been approached before. If you can, try to find out why they haven't responded to past appeals. Do they have political or philosophic differences? Are they committed totally to some other cause? Are they known as "Scrooges"? Or have past appeals to them been inadequate?

What about those prospects on your list who've never been approached before? Maybe they've never made a contribution because no one ever took the trouble to ask, or to find out if they were interested. What better way to find out than with a personal visit?

Women as donors. More and more, women are coming into their own as substantial givers to a variety of causes that interest them. A woman prospect who has never given before may not think that she is able to give, especially if she's married and has not yet given to any cause independently of her husband. Even if the cause is one her husband also supports, she may want to give as Mary Jones, instead of as the Mrs. part of Mr. and Mrs. John Jones.

Part of the solicitation process, then, may be to help the woman prospect find a way to give (or to increase her gift) if she genuinely wants to.

Since the volunteer has already made her own contribution, it might be helpful if she uses her own experience as an illustration. This is what one volunteer we know did when talking to women who wanted to become givers, but who did not feel that they had access to money.

"I once made a pledge early in my marriage," she told us. "It was a bit too large, and my husband wasn't exactly thrilled. He said it was up to me to fulfill that pledge. So I stuck a shoebox in my front closet.

"Whenever we were out for an evening and came home earlier than we'd planned, I put the extra hour's baby-sitting money into the box. If my golf game was cancelled because of rain, I put that money in the box. If I got back a couple of dollars at the supermarket by turning in coupons, I saved that, too. Where there's a will, there's a way."

Another volunteer solicitor told us, "Lots of times a woman I call on will use an excuse for not giving in her own name. She'll say, 'Oh, my husband gave at the office.' I suggest that she can think for herself and give for herself. If she wants to support the project, she'll find the money to donate. I know women who have gotten cash gifts and have chosen to donate them instead of spending on themselves."

"The woman's interest in the cause can get the whole family interested," says Ed Grefe. "Lots of times, women who really don't control the family income will sit down with their husbands and turn them on to a particular cause."

Free-lance consultant Dale Ahearn says, "Women are excellent givers, and should not be overlooked. Give them a reason and they'll make a contribution. As a group, their contributions are not usually so high as men's contributions.

That's because women aren't used to giving yet. But we're getting there."

2. *Setting up appointments.* Those people in the constituency who are most capable of giving substantial contributions are probably quite busy. Unless the volunteer knows the prospect very well and has an "open door" relationship with him or her, an appointment should be made. Even with an open door relationship, it's a good idea to make an appointment specifically to discuss the case. An appointment says that this is an important issue, which merits serious attention.

When the volunteer doesn't have an "open door" relationship with the prospect, setting up an appointment also says something else. It says, in effect, that the volunteer respects the prospect's time, respects his or her own time, and respects the case itself.

What's the best way to get an appointment? First, decide whether it is more appropriate to visit a person at home or at the office. Is that person's connection with your case related to business or personal interests? Is the volunteer's relationship to the prospect more social or professional?

Mr. Moneybags, president of the First National Bank, is one of your prospects. Are you looking for a contribution from Mr. Moneybags or from the bank? If you're raising funds for your church, it would be better to visit him at home. If you're trying to raise money for the town's new cultural center, a visit to the bank might be more appropriate, especially if you also intend to call on Mr. Goldenpockets at the Second National Bank.

People who are being called upon because of their positions as business leaders or community leaders are best seen in their offices.

If you think you'll have trouble getting an appointment, because you are not personally known to the prospect, consider having someone write a letter of introduction for you. This "someone" might be a past contributor, the president of your organization, a trustee—someone who is already committed and who knows the prospect well enough to influence him or her to see you.

You can also fall back on the letter of introduction if you have attempted to get an appointment and have failed. And if you have someone write a letter for you, be sure to wait until it has been received. Find out when it was mailed, or better yet, pick it up from the introducer and mail it yourself.

The impression you make upon the prospect begins *before* you have your meeting. It starts with making the appointment. What day you call, what time of day, how you treat the secretary, your telephone manner—all are important.

Make the appointment directly with the prospect, but do not cave in if he or she asks for the information over the telephone. Insist on a personal meeting and let the prospect know that you will do it at his or her convenience. Be willing to adjust your schedule.

William Lampton, in his column in *Fund Raising Management Magazine,* suggests calling a day or two in advance. Setting up appointments weeks ahead of time, he suggests, makes the occasion too formal, and subject to cancellation as the prospect's schedule is likely to change. Lampton also says that Monday mornings and late Friday afternoons are bad times to call. Late Monday through Thursday seems to work best.

Here are some of Lampton's tips for appointment-making protocol:

- DO ask *when* you can have an appointment, not *if.*
- DO accept appointments at hours or places that may not be completely convenient for you. We once had a prospect tell us, "I'm leaving the country for three weeks and my only free time is in the taxi to the airport." He was probably trying to turn us off, but we knew it was then or never.
- DO be truthful about the reason for the appointment. What do you say if the prospect asks if you're after a contribution? Lampton suggests that you tell the prospect you'd like to tell him or her about the project and hear his

or her opinion. Let the prospect know that you might ask, but that if she or he does not want you to ask for a donation, you will not. Then say that you'd like the appointment anyway. If you don't get the appointment, so be it. But if you do get the appointment, it will go a lot easier if you have not misrepresented yourself.

- DO figure out before you call how much time you'll need. Rehearse your case presentation and see how long it takes. Add some time for initial getting acquainted, for answering questions, and for a brief closure. Then let the prospect know that you want fifteen or twenty or thirty or sixty minutes and don't overstay unless the prospect lets you know he or she wants you to.
- DO try to agree on a flexible time for the appointment to begin. Ten or fifteen minutes of leeway will keep you from being late if your previous appointment runs overtime or if you're stuck in traffic.
- DO keep in mind that your prospect isn't obligated to see you. He or she's doing you and your organization a favor. The prospect should never get the impression that you think he or she *owes* you an appointment.
- DON'T be demanding or intimidating, and DON'T be subservient either.

When soliciting a business (rather than a specific individual who is a business person), it's crucial to get an appointment with the right person in the company, and, of course, that's the man or woman at or near the top: the owner, the president, or executive vice president.

No doubt, someone will try to put you off and get you to agree to see someone lower in the chain of command. Be persistent.

Sally Berger, one of the two women who raised $1.4 million for Michael Reese Research Institute in Chicago through a direct solicitation campaign, tried unsuccessfully to make an appointment with the executive vice president of Montgomery Ward. Finally, after several attempts, she told him she'd seen his counterpart at Sears. When the man from Ward heard that, she got her appointment.

You can use one success to generate another when making appointments. Maybe you're not asking for donations at Ward's or Sears' national headquarters, or at huge outfits like Macy's or Gimbel's. But the principle applies nonetheless.

If Mr. Diamond, owner of the jewelry store on First Street gives you a hard time when you ask for your appointment, there's nothing wrong with telling him you saw Mr. Ruby of Ruby's Broadway Jewelry Store yesterday.

Again, don't use this information to make demands or to twist arms. Just remember that if Mr. Ruby was interested in seeing you, then Mr. Diamond will probably have a genuine interest as well.

When you're asking for an appointment with somebody, be aware that this person is probably flooded with requests and sales pitches of one type or another. He or she long ago learned to try to turn off those people he's not really interested in.

It may help if you communicate this awareness. Many times we've said to a prospect reluctant to give us an appointment, "I know that a lot of people are coming to you time and time again and that you can't possibly see everyone. I realize that it is not easy to separate quickly who really does have something interesting or unique and that most of them don't. I've already seen Mr. X, Mrs. Y, and Miss Z. I was hoping to see you, too."

Sometimes you need more than one try to get an appointment. Any salesperson will tell you that giving up too easily is a mistake. This doesn't mean you should make a pest of yourself. But it does mean that you don't slink away at the first discouraging sign. Don't act like you expect a refusal, but be prepared to deal with discouraging words from your prospect, or even from the prospect's secretary.

3. Getting ready for the meeting. In preparing for your prospect meeting, you should think about preparing both yourself *and* your prospect. If you have background material that might answer some of your prospect's questions, consider sending it or dropping it off before the actual meeting. Don't burden your prospect with hefty reading, but if you have an informational, eye-catching, and attractive brochure about your organization, send it.

Sally Berger and Alice Pfaelzer (who raised money for Michael Reese Hospital) sent their prospects a brochure about its twenty-three research programs and a program book from the gala ball that was held the previous year, along with a letter confirming their appointment. The program book let prospects see who'd made sizeable gifts the previous year, since those people's pictures appeared in the program book.

You can also pave the way for an appointment with some pre-campaign publicity. Some campaign managers take space in the newspapers for a splashy public announcement of the campaign opening. Others send letters announcing the campaign to their prospects. Either way, the message is that the campaign is starting and a volunteer will be calling for an appointment to discuss the project further.

Part of your own preparation involves deeper prospect research. Learn as much about the prospect as you possibly can. The primary purpose of a personal solicitation, according to Arthur C. Frantzreh, writing in *Fund Raising Management Magazine*, is "to get the prospect to the point of *wanting* to give, to be part of a program, to gain *personal* satisfaction from doing so."

This means that every prospect must be approached as an individual. There should be nothing mechanical about your meeting. Frantzreh says, "99 percent of all solicitations proceed without the volunteer's knowing the prospect's true interest, concerns, hopes, constraints, philanthropic desires, and hangups or eccentricities."

But, if you take the trouble to find out about the prospect's hobbies, political and philosophical views, serious interests, people you know in common, clubs, schools, favorite vacation spots, ages of his kids, or something else, you can help increase your chances.

If the prospect gives speeches in the community, has had

articles written about him or her, or appears in *Who's Who* for his or her particular field of work, you can get some background on the prospect. Otherwise, ask the person in your organization who has the closest contact with the prospect.

What you know will make it easier to break the ice, and you will be better able to figure out which elements of your case will most make your prospect *want* to give.

Preparation for your meeting also involves becoming thoroughly familiar with your subject, your case. Facts and figures should be on the tip of your tongue. Your argument, or sales pitch, should be planned and rehearsed.

Use your knowledge of the prospect to figure out what your strongest argument is, and start there. Play devil's advocate with yourself. Think about the possible objections and counter-arguments the prospect may have and see if your case can provide positive answers.

Your prospect is going to look at things from his point of view—not yours. Prepare your argument so that from his point of view, he or she wants to give. The more you know about the prospect and about your case, the better able you'll be to find common ground.

It might help if you think of your meeting with the prospect as a planned conversation. Successful solicitation does not happen by chance.

Above all, you must appeal to reason, not to emotion or duty. You are not likely to receive a contribution otherwise. If you try to make the prospect feel obligated, he or she will end up feeling guilty, not generous. If you appeal primarily to the emotions, the desire to give may not last very long, and the prospect may feel foolish in trying to explain the gift to others. Your prospect will be making a decision based on reason, and the personal pride he or she can feel in becoming connected with your case.

4. *The meeting.* It goes almost without saying that you should arrive at the prospect's home or office on time and dressed in a dignified manner. You're representing an organization you are proud of and one to which you're committed. If you're late or sloppy, it may appear to the prospect that the organization you represent can't administer money or programs efficiently.

Do everything you can to make the meeting enjoyable for yourself and your prospect. If you go in with "get-a-contribution-or-else" attitude, with clenched teeth and defensive posture, you won't be able to relax enough to communicate effectively. Take the meeting seriously, but have a good time with it. Your success or failure as a person is not at stake.

Remember, you don't *have* to walk away with a check in your hand. You may receive one a few days later. You might get one next year instead of this year. Or the prospect may decide that his philanthropic interests and your goals don't match up after all.

You should, however, be aware that this is probably the only chance you're going to have, and you will want to make the most of it. Since you've called this meeting, you should have a *plan*.

There are three parts to the meeting. If you're going with a partner, rehearse a role for each of you during each part. Maybe one of you will best be the rapport establisher, attempting to draw the prospect out, making personal conversation, telling anecdotes, changing the subject if anything gets uncomfortable. The other can provide hard facts and data.

During your rehearsals, see how your style and your partner's style complement each other. What can each of you do best? Practice together with a third person—your spouse, or your mother, your sister or brother, or with a more experienced fund raiser from your organization. Create a drama. Give the third person all the data you have on the prospect and ask him or her to get into character. This rehearsal needn't be long or dramatic. But do it even if you're after a relatively small amount of money. It will do wonders for your self-confidence.

The first part of the meeting is the introduction. Its purpose is to establish rapport between the solicitors and the prospect. It's a get-acquainted period during which a general charitable feeling should be generated.

The introduction should take up about a quarter of your meeting time, or possibly a third if you and the prospect are complete strangers. Of course, you're not going to be checking your watch throughout the meeting, but you should be able to estimate how much time is passing. Do this during your rehearsal sessions, and you'll get a feeling for how much time is going by and for the appropriate moment to swing into your argument.

The second segment of the meeting is the argument. Its purpose is to motivate the prospect to *want* to give. During this portion of the meeting you should demonstrate that your case merges with the prospect's own interests and that a donation to your organization is a rational way for the prospect to meet his or her own needs, as well as the organization's.

The argument is not a monologue, however. The prospect should be talking, asking questions, and feeding you opinions. You should pay attention to what the prospect is saying, the tone of voice, nuances of expression.

Stress the positive aspects of your case—problems that it will solve, rather than those it can't, or other problems that may arise later. Any elements of your case that match your prospect's point of view are important. Build your argument from the prospect's position.

Fund Raising Management Magazine columnist Arthur C. Frantzreh says: "Let the prospect spin his dream. Listen to the true person beneath and between the words. Analyze perceived strengths and weaknesses, then proceed positively. Not in defense. Not with argumentative tone."

You may want to use some visual aids during this portion of the meeting. The solicitors for Michael Reese used a slide presentation. Slides are surprisingly inexpensive to produce, and are an effective way to give your case visibility and back up what you are saying. Photographs or illustrations should almost always be used in case presentation. Don't underestimate the impact of something visual.

But don't go overboard in expenditures on visual aids. If your presentation is too slick, glossy, or expensive for your monetary goal, it might arouse the suspicions of a prospect who wants assurance that his or her gift is going into a program and not campaign expenses.

But your visual aids, although inexpensive, needn't look shoddy. An album of black and white photographs, for example, makes a far better impression than a dog-eared set of loose prints.

The argument portion of your meeting should take up roughly half of your time, or maybe a third if the prospect has some knowledge of your organization and the case to begin with.

Every fledgling solicitor is concerned about the subject of money. When do you mention a contribution? Do you ask for a specific amount? If so, how much? How, finally, do you ask for money?

Actual money discussions should occur during the summation or closing segment of the meeting. Sometimes the prospect will give you an opening by asking what kind of money you're looking for. But if the prospect doesn't bring it up, then you'll have to bite the bullet.

Either way, the pledge card, which can be shown to the prospect during the summation, is an excellent device.

The pledge card is a simple card with space for the donor to write in his or her name, the amount of his donation, and the payment plan. You can have printed on your pledge card the gift amounts you've previously set, thereby establishing a lower limit for people who've been personally solicited. The donor can merely check off a box next to each suggested gift.

You can also have payment plans, with boxes to check. Payments can be made all at once, or in two, three, or four installments, or over a three-year period, if it's a capital campaign lasting for that time span.

The pledge card not only helps bring up the subject of money, it also can be left with the undecided donor as a reminder to take action soon. Your pledge card should be left with an envelope for mailing—and that envelope should be pre-addressed in handwriting to the volunteer herself (or himself), not to a business office or campaign headquarters.

In the case of Sally Berger and Alice Pfaelzer, contributions to Michael Reese ranged from $500 up, and the prospects did not know before presentation of the pledge card that they were going to be asked for $500 or more.

Sally Berger says, "If we had mentioned at the start that we were going to ask for $500 or more, many people would have told us not to come. But by the time the visit was over we had built a climate of receptivity for a gift of at least that size."

During the first two segments of your meeting you're establishing that "climate of receptivity," and giving your prospect the chance to assess his or her interest level. The summation's purpose is to present the various ways that the prospect can contribute according to the interest level.

Since the prospect is not obligated to give anything at all, it is presumptuous to tell him or her how much to give. However, it is helpful to both of you to suggest giving ranges. This keeps you—and the prospect—from floundering in the dark.

And don't undermine the importance of your case by asking for too little money. Says Lynnette Teich of the Oram Group, "Don't badger big givers for small gifts. Make sure the first time counts."

Also, a prospect who is capable of giving $100—and is interested in doing so—may be insulted if he or she gives you his or her time and then you follow up with a request for only $15.

If your case addresses itself to a large need, then there is a correspondingly large need for money. Your prospect won't feel relieved that, after all is said and done, you don't want much from him or her. If you've brought the prospect to the point of wanting to contribute, then you must request a substantial and meaningful contribution to make your prospect feel satisfied.

Part of that satisfaction, as you know from your own contributing experience, comes from being aware of the impact created by your individual gift.

For this reason, it sometimes helps to relate various *gift levels* to specific parts of your package. If you're raising money to build a children's room for the library, for example, then a $50 gift might be a chair, while a $200 gift might be a table, or a set of reference books.

Finally, when the meeting has come to an end, be sure to say good-bye on time. The meeting should not drag on after the pledge card is presented. Don't stall around waiting for a contribution. If you're going to get one then and there, the prospect will let you know. Bring the summation to a close, shake hands, and say thank you.

5. *Follow up.* If you've received a contribution at your meeting, then follow up with a handwritten thank you note.

But also write a thank you note to those prospects who did not give an immediate contribution. This note can also help to get a gift from an undecided prospect. It will be much more difficult for him or her to throw your pledge card in the garbage after receiving a note of appreciation.

Sometimes people will make a pledge without immediate payment. You will have to devise some system for pledge follow-up, and for recording contributions as they come in. Pledge follow-up can be done by letter or phone. Basically, this involves waiting for a pre-determined period and then reminding the prospect that the pledge has not yet been paid. Keep in mind that most people eventually pay their pledges. Some wide-based charities allow for a 4 percent shrinkage rate, but this is not so much the result of nonpayment, but because people get sick, or die, or lose their jobs, or move away. Experience has shown that most of this shrinkage is in the smaller gifts and, for that reason, shouldn't be of great concern.

Corporate and Foundation Giving

Since most giving is from individual contributors, we've made the approach to the individual the main subject of this book.

But this does not mean that you should overlook corporations and foundations. If your fund raising among individual constituents is functioning smoothly, and if you need larger sums of money, you should aim for larger donations (grants) from corporations and/or foundations.

Grant solicitation is an art form in itself. Many, many books have been written about how to do it, and we've recommended some of them in the Appendix. Read them if you're thinking about trying to get a grant.

The following information is included because it might give you some idea of whether you should pursue these areas.

Corporations. If you live in an area where there are large or small corporations, they are probably worth pursuing if you have something that will interest them or benefit them in some way.

"A corporation is a profit-making organization, not a philanthropic one," says C. Lloyd Bailey of UNICEF. "If it spends money, it must get something in return. It may want to improve its image, or create new consumers, for example."

This means you've got to do your homework with corporations just as you do with individual givers.

"The way I start my homework is by sending for annual reports from corporations," says CARE's Fannie Munlin. "Then I know what countries they're operating in, which is important for CARE to know. I look at the kinds of programs this corporation has supported in the past, and I pick those which would probably have an interest in what we're doing—in one of our specific projects.

"The next step is to make an appointment with the corporate contributions officer. I have a film which I show, and some support material. I give the officer a chance to ask questions, and I try to relate our needs to the corporation's interests as I've been able to determine from my homework."

Corporations that have set up departments for philanthropy are ready for your approach. If there is a corporate contributions department, you will be able to get an appointment. That's what they're there for.

"Corporations are much easier to deal with than individuals," says Lynnette Teich of the Oram Group. "They know the name of the game, don't give you a hard time, and behave like gentlemen."

"You can begin an approach to business in your community by getting one business person to help you," says Ruth Logan of the Federation of Protestant Welfare Agencies. "For example, maybe there's a farm machinery business in your area. You can ask the head of that company to chair a letter-writing campaign. He or she would write on his or her letterhead to his or her vendors and other people he or she does business with. Basically, the letter would say that he or she's interested in the local Boys' Club or whatever the organization is, and he or she asks others to help support this charity. If a letter like this goes to twenty or thirty people, it can bring in some good money, and get you new donors at the same time."

If a nonprofit organization has a person who is specifically in charge of getting corporate donations, you can be flexible about the peer-asks-peer principle. The person in charge of the corporate giving program, even if he or she is a volunteer, has the status of a professional, and can request a contribution from a business executive who is a total stranger because that is the volunteer's job. (If he or she is a volunteer, he or she should also be a high-range giver, however, to approach other high-level donors.) Peer contacts should be used if possible, though, just as when approaching individual givers. So part of the corporate chairperson's job is to do the homework and find out who, if anyone, on the organization's board has some entry or access to the prospect.

If there is no one who can provide an introduction, then the volunteer should make the contact. Sometimes the thought of visiting a business executive who is a total stranger can be intimidating. Perhaps what David Mahoney, chairman of the board of Norton Simon, Inc., said in a recent speech will help you feel more at ease.

"Everyone has a special interest, whether it be the local hospital or school board, a university or museum, a minority business workshop or a center for the handicapped . . . Too often we allow ourselves to be stereotyped as business executives who forget our multiple and equally important roles as husbands, wives, parents, neighbors, consumers, voters, and taxpayers."

So you do have something in common with that business executive, no matter how important or busy he or she may be.

Foundations. You don't have to visit Ford or Rockefeller to get foundation money. "There are thousands of small foundations, family foundations, and community foundations," says Lynnette Teich. "They are in the business of giving away money. The law says that if they don't give it away, Uncle Sam will get it. But if you don't ask, you won't get it."

Grants are made in response to a written proposal. Again, writing a grant proposal is a specialized skill, and many books have been written about it. (See Appendix.)

In grant-getting, contacts are all-important. Search out the connection between your organization and the foundation, and use it. Personal contact will most likely not eliminate the need for a written proposal, but it will help you to prepare the proposal in the best way, and can help insure a careful reading.

Other sources. "The government is a major source of giving," says Lynnette Teich, "and most people don't realize that so many government grants are around. You must research them and try to get whatever money is there. The government will not come looking for you. You must go to them. Contact your local politicians and ask them to help you find out what's available and how to apply."

Educational programs are often eligible for grants from the state. One Maine eighth-grade Earth Science class recently obtained a state grant for a conservation camp environmental education program, during which they spent one week of normal class time in a nearby state park. The grant, nearly $1,500, allowed the purchase of equipment needed to conduct on-site tests and studies.

DOOR-TO-DOOR CANVASS

If your case affects the community at large, door-to-door solicitation may be the best way to raise funds. It gives everyone a chance to participate and makes them feel an identification with your organization that will not only help you now, but also in the future.

We've all been called upon by volunteers from the American Cancer Society, or the Heart Association, or the March of Dimes, so we're all familiar with residential canvass—at least from the prospect's point of view.

Such campaigns work well for annual appeals, capital campaigns, and memorial campaigns, not to mention fund-raising affairs that depend upon a large number of tickets being sold to the public.

The residential canvass is also the method of choice when you're educating as well as fund raising. The American Cancer Society, for example, wants to create an opportunity for people to ask questions and to become more aware of the Seven Signals. So distributing literature and being available to answer questions are as important as getting a donation. The volunteer who is going from door-to-door knows this. This type of canvass can't fail as long as the literature is left with the prospect.

Residential canvasses should be treated and organized as serious campaigns, not haphazard collections. Before you decide on a door-to-door campaign, check city ordinances. Some locales require solicitors to register. You can ask the town attorney about this.

Publicity is a very important element in this type of campaign. Try to get the chairperson or a couple of volunteer solicitors interviewed on the local television news program.

This will alert the public to the campaign and prepare the prospects to answer the door when volunteers arrive. If you get television publicity, make sure you mention the hours and days your volunteers will call and display the identification they'll have.

Residential canvasses are organized to cover an entire geographic constituency. Using census tract maps and reverse telephone directories (which have listings by street and street numbers), you can make sure a volunteer is assigned to each household or apartment building. Ask your municipal office to supply or help you obtain maps and directories.

Getting enough volunteers for a residential canvass can be a problem, especially if you have a large area to cover and don't want to overburden the volunteers with too many prospects. (The American Cancer Society recommends fifteen households per "Crusader," as the door-to-door volunteers are called.) Each individual solicitor may have a block captain, or neighborhood chairperson to report to, give money to, and discuss problems with. This person should be a more experienced volunteer who can help train and recruit new people for this job.

It is very important that each volunteer know which households to visit. There should be no duplication, and if someone in her area is being personally solicited or has already given a larger gift, that prospect's house should not be on the list. The volunteer should understand why she is not to go there, and should not be left thinking that one particular home is missing from his or her list by mistake.

It is also useful for volunteers to know how much each prospect gave last year, if you have these records. And donors very often want to know how much they gave the year before. Having this information at hand increases the chance that the person will give no less this year than last. It also gives the volunteer an opportunity to stress the greater need now, which may cause the prospect to increase his or her contribution.

The spirit of the volunteers is very important in any campaign, and door-to-door is no exception. Some agencies like to kick off with a brunch or supper for all the volunteers or having counting parties afterward, where the funds collected are turned in, refreshments are served, and stories exchanged.

If you're considering a residential canvass, you might check with one of the local units or chapters of a national health agency that uses this method. You could learn a lot by volunteering to work for them during their door-to-door canvass. If you can offer them something in return, and promise not to hold your own canvass just before or during theirs, chances are they'll be more than happy to help you.

Every door-to-door canvasser should be well informed about the organization and be familiar with the facts and figures of the case. The canvasser should visit each home on the list and see an adult. If an adult is not home, the solicitor should return another time. If, after several attempts, an adult is not there, a phone call requesting an appointment is in order. Any educational information should be left with the adult, and the volunteer should answer questions or take the time to explain the information if the prospect is interested.

Then the volunteer should ask for a contribution, and should be ready with some kind of answer if the person would like an indication of how much is expected. "Any amount will be fine," is not good fund raising, and it's not even true. "Any amount is better than nothing," is closer to the truth.

The volunteer can remind the person of the amount he or she gave last year and express the need for even more support now. The volunteer can tell how much the neighbors have given, if not a specific neighbor, then something like, "The people in this area who are most concerned with this problem have been giving $10 or more."

But don't lie. And don't suggest amounts that are clearly outside of the capabilities of the prospect. In some neighborhoods, 50 cents might be a sacrifice and if that's so, then it can be disastrous to ask for more because the 50 cents contributor will think his or her gift has no value, which is not the case.

Going door-to-door with a donation can is not a very efficient way of building and strengthening the contributions of regular donors. First, the can encourages people to give change, when they might be just as able to give a dollar bill. Second, it doesn't provide you with a way to keep contribution records. These are very important, for they're how you assess interest and capability of prospects you don't otherwise know much about.

For example, if you're doing a neighborhood canvass and nearly everyone gives $1.00 to $5.00, but one person gives $10, that donor is a potential prospect for a larger gift. If he or she folds up the $10 and sticks it into your can, you might not know where it came from when it comes time to count the money, especially if others have given you folded $1.00 or $5.00 bills.

Checks are easy to record, of course, and if people ask if cash or check is preferred, say check. If your organization is tax-exempt, you must always write a receipt for a cash donation and then you also have a record. In some cases, people will just give you cash and you should write it down as soon as you leave the house.

If your prospect declines to make a contribution, then leave a pre-addressed envelope so the prospect can make a contribution later. Your organization can have these envelopes printed, with a little message, "Yes, I support the Centerville First Aid Ambulance Corps. Enclosed is my donation of . . ." There can be gift ranges on the envelope, too—or a description of how various sizes of gifts can be used. Also there should be a place for the donor's name and address.

After the canvass, the volunteer should turn in the money collected to the block captain, or neighborhood chairperson, or whoever is designated. Prospect lists should also be turned in, together with amount of contribution, and all information should be recorded for your organization's donor and prospect files. We cannot stress enough the importance of maintaining complete records, no matter what the size of your organization or your fund-raising goal. Your best prospects are always those who have given before, and knowing their giving patterns puts you a step ahead when you plan your fund-raising strategy.

If you're fund raising via the direct solicitation method, nothing is more direct than seeing your prospect in person. But there are other ways to do it—by telephone and by mail. Let's turn now to the first of these—telephone solicitation.

13

TELEPHONE SOLICITATION

WHAT's the next best thing to being there? Your telephone, of course. Use it during annual appeals, capital campaigns, or memorial campaigns, whenever you have too many potential donors to visit. Again, as in any fund-raising effort, telephone fund raising requires careful planning.

Because the telephone allows direct interaction between prospect and volunteer, it's far more personal than a mail appeal. Tests have shown, in fact, that people who don't respond well to mail promotions will often respond to a phone call.

Chances are your organization can make better use of the phone than it does now. You should consider the telephone especially if you have a batch of former contributors who have dropped or lowered their support, or who have not renewed memberships in your organization.

For example, the Los Angeles PBS station, KCET, decided to telephone subscribers who had not renewed, particularly those who had subscribed initially by calling in a pledge in response to on-the-air appeals.

During the first calling month of the campaign, 3,000 calls

were made—half to people whose subscriptions had lapsed for one year, the other half to those who hadn't renewed for a longer time. Twenty-eight percent of those called responded.

Of course, telephone solicitation can be used with people with whom you've had no prior contact. Two League of Women Voters chapters used this method to raise funds for the effort to pass ERA. One of them, in Highland Park, Illinois, took in $3,000 in pledges in one night. The calls were made by city officials, whose help had been solicited, and by some League members. Businesses were also solicited—the League asked them for use of their business telephones for one night to keep their phone costs down. If you're in an area with a message unit system, or a per-call charge, then you might consider this idea.

Among the kinds of organizations that have recently turned to telephone fund raising are colleges, universities, and private schools. It may be the best way to boost alumni giving.

In 1978, St. Edwards University in Austin, Texas, held its first "phonothon." Previous fund-raising efforts, by personal and mail solicitation, had bombed, largely because there were very few volunteers and even they weren't enthusiastic enough to make their efforts pay off in any big way.

Under the direction of the university's new annual funds director, Margie Kintz, the telephone campaign, with 140 spirited and determined volunteers, brought in nearly $800,000 in pledges—an incredible sum of money considering that the goal for this campaign had been set at $50,000.

A *Fund Raising Management Magazine* interview with Margie Kintz is available on cassette for $8.00 from the magazine. It will tell you most of what you need to know to do a telephone campaign. See the Appendix for how to order.

A list of past contributors, or names of anyone who has some connection with your organization, gives you a readily identifiable constituency very likely to respond to a phone call.

If you're trying to get new donors you can still consider a

phone campaign if you take the time and effort to compile high quality prospect lists.

Get names from other people in your organization, or recommendations from other contributors of people they think might be interested. Members' Christmas card lists are one good source of names.

Make one phone call per prospect, being careful to avoid duplication. If you decide to attempt a community-wide phone appeal, you'll still be better off if you can create some connection between volunteer and prospect. Often the name of a mutual friend or acquaintance is enough to establish similar peer levels between the solicitor and the prospect.

Some experts believe that good friends should not solicit each other by phone. Suppose Joyce Answer and Jill Caller are best friends. Jill can telephone Joyce and ask her for a donation, but Joyce can easily say no because of the nature of their friendship. Enter Jane Intermediary, who knows Jill but not Joyce. She can call Joyce Answer at the suggestion of Jill. Now the request is less casual. It comes via a special phone call. The case has worth. It commands attention. It is not presented as a "By the way, why don't you send a couple of bucks to the XYZ Fund," in the midst of a conversation about other things.

The KCET campaign also incorporated a taped message. In this case, it was a recording made by Charlton Heston talking about the importance of memberships to the station.

If you know of someone who can deliver a message effectively, and whose identification with your cause will influence other people, you should consider asking that person to make a tape to be used in a telephone appeal.

Most prospects won't hang up if you ask for thirty seconds of their time to hear a message from someone whose name they know and respect.

You should also consider scripting your telephone solicitation calls. In chapter 8, we suggested having something written in front of you whenever you make a phone call to ask for publicity. The same thing applies here.

Of course, even if your part is scripted, you should use a conversational tone. The prospect should not think he or she is being read a speech. Above all, you've got to listen to what your prospect is saying. Your script might have variations to allow for the different responses your prospect might make. And after the first five conversations, you can let your common sense take over (but keep the script handy).

The interaction between volunteer and prospect is important. It's not hard to establish rapport if the volunteer is friendly, enthusiastic, informative, undemanding, and interested in what the prospect is saying.

Telephone solicitation, like person-to-person solicitation, involves listening as much as it involves talking. And it also involves asking for a specific dollar amount. The St. Edwards University volunteers started out with a request for $120 a year or $10 a month. If a prospect found that figure too high, the volunteers suggested $50 a year or $5 a month. Finally, if the prospect refused that suggestion, the volunteers asked for $45. The campaign leaders had figured previously that the goal of $50,000 would be reached with an average gift of $45.

Remember to publicize any community-wide telephone campaign. If this is your organization's first phonothon, that's news. Who will be calling? When? Who has donated the use of the phones? Where will the callers be when they're making the calls? That's news, too.

A phone campaign will be more successful if all callers call from the same place at the same time, rather than at their leisure from home phones. Why?

First, the group endeavor gives callers moral support. They're not alone but part of an exciting group process, and this excitement gets conveyed to prospects.

In the St. Edwards University phonothon, phoning hours were from 7-10 P.M. Volunteer callers ate dinner together before calling began, and after dinner met for a half-hour group training session. Both of these activities stimulated group spirit and helped give callers confidence.

Second, it gives the phone volunteers the push they need to dial the phone. If you have a list of prospects to call at your leisure from your own home, you can delay and delay and can use the excuse that the people weren't home, or the line was busy.

Third, it lets the campaign chairperson control lists and arrange those useful early successes. If a phone volunteer isn't getting good responses, the campaign chairperson can immediately provide a different list, one which has some certain successes in it, and reassure the volunteer.

If you're going to set up a phone bank somewhere, you'll need some seed money. The phone companies require deposits and even if they didn't, it's not a good idea to go into debt in order to raise funds.

But, if you don't have the money, see what you can get for free. Try soliciting the use of business phones. Any kind of office with a switchboard or at least five lines is good, as are real estate offices, insurance offices, large stores, et cetera.

You don't need dozens of phones. Five, or even three or two volunteers can work together. If you have more phone volunteers than phones, set them up in shifts. Try to make the atmosphere festive. You can have coffee available, and some non or off-duty phone volunteers to keep track of the amounts of pledges received.

Keep background noise to a minimum, so that the volunteer and prospect can hear each other easily. If you're having a one-night phone campaign, the aura of excitement in the phone headquarters can add a sense of drama to the campaign and motivate the prospect. But communication should always be clear.

What do you need, in a telephone campaign, besides phones, callers, and lists?

You'll need a telephone pledge form in duplicate (or triplicate, whichever you need), so that one section can be mailed immediately to the donor and the other retained for your records. Callers should verify the address with each person who pledges.

The donor should find it easy to send in a pledge. The form should have the amount of the pledge on it, in case the donor has forgotten how much he or she pledged. The donor should be able to write the check, insert it into a pre-addressed envelope and send it off.

Of course, you will have to budget enough money in your campaign to cover mailing costs if you're planning a phone campaign. If you're a nonprofit organization, you can get a bulk mailing permit. But some small organizations have found that it's cheaper to pay the first class postage than to buy a permit, especially if they send a small amount of mail. Do not have your pre-addressed return envelope pre-stamped. The person who has made the pledge wants to give and will be more than willing to use his or her own stamp.

One of the big benefits of a telephone campaign is that you know by the end of the night how much of your goal has been reached, and whether you'll have to do any more fund raising.

A word about refusals from donors: If the prospect does not pledge, the phone volunteer should write down reasons for refusal on a pledge form. If the prospect does not volunteer this information, the phone volunteer can ask politely, again communicating the awareness that the prospect is not obligated. The volunteer is merely seeking information. If the volunteer is truly interested in the reasons for refusal, and not trying to badger the prospect into making a donation, the prospect will probably give an answer. Among other things, these reasons will let you know whether to try that prospect again sometime.

Use the telephone solicitation not only as a fund-raising method but also for assessing donor attitudes. Remember, the more you know, the better directed your future fund-raising efforts can be. If you've made mistakes (and you will), you can correct them next time—if you know what they are. Your prospects are a valuable source of information, as well as money.

A successful telephone campaign should also be well-publicized *after* the fact. News releases can be sent out as the money comes in. If use of business telephones was donated, then a personal thank you note to those people should be written by the campaign chairperson or whoever solicited the use of the phones.

All phone volunteers should receive a special, handwritten thank you note as well. A party for the volunteers is also in order. Why the fuss? Because any volunteer who has been properly thanked and appreciated is likely to work again for your organization.

14
DIRECT MAIL

How MANY appeals for money did you get in your mail today? Who sent them? Why did they choose you, do you suppose? How did you respond?

If you sent in a contribution, then take a few minutes to study the letter and why it appealed to you. And fish those other letters out of the wastebasket and try to figure out just what turned you off.

If you think of appeal letters as "junk mail," then become a junk collector. Encourage everyone else on the fund-raising committee to save mail appeals. By studying them, you'll be able to design a more appealing mailing for your own organization.

How do you know if your cause lends itself to a mail appeal? "Mail can be used for any cause under the sun," says Francis Andrews, president of American Fund Raising Services, Inc., Waltham, Massachusetts, a firm specializing in direct mail appeals.

Mail appeals can be used for annual campaigns, capital campaigns, memorial campaigns, and to promote bequest programs. You can even use the mail to sell tickets to special fund-raising events. You can also use a mail appeal in an emergency or a disaster.

But the mail appeal should not be thought of as a one-shot deal. When your organization sends out a mailing, it is making an investment in its own future financial health. To get the full benefits, you should repeat the appeal several times, refining the list each time.

"There are two types of mailings," says Andrews. "One type is for new donors, new people, and new money. That means mailing to a lot of people and taking a chance. It also means a low response—something between 1 and 4 percent is typical."

Andrews continues, "The second type of mailing is to people who have already responded to a previous mailing. These are the people whom you've put on your list, because they've already contributed. Once you've built yourself a list of donors, you can send mail appeals to them several times. Eventually, as you weed out the names of those who don't respond and add names of new prospects, you'll have a good list—the sort that will draw a 50 to 85 percent response with any given mailing."

This mailing list might turn out to be your organization's most valuable possession, since it will continually help you replace those contributors who've retired or gone on Social Security with younger donors—people who will support your organization for years. It will also help you increase the number of people who donate funds to your organization. And that's vital, in this age of increasing financial needs and inflation.

If your organization deals with issues of national concern and you want to reach a constituency beyond your own community, you might consider speaking to a direct mail fund-raising consultant. They have the lists, they have the experience, and, in the end, they can save you money on a first mail appeal.

But if you want to do a community-wide mailing in an

effort to find new money among your own geographic constituents, you can certainly do it without professsional help.
Churches, scouting groups, PTA's, social service clubs, school
bands, civic groups, hospitals—groups of nearly every type
have successfully used mail appeals—and you can, too.

Mail appeals have five distinct advantages:

1. *You don't need an army of volunteers.* It takes just a few
people to conduct a mail campaign, although those people
will have to work hard. Lists must be compiled by volunteers
or purchased from a list broker. The letter must be written
and printed. Envelopes must be addressed. But, in comparison
to a door-to-door canvass, a telephone solicitation campaign
or a huge, special event that takes lots of work hours to pull
off, mailings take fewer volunteers to reach more prospects.

2. *The prospects are contacted.* Almost everyone opens the
mailbox and, at the very least, glances at every piece of mail
received. A telephone campaign can miss prospects if they're
not home during calling hours. Door-to-door volunteers might
not be so diligent as they should be. (Some of the national
health agencies estimate that their volunteers actually visit
just 30 percent of the households, and, for this reason, more
and more of them are using the mail.)

3. *There's no hesitation about requesting a specific amount.*
In spite of training, volunteers may be timid about mentioning
a specific sum of money. So they're likely to settle for anything. Studies show that people tend to give the lowest requested amount, if it's reasonable. The volunteer who has no
trouble requesting $1.00 may find it difficult to ask for $5.00.
If $5.00 is reasonable, you may be better off asking for it in a
letter than trusting volunteers who don't feel comfortable asking for that much.

4. *It's easy to suggest several gift amounts.* When the Columbus League of Women Voters did a special appeal to raise
money for the passage of ERA, they decided to use the mail.
They designed a "nonevent" event, which they called a "non-
Party." The mailing was done in the form of an invitation to a

"nonNew Year's Day Gala party," giving prospects the opportunity to make a contribution without leaving the comfort of their own homes on New Year's Day.

"We need financial support and we have figured out a uniquely painless way for you to give," said the letter of explanation. "You are invited not to come to a cocktail dinnerdance. Watch the Rose Bowl or the Orange Bowl and recover from the previous night in your bathrobe, all courtesy of the League and for the benefit of Equal Rights for Everybody."

Prospects were given three different gift packages to choose from: no cocktails for $10 per person; no four-course dinner with domestic champagne for $25 per person; no dancing til dawn to the strains of Guy Lombardo for $50 or more. The net profit on this event was $3,500. Costs were $500 (printing and postage). Invitations were sent to 2,500 people, and 212 responded. This is an excellent response for a first-time mailing, due to a good list.

The party was scheduled to be held in the Columbus Convention Center—which was under construction. At the time of this mailing, in fact, it was a hole in the ground. The reason for this was so that no one would make a mistake and actually go to the nonexistent party.

5. *The quality of salespersonship is uniform.* All prospects are told the same story in the same way. If you're doing a door-to-door or telephone campaign, each volunteer is likely to tell a slightly different version of the case.

If you've been concentrating on raising your funds indirectly, a mail appeal can get you started on direct fund raising. It's very easy to attract event-minded supporters by mail. This is, in effect, what the Columbus League of Women Voters did with their nonNew Year's party, which was a nonevent. The United Methodist Women of Christ United Methodist Church, Bradenton, Florida, used a similar approach when they did a mailing for an "Imaginary Bazaar." Letters asking for contributions were sent to all members of the organization and $2,000 was raised.

The letter was in the form of an announcement describing what an Imaginary Bazaar is. "No aprons to make, no cookies to bake, no candy bar, or gifts to take, no fishponds, or cakes all covered with cream, honestly, doesn't it sound like a dream?"

No specific amounts were suggested, but donors got the idea from the following shopping list that was also provided. Contributors were asked to fill in the blanks.

Estimated cost of running car back and
forth to bazaar $_____

Money for apron NOT bought   _____

Money for food and coffee NOT eaten   _____

Money NOT spent for candy, cookies, cake   _____

Money NOT spent at gift booth and fish-
pond   _____

Thank you money for feet NOT sore from
kitchen work   _____

Special thank-offering for being privileged
to participate in this unique enterprise   _____

Money not spent for baby sitters   _____

GRAND TOTAL   _____

Everything about this bazaar is imaginary except the earnest need for money.

The two basic elements in every mail campaign are the *list* and the *letter*.

LIST

If you're going after new money, then you'll want to consider a community-wide appeal. You can use voter registration lists, or census lists, or the telephone book. Civic organizations—symphonies, theatres, museums—often have lists which they will share with you. Either they will exchange their list with yours, if you've got one that can be valuable to them, or they will rent you their list.

If you live in a large community or if your budget doesn't permit a mailing to everyone, then you should mail to a selected group. Develop your prospect list in the same way you would for other fund-raising methods. Sit down with your committee and write down names, or ask everyone in the organization to give you ten or twenty names. Christmas card lists are a good source of names.

You can also select a certain group to mail to. One time, you might mail to people who have small businesses, another time to doctors, another time to parents of twelfth graders, or whichever group you want to reach.

Should you buy a mailing list? This depends on how valuable that list can be to you and whether your budget allows for this expenditure. In fund raising terminology, a list can be "hot" or "cold" depending on whether it's been tested and what the response has been. A wide variety of lists can be purchased and the price range is also wide.

It takes time to build a "hot" list of your own, especially when you're looking for new money. If you can purchase a list of names—people who are similar in many respects to regular contributors, and who therefore are likely candidates—it may be worth it. If you live in a metropolitan area where there are list brokers, then you may be able to get a computerized list that comes very close to filling your requirements.

Unless you're planning a really massive mailing, though, you can cut costs by doing everything yourself—preparing the list, writing the letter, addressing the envelopes, recording the responses.

Although some fund raisers use bulk mail, we think mailings should be sent first class if possible. (Incidentally, on all mail solicitations, federal law requires that you use a return address with a full street name and number rather than a post office box number.) If your organization can't afford postage, you can consider soliciting a gift of postage from some business in your area. (That gift, of course, should be personally solicited.) Printing and paper costs can also be solicited from businesses. So can the use of a copying machine, if you decide against printing.

You can also consider using a "mag-card" typewriter to print the body of your letter. The individual names and addresses can be typed in later, as long as the typefaces match. Again, many businesses have these typewriters, which make any number of *originals* automatically. Many businesses that refuse outright contributions may be happy to help you by leting you use their "mag-card" typewriter.

Use common sense when you prepare your list. If people in one area of town are known to be having trouble making ends meet, it doesn't make much sense to send them appeals. If there's a strike going on, it doesn't make much sense to mail to anyone in the union or the management, since they all have financial worries. In fact, the economy of the entire community may be affected, so you might want to postpone your mailing until the strike is settled.

"Most money is given by educated people of middle income—about $20,000 a year or more in family income," says Francis Andrews. It makes sense, then, to aim your mail appeals to people in this group.

LETTER

Fund-raising letters have five main aspects: content, readability, length, enclosures, and salutation/signature.

1. *Content.* So many gimmicks have been tested in direct mail appeals that no one could ever hope to count them. The final result of all these tests: Literate, middle-income individuals respond best to a simple, intelligent, direct appeal.

When fund raising by mail, you must give people a good reason to contribute to your cause—just as in any other kind of appeal. You can't beg. People won't give because your organization is poor, or in debt, or badly managed. "They want to feel that their money is given for a logical reason," says Francis Andrews.

According to Andrews, "Readership studies show that you've got about thirty seconds to catch the reader's attention—that's a little way through the first paragraph."

The first paragraph of your letter, then, is of prime importance. It doesn't have to be tricky. In fact, coming quickly to the point is probably the best way to catch the reader. "Almost everything going into the home is at least opened and glanced at," Andrews says. "Get the story right up front. Play it straight. Don't ramble, or you may lose the reader."

Andrews suggests that you make your first paragraph like a newspaper lead. "Use any news you can. State your reasons for wanting money. Usually you begin by presenting the problem, or a solution to a problem that everyone already knows about.

"For example," Andrews says, "you might say that a major cancer discovery at our local hospital makes it possible for people with skin cancer to be treated closer to home. That's a piece of news."

Your letter might continue saying something like, "Now that we can treat skin cancer here at home, we need a laboratory to do it."

Finally comes the appeal itself, or the request for a specific sum of money, and one of the keys is to ask for the right amount. "Make sure the amount you ask for is reasonable," says Andrews. "For example, if you're collecting for Red Cross, you can't ask for $1,000 in a letter because people don't normally give $1,000 to Red Cross.

"But if your letter states the problem, and then says that if a reasonable number of our townspeople send in $10, we will solve the problem, then if that's true, you'll end up with $10 gifts."

The specific dollar amounts are usually best mentioned toward the end of the letter.

2. *Readability.* Before you go any further with this book, try writing a fund-raising appeal letter for whatever case you're currently concerned with. Be sure to put the news, the problem, or the solution in the first paragraph. Put any further explanation later on, and make the request for a specific amount at the end.

Then come back to this book, and you'll find out how to check your letter for readability.

If something is readable, it's neat, legible, easy to read and understand. It won't make you feel confused and won't force you to backtrack.

One key to making your letter readable is your choice of words. Avoid long words or technical or unfamiliar words. They hinder communication. Avoid any jargon of your organization. Don't write a letter to raise funds "to implement a program for raising students' reading quotients." Say instead you're raising funds "to teach children to read better."

Don't be afraid that by using short words, you'll be talking down to the reader. The reader may well be able to understand long words, but why force him to?

Jerald E. Huntsinger of *Fund Raising Management Magazine* has developed a formula to help you check the readability of your letters:

First, count *all* the words in your letter, including salutation, closing, names, numbers, hyphenated words.

Second, go back and count the words that have five letters or less.

Third, divide the number of five-letter or under words by the total number of words to come up with a percentage figure.

How did you rate on your test letter? According to Huntsinger, "75 percent is extremely readable; 70 percent is acceptable; 65 percent is a sign of trouble; 60 percent is bad news; 55 percent is unacceptable."

You might also want to test out some of the letters you've received in the mail from other organizations. See whether your response to them has anything to do with their read-ability—percentage of short words used.

3. *Length*. Unfortunately, there aren't any set rules. There's Huntsinger's readability formula, but no length formula except common sense. And common sense says to take as much space as you need—but no more.

Obviously, if you're an organization that everyone knows about, or you're dealing with a problem everyone is familiar with, it will take less space to tell your story and state your reasons for wanting money than it will if you're dealing with something that's completely new to the reader. But, even so, telling too much can be fatal. If you lose the reader before he or she gets to the end, you've failed.

Our own feeling is that shorter is better. Most inexperienced fund raising letter-writers try to tell too much, more than is really needed. Pick out the *most* newsworthy or dramatic elements and leave out the nonessentials. People who are interested will most often be sold by what you say first anyway.

4. *Enclosures*. There are two kinds of enclosures you may send along with an appeal letter. One is an essential enclosure—something for the donor to send back to you with his contribution.

The other is an optional enclosure—promotional literature that tells more of the story than is contained in the appeal letter. It provides the donor with additional information. It is not returned to you.

Let's talk first about the essential enclosure. There are two parts to it. First is the contribution reply form. This tells you the donor's name and address and how much he or she is giving you. The donor fills it in when writing out the check. If you've used a computer service to do the mailing, the name and address are probably already on the form and the donor will only have to fill in the amount of the contribution. Otherwise you will have printed on the form lines designated for the donor to write in this information. Or you can write the donor's name if you are stuffing and addressing envelopes.

Second, is the return envelope, *pre-addressed* to the organization. You don't have to stamp the return envelope. Your donors can put on their own stamps. In fact, they'll probably prefer it if a nonprofit organization does not spend money on stamps. They want to give, remember.

You can have a message printed on your envelope in the space for the stamp. It can say something like, "Your stamp will help." We found that message on a recent return envelope in a Salvation Army mailing.

Sometimes the contribution form and return envelope are combined in a one-piece mailer. In this case the flap of the envelope contains the contribution form. It is usually perforated and can be torn away from the rest of the envelope, placed inside with the check, and then a smaller flap remains on the envelope for sealing.

We've mentioned that the essential information for the contribution form is name and address of donor and amount donated. What else can you put on it to help make a sale to the donor?

There are two other things that you should include on a return form. One is suggested gift amounts, plus a blank line for "other" amounts not suggested. Have a check box beside each dollar amount and "other." The lowest suggested gift should be the same amount as is mentioned in your letter. If each dollar amount is related to a certain type of membership, or a certain part of the case, then you can state that as well.

CARE, for example, tells you that $5.00 gives one hundred children a bowl of porridge for a week, and $10 buys a glass of milk for 2,000 children, et cetera.

If your organization is a membership organization, then you should offer several types of membership at various prices. We recently received a mailing from a marine museum that offered ten different types of memberships ranging from student at $5.00 to benefactor at $5,000. You can probably do with three or four types of memberships. In order of increasing donation, these are usually called: individual, family, contributing, sustaining, patron.

If you're offering memberships, then your return form should also include the privileges of membership, such as newsletters, discounts, meetings, et cetera. That marine museum, for example, has several membership advantages, including free admission to the museum and whatever lectures, films, or other kinds of entertainment are offered there.

In addition to the gift ranges, there should be a simple subscription message on your return form. "Yes, I do want to help feed the world's starving children. Enclosed is my contribution of $_____," or whatever message is appropriate. This message serves to reinforce the donor's commitment.

Now, for the *optional enclosures.* If you need to give the prospective donor any other information about your organization or its program—background that would make your letter too long or that is not directly related to the fund-raising appeal, this, too, can be included as an enclosure. It might be a four-page promotional brochure, or a one-page fact sheet, or a copy of a recent newspaper story about your organization.

Sometimes fund raising envelopes are stuffed with so many enclosures it's hard to figure out just what the message is. So keep your enclosures to a minimum. If the prospect's confused by too many pieces of paper, he or she is likely to toss them all into the wastebasket.

Refer back to the Case chapter if you need to, and remind yourself of the questions a donor is most likely to want answered about your organization. Limit your promotional enclosures to answering these questions.

One word of warning is in order about enclosures, however. They add to the weight of the package you'll be mailing. They may increase postal expense—and it could be a make-or-break difference when you make a final tally. Be sure to check this out in advance.

5. *Salutation/signature.* Although the salutation comes first in the letter, your decisions begin with what comes last—the signature.

Who should sign your appeal letter? Should the same person sign every letter, or should different people sign letters going to their own personal mailing lists?

If you have the personal mailing lists of some of your own officers and members, then those people who gave you the list may put a personal message at the bottom of the letter. Let's say that George Prexy, president of your organization, has written to Alice Prospect, whom he does not know personally. Your organization's vice-president, Laura Veep, however, does know Alice. Laura Veep might put a "P.S." on Alice's letter. "Dear Alice—I do hope you'll join me in supporting the Acme Museum. Laura."

Who will you be appealing to? For example, are you sending an appeal to all the merchants in town? In that case, you might enlist the aid of an influential merchant who has supported you, asking him or her to sign the letter. The salutations, then, should be whatever the merchant calls the people on the list. Some letters might have "Dear Joe," while others, to merchants he or she knows less well or does not know personally, would be "Dear Mrs. Black."

In cases like this, it's best to use the signer's personal letterhead, not the organization's. But the organization does all the work; it writes the letter, subject to the signer's approval. It types in names and addresses and greeting, and it addresses the envelopes. All the signer does is put his or her signature on the letter.

If no member of the group you're appealing to is willing to sign, then the letter should be signed by the leader of your organization, the president or the executive director, or perhaps a prestigious past officer. (And, of course, the letter should be written on your organization's letterhead.) Again, make sure that people the signer knows personally and calls by first name are not called Mr. or Mrs. or Miss in the letter.

If you're thinking about using a "Dear Friend," salutation, consider your own response to such a letter, and ask others on your committee. Maybe you and others you know will just as likely respond to this as to a letter with your name on the inside. Again, these decisions will be influenced by the size of your list, number of people working, access to typewriter with the same typeface as the body of the letter, method of reproduction of the letter (printed letters or mag-card originals are most suitable for personalizing the inside address and salutation).

"In general, the more personalized the letter, the more clout of the signer, the greater the percentage of return," says Lynnette Teich of the Oram Group.

Donations that come to you in response to a direct mail appeal should be recorded on a donor card, and that donor added to your contributor list for next time. And, of course, thank you notes should be sent for all donations, however small.

Thank you letters can be composed at the same time you're writing the appeal letter. You can have some typed in advance, and when the donation is received, add the person's name and mail the thank you note. Some organizations have cards printed, but our own preference is for a personal note.

If you're appealing to long-time supporters, check your records so you can acknowledge their past support in your latest appeal.

When appealing to previous contributors, stress the urgent need. Tell the person that you are appreciative of past gifts, then remind him that the need continues and that his continuing support is vital. Mailings, then, to previous donors will be different from mailing for new money.

If you're starting a direct solicitation campaign for special gifts, be sure to check those who responded last time, especially those who gave more than the lowest suggested amount. They're your best prospects.

MAILING DATES

Timing a mail campaign is like timing any other campaign. You've got to make sure you're not competing with too many other demands for your prospects' money. You have to set your mailing dates early and work backward when establishing other deadlines—letter written, copy to printer, envelopes addressed, et cetera.

If you're mailing an invitation to an event, then you must make sure that the invitation is received far enough in advance, but not too far. If the person must purchase a ticket by mail, then make sure there's time for your invitation to reach the person, for him or her to send the money back, and for you to send back a ticket.

Some experts think the day the mailing arrives is important. If people go away for the weekend, then the letter should not arrive on a Friday, when they may be busy getting ready to leave. Other people say that Saturdays are good because business people are at home when the mail comes and are likely to give the mail more attention. Others say have your letter get there on Thursday because people who get paid every Friday will respond best to letters that come on Thursdays. And on and on and on.

Francis Andrews of American Fund Raising Services, Inc., says, "Most people look at the mail and if something interests them, they put it aside and act on it when they have time or when they pay their bills. It really doesn't matter which day of the week it arrives. Besides, you can't control that because you have no control over when the post office delivers it."

SUMMARY

To sum it all up, mail appeals have a lot going for them. They're an excellent way to find new donors and they're an excellent way to get additional donations from those who have already contributed.

Mail appeals don't require an army of volunteers. They're a way of being absolutely certain that each prospect *is* contacted. They're an easy way to ask for a specific amount, in fact, to suggest several specifics. They're a way to make sure your message gets across exactly as you want it to.

What mail appeals do require is a *list* and a *letter*. You can put together a list on your own or you can rent one. You can get professional help or you can do it yourself. But whatever you do, time it carefully.

So there are three ways to solicit directly: in person, by telephone, and by mail. Which to use? As we've been saying all along, it depends on the circumstances.

But whichever method you choose, your campaign isn't over when the last dollar is in. There's still a lot of work to do—work that can guarantee an even better campaign next time.

$
$
$

PART FIVE

Ending a Campaign

15
THE WRAP

ACCORDING to *Designs for Fundraising* author Harold J. Seymour, "the post-campaign period is more a time for embracing rich opportunity than a time for complacent convalescence. . . . There is nothing here to be lost except by delay or self-deception. There is everything to gain."

So, let's zoom in for a closer look at ending the campaign.

WHEN TO STOP

The first question is when to end it. And that depends on what kind of campaign you've run.

Self-contained special events campaigns have built-in deadlines, with the closing date or time established right from the start. When the party's over, it's over. If you haven't met your goal, you can't prolong the campaign. All you can do is to give another party or plan some other type of campaign.

Annual campaigns also have a built-in closing date, and the best policy is to stick to it (although you may keep the books open for thirty days or so for stragglers). If you've arrived at your goal, you can put late donations on the books for next year.

Even if you haven't reached your goal, stop. Seymour's book advises announcing your results without a comparison to original goals or last year's success. "Any additional fund raising should then be done quietly and more as a cleanup than as extended campaign," he says.

If you are far short of your goal, "organize a new and special fund raising apparatus—with a name and goal all its own and all the power-structure type of personnel that can be mustered. . . . Change of pace and change of approach are the vital factors here," Seymour notes.

The important thing is to close an *annual* campaign on schedule. Then begin a special campaign if necessary. Who's your best source of new funds? Exactly those people who've given previously. The best source of all: those hard-working volunteers who were also among the top givers.

Ending a *capital* campaign is different. Most capital campaigns run for three years, and the closing date established at the beginning may not hold. That decision should be made as you approach the closing date set way back when. Few, if any, capital campaigns really end on the specific date assigned at the outset.

Why? Because, according to Seymour, "there are always a number of important solicitations still hanging fire." This is usually true whether or not the money goal has been reached.

Seymour advises "a special plan for the homestretch" to take care of outstanding solicitations. As for capital campaigns that have not attained the money goal, you can decide merely to extend the campaign, or to take the unraised portion and "tuck it in with other needs to make a new goal, with fresh identification." Your decision will be based "first on the size of the problem but most of all on how much steam there is in the barrel," says Seymour.

What if . . . It's probably clear by now that all campaigns don't succeed. Some lose money. Some break even. Some simply don't reach their goal—either by a lot or a little.

If you haven't met your goal, decide whether to end or

extend (if a capital or special campaign) or close (if annual or special event campaign). What not to do? Mope, moan, and blame. It will get you nowhere.

Instead, hold a committee meeting as soon as possible. Two things must be discussed—what went wrong and what to do next. But don't start blaming people.

Even if you haven't made money, you have gained experience. An unsuccessful campaign is a challenge to your spirit. If you make the most of it, you'll learn enough to carry on. You'll see your mistakes and won't make them again.

Instead of blaming someone, analyze all the fund-raising elements (case, leadership, volunteers, constituency, and the campaign itself—with all its elements). You may find a weakness somewhere—anywhere—from a poorly presented case to not enough publicity, to a goal set unrealistically high.

THE POST-CAMPAIGN

According to fund-raising experts, the post-campaign period can be divided into eight elements:

1. *Loose ends.* Loose ends are bills to pay, equipment to return or sell, bank accounts to close, et cetera. You can have many or few.

One of the loose ends you're sure to have if you've run a direct solicitation campaign is reaching all those people who said they'd give "later." (Not counting those who have actually pledged previously.) Each person who said he would respond "later" should be evaluated individually. Should the person be approached again? If so, should the original solicitor do it, or should someone else?

Make a list of your loose ends, so you can take care of them quickly and efficiently. The more details you have hanging over your head at the end of the campaign, the less able you are to give your attention to the future.

Furthermore, leaving things undone doesn't help your group's image, especially where other people are concerned.

If you've borrowed five dress racks for your rummage sale, the store that you borrowed them from will appreciate a speedy return. If you've rented the American Legion Hall for your dinner, sweep up and take all your stuff out of there, pronto. When you go back next year, you don't want to hear, "Last time, we had to store your tablecloths for two weeks."

2. Evaluation and records. Don't hesitate to take care of this loose end. More than likely, everyone will protest about having yet another meeting, but evaluations must be done while the memory is fresh.

Things you should discuss and keep on record include (for an event) which brought in the most money (the raffle? the cash bar?), how many people attended (pre-sold ticket-holders vs. tickets sold at the door), how many workers were there, how many people-hours were spent, who were the volunteers (students, housewives, working men and women, members, nonmembers). If this was an annual campaign, be sure to compare all data with last year's and earlier.

Says Linda Abromson of the United Jewish Appeal, "Comparisons are important because you get perspective. Did the pot luck supper do worse the sixth year? Maybe the time limit on pot luck suppers is five good years and you need to consider a change. Or maybe you'll find another reason for a not-so-great sixth year."

Each committee chairperson should turn in a detailed written report. It should have a description of the job and responsibilities, a list of people on the committee, a schedule of what was done first, second, and so forth.

An evaluation should also be included in the report. What was easy and went along with no problems? Which things took longer than expected? What, if anything, should be handled differently in the future? What suggestions does the chairperson have for the person in charge to consider next time? Was the committee too large, too small? Should this job be handled by two people instead of one? Can this job be combined with another one? Have new suppliers come into the area who can give you better service or better prices?

Should your organization consider buying some equipment rather than renting it year after year? Are there any procedures that need reviewing or revising? How many hours did the chairperson and each committee member put in? From the point of view of this person, was the event time-efficient? If not, is there a more efficient way of handling this job? Can the number of work hours be cut down, or can the profit be raised? How?

Many of the above questions will also apply to direct fundraising campaigns. But there are others you should ask yourself: What was good, what was worthless? What money was well spent, what was wasted? What publicity ideas worked, which failed? What meetings worked—when and where?

Which approaches brought in the highest responses and the largest gifts? Which younger volunteers should be moved up in the next campaign?

Write all of this up in a report—a simple one, if you like. Include figures for the sizes and numbers of gifts sought and obtained. Also include a final budget report on what you spent. And do a complete chronology, showing the timing of everything, from publicity contacts to campaign events.

All this will take time, of course. But it's part of the job. And imagine the time it will save you next time.

To make sure every committee chairperson turns in her report, set a deadline—say a week after the campaign ends. Then have a party on deadline day, to turn in reports, to analyze them, and to celebrate your accomplishment.

3. Rewards and recognitions. *Donor letters.* These include not only thanking contributors but also letting them know what their gifts have accomplished. Periodic news bulletins or releases sent to donors—not requests for money—encourage them to remain interested. The post-campaign period is a good time to discuss starting a newsletter.

Keeping your organization and its programs in front of the donor's eyes is good preparation for future fund raising. You can communicate with your contributors once a year, or whenever something significant has happened that will be meaningful to the contributor.

If your organization has made news, be sure to have news stories reprinted. A packet of press clippings is another good way to keep in touch with your donors. Press coverage says that your organization is doing something newsworthy, that your programs are valuable, that the money you raised is indeed being well-spent.

Of course, donor thank you notes are vital. A thank you letter to a contributor should not be routine if you expect it to aid you in future fund raising.

A properly written thank you letter does four things, according to Jerald E. Huntsinger, a columnist for *Fund Raising Management Magazine:*

First, it "completes a warm and positive experience." The thank you letter is "proof of your personal appreciation."

Second, it "conveys official thanks." This is especially important if your organization is large. Good thank you letters personalize even a giant-sized institution.

Third, it "educates the donors." In a thank you letter, you have the opportunity to "communicate concepts that the donor would not bother to read in a normal fund-raising letter." But keep it brief.

Fourth, it "raises additional money." If the donor feels fulfilled in making a small gift (and he will, if you send him a warm, personal thank you), he may be ready to go on to an even more gratifying experience.

But make sure the thank you letter doesn't sound like an appeal letter. "Set the tone by expressing appreciation for the gift," Huntsinger advises. The donor should know right away that he is being thanked—and not asked for a contribution.

New donors should get a new donor thank you letter that

serves as a welcome. Say it right out front, Huntsinger advises. "I am so pleased to welcome you to our family of contributors," is one way to put it.

People who've contributed goods or services should also get thank you notes. In fact, any business person or private individual who has underwritten or sponsored any part of your campaign, loaned you equipment, given you discounts or "free-bees" deserves a sincere letter of thanks.

Workers. Workers need recognition. Don't slight them in favor of donor recognition. There's nothing like recognition to make a volunteer feel that doing the job was worth the time and energy.

"Thanking workers is one of the first things that needs doing," says Linda Abromson. "The president of the organization, the chairperson, or the one who did the recruiting must send a thank you note.

"And that note had better be good. I don't care if the worker did a lousy job, she or he must get a good note— because that's all she or he has."

A good letter is one the worker will feel proud to receive. In your letter, mention specific things and point to services performed. But don't gush.

Workers who did spectacular jobs (difficult solicitations, higher-than-average ticket sales, et cetera) can receive special recognition, in the form of mementos, certificates of achievement, or prizes.

A party given for the workers by the leaders is also a nice way to express your appreciation. Luncheons or brunches are often appropriate.

4. *Ensuring the continuity.* If you're involved in an annual campaign or annual event, now is the time to make sure you've got someone to head up the next campaign.

Many organizations have a system for bringing people up through the ranks. In some, for example, the first vice president automatically becomes president, second vice president becomes first, et cetera. The board and officers also make it a habit to nurture potential leaders and recruit members with leadership capabilities.

According to Seymour, if you expect to leave the fund raising in good hands next year, don't talk about how hard it was and about how you got no cooperation. Your message to your successor should be, according to Seymour, "one of hope, confidence, and good cheer." The last thing you want to do is discourage future leaders from taking on the responsibilities. Stress the rewards that come with the job.

5. *Repairs and replacements.* The post-campaign period is a good time to examine your list of contributors, potential contributors, and your ways of reaching them.

Review your list of contributors, up-date it if necessary. If you have not been keeping donor cards, start now.

See if your constituency is changing. What new people might be interested in your organization now? Children of older donors? Young people out of school and beginning in business? Young people beginning their own families? New people in town?

How can you reach these people? Does your organization need new programs, more members, more community outreach? Should your publications be re-designed—or eliminated? How can you provide more effective leadership? How can you replace contributors who have lost interest? How can you regain donors who have not continued to give?

Study the image of your organization or institution. Does it suit your current purposes?

6. *Reappraisal of needs.* Your need for funds is not over, even though you may have just ended a successful campaign. If your organization is going to continue, so must your fund raising. Whom does your organization serve, and what are their needs? What are the organization's needs? What will be your organization's role in the future, and what can you do to raise the funds needed to carry out the role? The time to begin raising additional funds is now.

If you don't have an annual giving program, consider starting one. If you do, work on getting increased gifts. What about starting a special gifts program? See how your program and the interests of the top givers match and work to build the connection stronger.

7. *Pledge collections.* Most people who make pledges honor them. But there's always the few who pose a collection problem. Some people need to be reminded again and again. You must follow up on pledges. Sometimes you'll have to follow up at the end of a campaign and again several months later if the money has not come in.

The most important thing is to devise a system for collection, which involves an initial letter and then a second one, if necessary. Most people who pledge intend to pay. Sometimes it's just a matter of a phone call to a friend who is forgetful or slow. If that's inappropriate for your relationship with the donor, then the letter approach should work. But don't neglect to follow up on pledges. And in doing so, never insult or threaten the donor. There may be a small number of people who simply don't respond, and chances are good that the pledges are small. At some point, the cost of collection will become too great. Use your best judgment. You simply may have to cross some of them off the list.

EPILOGUE

IN THIS book, we've tried to give you as complete an idea of how to go about raising funds as possible—without knowing your exact circumstances, resources, and needs.

We've talked about the science of fund raising and the art. We've described how to work up a good case, how to find a leader, how to get volunteers, how to identify your constituency, what types of campaigns exist, and how to get publicity for them.

We've explained the difference between indirect fund raising and fund raising of the direct type. We've reviewed the thirteen major types of indirect fund raising. We've discussed the three types of direct fund raising: person-to-person, mail, and telephone.

And, finally, we've described how to go about ending your fund-raising drive.

What have we left out? Only the single most important thing: *you.*

Will you be able to raise the money you need? Will your event be a success? Will people get the satisfaction they should? Will your organization be strengthened as a result? Will you accomplish the philanthropic purpose that motivated you in the beginning?

It's up to you. Why? Because there's no substitute for energy, dedication, and determination. And that's something no book can supply.

But, if there's one thing we discovered in our research, fund raising is an activity that seems to draw people with the ability and desire necessary to do the job. Far more often than not, the people we talked to had risen to the occasion, exceeding their hopes, raising more than they needed.

You can do it, too. And, in the process, you can gain a great deal of satisfaction—for yourself, for others in your organization, for your volunteers, for your donors, and, finally, for those who benefit from your efforts.

Go to it.

Appendix A

EVERYBODY'S BASIC FUND RAISING LIBRARY

THERE's no one book that can tell you everything you might want to know about fund raising. Put the following books and publications next to *The Woman's Day Book of Fund Raising* on your library shelf, and you should have just about everything you need. All prices are for the softcover editions.

MUST BOOKS

Grass Roots Fundraising Book, by Joan Flanagan. Send $4.75 per copy, plus 50 cents handling, to National Office, The Youth Project, 1000 Wisconsin Avenue, NW, Washington, D.C. 20007.

How to Succeed in Fund-Raising Today, by Helen K. Knowles. Send $6.95 per copy, plus 60 cents shipping, to The Bond Wheelwright Company, Porter's Landing, Freeport, Maine 04032.

Presenting Performances: A Handbook for Sponsors, by Thomas Wolf. Published by New England Foundation for the Arts, 8 Francis Avenue, Cambridge, Massachusetts 02138. Send $2.95 per copy or $2.00 per copy if ordering five or more. (Although this book was written especially for new performing arts groups, we think it's a must for everyone who needs to raise funds.)

Publicity: How to Get It, by Richard O'Brien. Published by Harper & Row in hardcover and by Barnes & Noble Division of Harper & Row in paperback. Order through your bookstore or from Harper & Row Publishers, Inc., 10 East 53rd Street, New York, New York 10022. Softcover price is $2.95.

MUST MAGAZINES

Fund Raising Management, Hoke Communications, Inc., 224 Seventh Street, Garden City, New York 11530. Subscription price $16 a year for six issues. This magazine, written by and for professionals, is highly recommended. Reading it is like having your own personal fund-raising consultant. Order a two-year subscription and request a year of it in back issues. Read them from cover to cover (columns, articles, news items, and advertisements) for a crash course in fund raising, plus hundreds of additional fund-raising resources.

Grantsmanship Center News, Grantsmanship Center, 7815 South Vermont Avenue, Los Angeles, California 90004. Subscription price

$15 a year for six issues. Terrific whether you're trying for grants or just fund raising in general. Order supply of back issues of this one, too.

Side benefit of subscribing to magazines: your name gets on mailing lists for other things that will help you in your fund raising—workshops in fund raising, workshops in grant proposal writing, other fund-raising publications, fund-raising consulting firms, et cetera.

MUST PAMPHLET

If You Want Air Time: A Publicity Handbook. Ask for it at your local television or radio station or order from the National Association of Broadcasters, 1771 N Street, NW, Washington, D.C. 20036.

Appendix B

PUBLICATIONS FOR SPECIAL INTERESTS

IF YOU want to know more about:

DIRECT MAIL

Donors & Dollars: Investing in Direct Mail Fund Raising and *How to Start and Manage Your Direct Mail Annual Appeal.* Free from John E. Groman, Senior Vice President, Epsilon Data Management, Inc., 24 New England Executive Park, Burlington, Massachusetts 08103. Epsilon is a direct mail consulting firm. If you don't want one of their sales representatives to call on you to discuss your fund-raising needs, say so. You can also order these booklets by calling toll-free 800-225-1919.

HOW TO COOK FOR GROUPS

Cooking for Small Groups, Agriculture Information Bulletin No. 370. 30 cents. Order from Superintendent of Documents, U.S. Government Printing Office, Washington, D.C. 20402. Terrific menu and recipe guide if you're raising funds with do-it-yourself group eating events.

GETTING FOUNDATION GRANTS

The Bread Game: The Realities of Foundation Fund Raising, Revised Edition, edited by Herb Allen. Send $2.95 plus 50 cents handling to Glide Publications, 330 Ellis Street, San Francisco, California 94102. (If you're thinking of trying to get foundation grants, this primer can get you started. Select other books on this subject from the bibliography in *The Bread Game.*)

DESIGNING PROMOTIONAL LITERATURE/SAVING ON PRINTING

Printing It, by Clifford Burke. $3.50. Published by Wingbow Press, Berkeley, California. Order through your bookstore or from Book People, 2940 Seventh Street, Berkeley, California 94710. (Everything you need to know if your organization puts out a lot of printed material, anything from flyers to posters to pamphlets or booklets.)

PHILANTHROPIC GIVING FIGURES

Giving USA. Published annually by the American Association of Fundraising Counsel, Inc., $8.00. Order this if you want more statistics on who gives and gets philanthropic dollars. Send check to American Association of Fundraising Counsel, 500 Fifth Avenue, New York, New York 10036.

RAISING FUNDS FROM CORPORATIONS

If you want to make a serious attempt to get money from corporations, send for information about how Standard & Poor's Register of Corporations, Directors and Executives can help you raise funds. Write to Standard & Poor's Corporations, 345 Hudson Street, New York, New York 10014. Be sure to include a request for price of a subscription along with your request for information.

HOW TO DO TELEPHONE CAMPAIGNS

Order Cassette No. 29-0052 SF from Fund Raising Management, 224 Seventh Avenue, Garden City, New York 11530. $8.00. Taped interview with Margie Kintz, Director of St. Edwards University's $800,000 phonothon.

HOW TO DO TELETHONS

Order Cassette No. 29-0029 JM from Fund Raising Management, 224 Seventh Avenue, Garden City, New York 11530. $8.00. Taped interview with Jim LaMont, producer of Chilton Memorial Hospital's first telethon, which raised more than $28,000.

HOW TO RAISE BIGGER BUCKS

The Planned Giving Idea Book: Creative Ways to Increase the Income of Your Institution, by Robert F. Sharpe. $19.95. Order from Thomas Nelson, Inc., 407 Seventh Avenue, Nashville, Tennessee 37203. If you're reluctant to invest this much money in a book you haven't seen, ask for the promotional literature about the book so you can decide whether or not to order it. As of this writing, the publisher was offering a sixty-day trial period with guaranteed refund. Inquire.

Appendix C

MISCELLANEOUS INFORMATION

For professional production and direction of your own fund-raising follies and cabarets: Jerome Cargill Producing Organization, Inc., 890 Broadway, New York, New York 10003. You provide the talent and Cargill provides the show and direction. Junior Leagues, hospitals, and other organizations throughout the country recommend Cargill without reservation. Write to the company for more information.

Cookbook publishers for nonprofit organizations:
Wimmer Brothers Books, P.O. Box 450, Memphis, Tennessee 38101. Write for free information package on this company's cookbook fund-raising program.

S.C. Toof & Co., P.O. Box 14607, Memphis, Tennessee 38114. Write for more information.

North American Press of Kansas City, 3947 State Line, Kansas City, Missouri 64111.

Merchandise for resale: The following are just some of the firms that offer every kind of merchandise imaginable (candy, greeting cards, pens, books, fire extinguishers, et cetera) for resale to nonprofit organizations. Find out what's available by writing and asking for more information on their fund-raising programs. A listing in this section doesn't necessarily imply a recommendation. Some firms offer merchandise on consignment; others require an outright purchase from the organization. Profits for your organization usually come to 40–50 percent of the retail sales price.

Many mail order houses have fund-raising programs. Look through the catalogs you receive in the mail and write to them as well, if you're interested in raising funds by reselling merchandise.

Abigail Martin, 1113 Washington, St. Louis, MO 63101

Akron Novelty MFG Co., 2181 Killian Road, Akron, OH 44312

Bee-Hive Family Popcorn, Blevins Popcorn Company, Inc., POB 171233, Memphis, TN 38117

Fund Raising-Made-Easy, 5 Railroad Way, Larchmont, NY 10538

Fund Raising Specialties, 21 Palmer Avenue, Cranston, RI 02820

Inter-All Corporation, 31 West State Street, Granby, MA 01033

J. H. Schuler Company, 1649 Broadway, Hanover, PA 17331

K. G. Gravette Publishing Company, 2969 Old Tree Drive, Lancaster, PA 17603

Kathryn Beich Candies, Bloomington, IL 61701

Michael M. Gilbert Enterprises, 6324 Warren Avenue, Minneapolis, MN 55435

Printing Specialty Co., Inc., 1300 Highway 8, St. Paul, MN 55112

Revere Company, Scranton, PA 18504

Standard Brands Confectionery, 365 West Passaic Street, Rochelle Park, NY 07662

Style-Craft Greeting Card Company, 5533 Troost, Kansas City, MO 64110

U. S. Pen Company, W. Caldwell, NJ 07006

World's Finest Chocolate, Inc., 2521 W. 48th Street, Chicago, IL 60632

Zokan International Supply, Inc., 474 W. Wrightwood, Elmhurst, IL 60126

INDEX